Around the World in *Fewer Than* Eighty Days

The Journeys of Nellie Bly and Elizabeth Bisland

Around the World in *Fewer Than* Eighty Days

The Journeys of Nellie Bly and Elizabeth Bisland

Edited with an Introduction by
Cassidy Weese

WHITLOCK PUBLISHING
Alfred, New York

First Whitlock Publishing edition 2017

Whitlock Publishing
whitlockpublishing.com

Editorial matter © Cassidy Weese
ISBN 978-1-943155-25-9

This book was set in Adobe Garamond Pro on 55# acid-free paper that
meets ANSI standards for archival quality.

Acknowledgments

The editor would like to thank

Dr. Allen Grove

Alfred University Libraries

and

Ms. Devon James

for their support and advice throughout
the process of creating this book.

Contents

Introduction

I N 1889, Nellie Bly challenged herself to turn the fictional journey of Jules Verne's *Around the World in 80 Days* into a reality. Elizabeth Bisland followed, and single-handedly put Cosmopolitan on the map. Together, these women shattered expectations and set the stage for the women's travel narratives, like Giblerts' *Eat Pray Love* and Savage's *Miles from Nowhere* that readers are familiar with today.

Nellie Bly

Elizabeth Cochran, who would later be known as Nellie Bly, was born on May 5, 1864 in Pennsylvania. After her father's death, the Cochran family was forced to sell the family mansion, and with it lost the wealth they once had. Elizabeth was the most rebellious of her five siblings and ten stepsiblings, but she worked hard to help her mother support the family. An avid writer throughout her childhood, Bly was first published as a teenager in the *Pittsburgh Dispatch* under the pseudonym "Lonely Orphan Girl." Bly was neither an orphan nor lonely, but felt the name would garner her sympathy as she penned a rebuttal to an article that she found misogynistic. After publishing her first book, *Months in Mexico*, at 21, Bly began writing for Joseph Pulitzer's *New York World*. Again Bly decided to write under a pseudonym, this time choosing Nelly Bly, after a Stephen Foster song. The name was misprinted as "Nellie," but she quickly became a favorite among readers and the spelling stuck.

Bly famously spearheaded "yellow journalism," or "stunt reporting," a style of sensationalist investigative writing. The 22-year-old reporter was a devoted fan of Jules Verne and spent several months attempting to convince her editors to allow her to take the journey described in the author's popular 1873 novel, *Around the World in 80 Days*. Finally, in 1889, Pulitzer approved Bly's outlandish plan, citing the inevitable sales and ad revenue this journey would bring to the *World*. The paper even held a contest in which people could write in and guess the length of Bly's journey to the minute. The trip lasted 72 days, 6 hours, and 11 minutes from the moment Bly's ship left Hoboken to the moment it arrived back in Brooklyn.

Bly did not know she had a competitor until several days into her journey. The two, though very similar in their beliefs and love of writing, were different in the way they presented themselves. Bly neither had the means nor the desire for the number of dresses that Elizabeth Bisland brought, packing lightly in a small leather bag. Bly did have her concessions, however, carrying a bulky and inconvenient jar of cold cream throughout her entire journey that often prevented her luggage from closing all the way. Bly also carried with her two self-winding watches— one on a leather band and one on a chain which remained set to New York's time zone— and a thin, gold ring that Bly believed to be good luck.

Bly may have been right to believe in her talisman, as she enjoyed tremendous luck on her journey, which continued after she arrived home. After circumnavigating the globe in record time, Bly continued her career as an investigative journalist until her marriage to 70-year-old millionaire Robert Seaman in 1895. Bly, at the age of 30, became a housewife and assisted Seaman with his factory, even obtaining a patent for the 55-gallon steel drum, an invention still used in factories today. After her husband's death, Bly took command of her Seaman's Iron Clad Manufacturing Co., and enacted the kinds of worker's benefits that she advocated for during her writing career, including access to a gym, libraries, and even healthcare. Bly was undoubtedly a far better writer and inventor than businesswoman. She did not take into account the full cost of the benefits, and her unwatchful eye made her vulnerable to embezzlement by employees. All of this depleted Bly's inheritance, and she left the factory to return to her true calling of journalism.

While Bly volunteered to report from the trenches of the war, her true interests remained with early feminist ideas. In 1913, Bly was honored at a suffrage convention in Washington where she was also honored in the subsequent parade because of her dedication to writing about social reform. Bly famously penned an article titled "Suffragettes are Men's Superiors," wherein she advocated for the importance of women's rights, but correctly predicted that the right to vote would not come until 1920.

In 1922, at the age of 58, Bly's innovative and progressive writing career would be cut short. On January 27, Nellie Bly died from pneumonia at Saint Mark's hospital in New York City. She is buried at Woodlawn Cemetery in the Bronx.

Elizabeth Bisland

In stark contrast to Nellie Bly's financial struggles, Elizabeth Bisland came from a wealthy and genteel southern family. Bisland was born on February 11, 1861 on Fairfax plantation in St. Mary Parish, Louisiana. The family briefly moved to avoid the battles of the Civil War, but eventually returned to Louisiana in 1873. At this time, Bisland began submitting poetry to the *New Orleans Times Democrat* under the penname D. L. R. Dane. Bisland held a deep interest in literature and the arts, which, like Bly's interest in journalism, would stay with her for her entire life.

In 1887, Bisland moved to the Upper East Side of New York City with her sister to pursue her a career in writing. Bisland's first writing job in her new home came from The Sun, though by 1889, her work was being printed in several publications including *The New York World, Atlantic Monthly*, and *The North American Review.*

Later that same year, Bisland became the literary editor for the struggling 3-year-old magazine, *The Cosmopolitan.* The monthly magazine industry was extremely competitive at this time, and *The Cosmopolitan* was dangerously in debt when John Brisben Walker purchased the publication. Like Pulitzer, Walker saw the idea of sending a woman around the world as a financial opportunity, and chose Bisland to make the journey.

On November 14, 1889, Bisland departed on her trip around the world from New York. Bisland believed that literature was much more valuable than sensationalist journalism, but nonetheless left just six hours after receiving her assignment. Bisland was much less frugal than Bly in her packing, and brought several custom-tailored dresses in her multiple bags. Her luggage also included several layers of hairpins so that she would not have any trouble keeping up her appearance over the next 76 and a half days. While this may seem frivolous, Bisland held the reputation of being the most beautiful woman in journalism at the time and never lost sight of her manners on her journey.

Bisland was not as interested in interacting with local culture as Bly, and her bigotry toward the Chinese is apparent throughout the narrative. Such bigotry was common at the time, and Bisland lived a relatively sheltered and privileged life. Her inexperience with poverty sometimes influenced her views of the countries she visited, believing that throwing money at begging locals was simply a game for tourists to play.

While Bly departed eastward against the current, Bisland chose to direct her journey westward. Bisland almost beat Bly's time, until January 18, 1890, when Bisland was wrongly convinced that she missed the final ship that would take her home. To this day, it is unclear whether this was a simple misunderstanding or whether the ticket-holder was a fan of Bly's popular writings. Whatever the reason, Bisland was forced to board the slow-moving Bothnia, securing Bly's victory and delivering Bisland home on January 30, several days behind schedule.

In 1891, Bisland compiled her monthly travel articles in a book titled *Seven Stages: A Flying Trip Around the World*. She continued her journalistic work, stepping beyond literature and writing several articles that, like Bly, supported the women's suffrage movement. During her trip around he world, Bisland found a deep love for Japan and later published *The Life and Letters of Lafcadio Hearn*, which focused on an author who shared her love for Japanese culture.

In 1891, Elizabeth Bisland married Charles Whitman Wetmore, and while she legally took his last name, she continued to publish her work under her maiden name. The two lived a comfortable life together in New York, and Bisland continued to write after marriage until she died of pneumonia in 1929. Bisland would join her competitor at Woodlawn Cemetery, but her *New York Times* obituary would not mention anything about the author's incredible trip around the world.

A Woman's Place in 1889

Until the 19th century, many families in the United States lived off of their farms. Prior to the 1800s, the men would labor outside in the field or with livestock, while women worked inside, making and mending clothing, cooking, and taking care of her family. As the country moved away from an agrarian system toward a market economy, with large-scale farming and factory-made consumables, women's responsibilities became less valueable. By the 1850's, cloth and food were premade and readily available in stores.

Changes in the economics of the home caused people to question gender roles. By the late 1850's, women began their fight to assert themselves as equal to men. Some women entered the workforce and generally sought a life outside of their homes, upsetting traditional values. Many argued that life outside the home corrupts, and that staying in one's house and caring for one's family was the only righteous way to live.

A proper woman at this time remained in the domestic sphere. She was educated enough to hold a conversation with her husband, but not enough to know more than him. A proper woman cared about the appearance of herself and her home, and practiced her embroidery or read novels in her freE TIME.

Neither Bly nor Bisland would really be considered a proper woman at this time, though Bisland is the closest. Elizabeth Bisland makes a point in her writing to mention the tea party that she was planning on hosting, the calm and orderly manner of her home, and the dress she was having tailored. Bisland also includes a detailed description of the contents of her bag, including several layers of hairpins and clothing for every type of weather she thought she might encounter.

While Bisland looked the part of a proper lady, she was far more progressive than she let on. By virtue of travelling the world alone, Bisland is breaking the rules. Additionally, over the course of her life, Bisland wrote many pieces calling for equal treatment of a woman, especially in marriage. Bisland was uniquely appealing to readers because she represented both types of women of the 19th century— she looked the part and behaved like a proper woman while standing up for the right of women to be independent.

Jules Verne and Nellie Bly

In 1873, French novelist Jules Verne published *Around the World in Eighty Days*, which would serve as the inspiration for Nellie Bly's travels. The novel follows newly widowed Phileas Fogg, a Londoner who wagers £20,000 with his gentlemen's club that he can circumnavigate the globe in only eighty days. Fogg is accompanied by his newly hired French valet, Jean Passepartout, whose name translates to "skeleton key" (literally, "passes everywhere"), and is a play on the English word "passport." Fogg completes his journey in exactly eighty days— from October 1 to December 21.

The novel was extremely popular and well-received, thanks largely in part to popular theatrical adaptations. Today, behind Agatha Christie, Verne is the second most translated author in the world.[1] Verne's work inspired countless authors and adventurers, including one of his most dedicated fans, Nellie Bly.

After finally approving Bly's daring trip, her editors at *New York World* helped to coordinate a meeting with Jules Verne. The paper was interested in the sales that would likely come from the meeting of the popular novelist and the journalist who brought his story to life, but Bly was far more interested in meeting an author she had read and admired for years.

The two met in 1889, in Amiens, France. Bly spoke no French, and Robert Sherard, the Paris correspondent for *New York World* who helped orchestrate the meeting, served as a translator. The two discussed Verne's novels, his travels and health, Nellie's plans for her journey, and favorite authors. The two got along very well, and Verne offered his full support. As Bly left his home, Verne offered his best wishes, telling her "If you do it in seventy-nine days, I shall applaud with both hands!"

1   United Nations Educational, Scientific and Cultural Organization "'Top 50' Author"

To the delight of the editors at *New York World*, the story of Bly and Verne's meeting immediately became popular. Other newspapers and magazines picked up the story, which meant more revenue for the *World*, as new readers bought the latest issue to follow Bly's journey. Nellie Bly, however, was not interested in how much money her evening had made for the *World*. Jules Verne inspired her, and provided her new hope during her often uncomfortable travels.

Reception

New York World and *Cosmopolitan* wanted to increase their sales by sending a woman on a solo journey around the world— and both exceeded expectations. Other magazines and newspapers across the country and the world were writing about the competing travelers. Everyone was fascinated with these daring women who seemed to be polar opposites but shared enough courage to circumnavigate the globe alone.

Though Bly and Bisland's travels were similar, and Bisland travelled faster than Bly for the majority of her journey, Nellie Bly's journey was far more famous. Cosmopolitan released new issues monthly, while the *World* printed Bly's travel writing weekly. It was easy for people to attach themselves to both women— Bisland's genteel appearance and personality appealed to upper-class readers while Bly's humble upbringing made her more universal. However, there was simply more of Bly's work for readers to consume. Bly wrote for *New York World* in its golden age, under the management of Joseph Pulitzer. While Pulitzer was not desperate for readership, Bly's journey certainly boosted the sales and widened readership of his publication.

John Brisben Walker, however, was pining for readership when he dispatched Elizabeth Bisland. *Cosmopolitan*, the self-described "first-class family magazine," was struggling. In 1889, when Walker acquired the magazine, its circulation was around 25,000. Bly's trip, combined with the inclusion of photos and fiction writing, reached 75,000 readers by 1892. Though Bisland did not consider herself a journalist, nor did she find the profession appealing, her writing helped to bring popularity to *Cosmopolitan*. Without Bisland's journey around the world, it is possible that *Cosmopolitan* would not have survived to its modern-day popularity.

Differing Tones

Elizabeth Bisland was a well-versed lover of literature. She found modern journalism to be a waste of time, and, after returning to New York, continued on as a literature editor. Because she was not interested in journalism, her writing does not reflect the writing that was often printed in magazines at the time. Instead, Bisland is influenced by literature, particularly romantic poetry. She cites John Keats and Samuel Coleridge often in her work, especially in moments when she is overcome with emotion. She often focuses on nature, and many descriptions of her surroundings read like pastoral prose.

Nellie Bly, however, had already started her career as an investigative journalist. Bly preferred adventure novels to popular novels targeted specifically toward women. Bly's accounts subsequently reflect the sensationalist writing that was popular in newspapers at the time. At times, her work reads like an adventure novel—Bly captivates her readers with gritty details and exciting situations. Where Bisland often prefers space between herself and locals, Bly is eager to interact. For example, Bly is careful to explain the different vocabulary she picks up in her travels. She is also open to having roommates and interacting with other people on the ship on every leg of her trip.

Neither writing style is better than the other. Bisland and Bly came from two different literary backgrounds, and had different goals in their writing. Bly was interested in understanding culture, while Bisland wanted to express to her readers the aesthetics of each country she stepped foot in. It is fortunate readers have access to both accounts, because Bisland describes her journey in exquisite detail, which provides context for reading Bly's attempts at interacting with different cultures. Together, Bly and Bisland paint a thorough and honest portrait of the world in 1889.

Lasting Cultural Impact

Though risky and sensationalized, Bisland and Bly made a lasting cultural impact with their individual trips around the world. Both women helped to carve out a place for female writers in modern journalism, and they set the precedent for the genre of women's travel books, a genre that is popular to this day.

The story of the race around the world continues to be told and retold to this day. In 2013, Matthew Goodman created a detailed account of the race in *Eighty Days: Nellie Bly and Elizabeth Bisland's History-Making Race Around the World*, which became a national best seller. Bly and Bisland were even recently the focus of the popular TV comedy series, *Drunk History* ("Journalism," season 3 episode 8). Bly was also featured for her investigation into the Blackwell Island asylum in an earlier episode of the same show ("New York City," season 2 episode 2).

While Bisland faded out of the public eye over time, Bly's life of investigative journalism makes her a popular figure even today. Many modern writers are still inspired by Bly, and consider her one of the mothers of investigative journalism. In 1981, *The Adventures of Nellie Bly* was released, a movie following the daring Nellie Bly as she exposes corruption in New York City. Movies about Bly are still being created, with films as recent as the 2015 adaptation of Bly's *10 Days in a Madhouse*.

Without the work of these two daring women, the role of women in journalism may have been drastically different than it is today. Though Bly may have become the more prominent historical figure of the two, the achievements of Bisland and Bly created a lasting impact on the culture of the United States.

CASSIDY WEESE

Timeline of Nellie Bly and Elizabeth Bisland

In this chronology, bolded events refer to Nellie Bly, non-bolded events refer to Elizabeth Bisland, and gray events refer to culturally significant moments that relate to the authors' works.

1861   Elizabeth Bisland is born on February 11 on Fairfax plantation, St. Mary Parish, Louisiana.

1863   During the American Civil War, the Bisland family flees their home, prior to the battle of Fort Bisland.

1864   **Elizabeth Jane Cochran (Nellie Bly) is born on May 4 to Michael and Mary Jane Cochran, in Cochran's Mills, Pennsylvania, a town founded by her father. Elizabeth would later add an "e" to the end of her surname.**

1870   **Michael Cochran dies suddenly without a will, leaving the family no legal claim to the estate.**

1871   **Cochran family is forced to auction their mansion to help with financial hardships.**

1873   Bisland family moves back to Natchez, Louisiana. After sending her poetry to the *New Orleans Times Democrat* as a teenager, Bisland begins writing for the *Democrat* under the penname B.L.R. Dane.

1879 Cochran attends Indiana Normal School to become a teacher. However, the school is too expensive to attend for more than one semester.

1880 Cochran moves to Pittsburgh, Pennsylvania with her mother, where she helps run a boarding house for five years.

1882 Cochran's first editorial printed in *The Pittsburgh Dispatch*, a response to an article that claimed girls entering the workforce were "a monstrosity."

1885 Cochran hired full time at the *Dispatch* with a salary of $5.00 per week. Adopted the penname Nellie Bly and focused on women's rights issues.

1887 Bly relocates to New York City and begins work at *New York World*. Goes undercover for 10 days in an insane asylum, Blackwell's Island. (Later republished in a book, *10 Days in a Mad House*)

Bisland moves to New York City and begins working for *The Sun* newspaper.

1888 Bly's reports on Mexican people and culture are published in *Six Months in Mexico*.

1889 Bisland becomes an editor of *The Cosmopolitan*, while contributing to other publications like *Atlantic Monthly* and *North American Review.*

On November 14, Bly departs eastward from Hoboken, New Jersey two days after receiving her assignment. Bisland departs westward from New York, just 6 hours after receiving her assignment.

1890 Bisland, though originally leading the race, is delayed in

China. Boards the slow-moving Bothnia on January 18.

Bly returns from her journey on January 25 at 3:51 P.M.

Bisland arrives in New York on January 30, completing her journey in 76 and a half days.

Bly's *Around the World in 72 Days* published.

1891   *Seven Stages: A Flying Trip Around the World*, the compilation of all of Bisland's reports for *The Cosmopolitan*, is published.

Bisland marries Charles Whitman Wetmore, though she continues to publish books under her maiden name.

1892   Bisland and her husband construct their summer residence, Applegarth, on Long Island.

1895   **At 30, Bly retires from journalism to marry 70-year-old millionaire, Robert Seaman.**

1904   **Robert Seaman dies, Bly becomes head of husband's company, Iron Clad Manufacturing Co., and obtains patent for 55-gallon steel drum.**

1906   Bisland publishes *The Life and Letters of Lafcadio Hearn*. The book is well received and considered her most notable work. Bisland also releases *The Secret Life: Being the Book of a Heretic* the same year.

1913   **Bly covers suffrage convention in Washington, D.C., where she is also honored at the parade. Bly publishes article titled "Suffragists are Men's Superiors."**

1914   World War I begins on July 28.

Bly, having returned to journalism, reports from the

trenches.

1920   19th Amendment is passed in the United States.

1922   **Elizabeth Jane Cochrane Seaman dies from pneumonia at St. Mark's Hospital in New York City on January 27.**

1929   Bisland dies of pneumonia near Charlottesville, Virginia on January 6. She is buried at the Woodlawn cemetery in the Bronx, where Bly is also buried.

1930   Bisland's final book, *Three Wise Men of East*, is published posthumously.

BIBLIOGRAPHY

Goodman, Matthew. *Eighty Days: Nellie Bly and Elizabeth Bisland's Historic Race Around the World* (2013).

Marks, Jason. *Around the World in 72 Days: The Race Between Pulizer's Nellie Bly and Cosmpolitan's Elizabeth Bisland* (1993).

Roggencamp, Karol. Cosmopolitan, Elizabeth Bisland, and Trips Around the World. American Periodicals: A Journal of History and Ctiticism 12 (1) 2007.

The Cosmopolitan, Volume 8. Schlicht & Field, 1890.

The Cosmopolitan, Volume 9. Schlicht & Field, 1890.

NOTES ON THE TEXT

The works in this edition are based off of the original 19th century texts. In the case of Elizabeth Bisland's book, the writing was compared with text from select original articles in *The Cosmopolitan*.

Outdated spelling and punctuation were preserved in order to ensure the authenticity of the works.

IN SEVEN STAGES:
A FLYING TRIP AROUND THE WORLD

Elizabeth Bisland

FIRST STAGE

IF, ON THE 13TH of November, 1889, some amateur prophet had
foretold that I should spend Christmas Day of that year on the
Indian Ocean, I hope I should not by any open and insulting incre-
dulity have added new burdens to the trials of a hard-working sooth-
sayer— I hope I should, with the gentleness due a severe case of aber-
rated predictiveness, have merely called his attention to that passage in
the Koran in which it is written, "The Lord loveth a cheerful liar"—and
bid him go in peace. Yet I did spend the 25th day of December steaming through the waters that wash the shores of the Indian Empire,
and did do other things equally preposterous, of which I would not
have believed myself capable if forewarned of them. I can only claim
in excuse that these vagaries were unpremeditated, for the prophets
neglected their opportunity and I received no augury.

On the 14th of November of the aforementioned year, I was awakened at eight o'clock as usual by the maid with the breakfast tray—
which also contained the morning papers and a neat pile of notes and
letters. Among the latter were acceptances of invitations I had sent to
half a dozen agreeable folk to come and drink five-o'clock tea with me
on the 15th, the usual communications from one's friends on casual
subjects; an invitation to dinner; a bill; and a notice from my tailor
that I might some time during the day have the final fitting of a gown
in process of construction. All as pleasantly commonplace as the most
mild-mannered individual could expect or desire.

I read the papers leisurely, made a calm and uneventful toilet, and
the very first intimation I received of the coming thunderbolt out of
the serene sky of my existence was a hurried and mysterious request

1

at half-past ten o'clock, that I would come as soon as possible to the office of the magazine of which I was one of the editors. My appetite for mystery at that hour of the day is always lamentably feeble, and it was nearly eleven before I found time to go and investigate this one, although the office in question was only a few minutes' walk from my residence. On arriving, the editor and owner of the magazine asked if I would leave New York that evening for San Francisco and continue from there around the world, endeavoring to complete the journey in some absurdly inadequate space of time.

If my appetite for mystery at that hour is not strong, my appetite at eleven in the morning for even the most excruciatingly funny jokes may be said to actually not exist, and this one, I remember, bored me more than most. But in the course of half an hour I had become convinced that the editor really wished me to make the attempt, and I had earnestly endeavored to convince him that I meant to do nothing of the sort. To begin with, I didn't wish to. In the second place, guests were coming to my house to tea on the following day; thirdly, I was not prepared in the matter of appropriate garments for such an abrupt departure, and lastly, but most weightily, I foresaw the notoriety that an effort to outdo the feat of Jules Verne's hero was likely to bring upon me, and to this notoriety I most earnestly objected. Though for some years I had been more or less connected with journalism, I had appeared in the papers only as the contributor of unsigned articles, and the amount of distress I experienced when I first saw my name in a headline was so far beyond even my anticipations that I then and there registered a vow – Throughout this voyage I had cause to owe much gratitude to journalists for all manner of aid and civility, but I resolved in the future to so endeavor to conduct myself that they would never have reason to put my name in a headline again.

The editor and I having passed the better part of an hour going over this matter, substantial arguments were finally advanced by him which persuaded me to make the experiment of lowering the circum-navigatory record. I then took a cab and drove to my tailor for the appointed fitting and for a vigorous interview in which he was ultimately convinced that I could wear that gown at six o'clock in the evening.

The next few hours were busy ones.

To the masculine mind there appears to be something strangely exhilarating in the thought of a woman being abruptly torn from her home without sufficient time to put her wardrobe in order, and to all the men responsible for this voyage the most delightful feature apparently of the whole affair was the fact that I should be forced to get ready in five hours for a seventy-five days' voyage around the world— why this should be so a woman cannot easily divine. It fails utterly to appeal to her sense of humor. It is one of those hopeless warps in the male mind that my sex no longer attempt to comprehend or to straighten, and, finding it incurable, have learned to bear with and ignore it as far as possible.

I finally managed to get all absolute necessaries of travel into a good-sized steamer trunk, a large Gladstone bag and a shawl-strap, but found, by experience, that my progress would have been in no degree retarded, and my comfort and happiness far better served, by carrying a second and larger box with everything I could possibly have required. I managed the trip on two cloth gowns, half a dozen light bodices, and an evening silk, but might quite as well have carried my entire winter and a large part of my summer wardrobe. Happily I took the precaution of carrying plenty of pins and hair-pins. I had had some previous experience with their vicious ways, and well knew that in critical moments in foreign parts they would get up playful little games of hide-and-seek that would tend to undermine my temper, and the only sure preventive was to have geologic layers of them all through the trunk, so that a shaft might be hastily sunk through one's belongings at any moment with a serene certainty of striking rich deposits of both necessities of female existence.

... To wake up in the morning to one's usual daily duties and find one's self at night voyaging round the world is an experience calculated to surprise even a mind as composed as that of Pet Marjorie's historically placid fowl;[1] and looking back now over the time of my departure I find that, though to outward seeming I also was

"…most exceeding ca'm,"

---

1 Reference to Marjorie Fleming (1803-1811), a popular Scottish child poet

in reality I was practically stupefied with astonishment for at least two days.

I remember thinking rapidly on all manner of subjects; telling my-self warningly that it would not do to forget anything or make any mistakes, as they could not be rectified... I remember thinking that my new gown fitted very well, and that, though my face was drawn and white with the excitement and fatigues of the day, my new hat was distinctly becoming... Then there were cabs and hurry— kisses— last directions— the bumping of the box on the stair— a big bunch of pink roses (which I felt was a nice complimentary touch to my travel-ling ensemble)— everybody talking at once and giving different advice and directions— the glare of lights— the coffin-like smell of a sleep-ing-car— and I was off for seventy-five days' travel round the globe.

Then no more distinct impressions until Chicago suddenly steps across my twenty-five-thousand-mile path and it is necessary to change cars.

Even this is vague. I remember that through some mistake there was no one there to meet me as had been arranged— that I wandered about a vast, gloomy, and rather empty station in the care of a friend-ly conductor— that I sat on a high stool at a counter and quenched internal cravings, caused by lack of dinner, with tea and ham; every mouthful regarded with wan interest by the person who officiated in the echoing lunch hall— that the conductor having bidden me a com-miserating adieu, I slid away into the night, very homesick, very cross, and haunted by the bitterest suspicions of the happy results of a tea-and-ham dinner.

But with that night's sleep I slept away my stupefaction of amaze-ment, and awoke at daybreak in my right mind, and, pulling up my window curtain, found the sun almost ready to rise.

I have never permitted a vulgar familiarity to dull my keen delight in the ever-varying pageant of the breaking of day; so that, consequently, on the rare occasions when I assist at this function, my pleasure has all the enthusiasm of novelty.
Now the lifted curtain showed me a New Jerusalem... As if to one who should rise to pray at the moment when God gave his great daily fiat

of "Let there be light,"[1] there should be vouchsafed a white, luminous foreshadowing of that which it hath not entered into the heart of man to understand... Not the strangely narrow and urban vision of Patmos;[2] no streets or walls, but a limitless Land of Pearl!

Soft undulations, full and tender as the bosom of a sleeping mother, rose and fell far beyond the eye's reach, and melted into the sky. No tree or thicket broke the suave outlines, but where the thin silver veins of the streams slipped through the curves of the plain, slim, leafless willows hung, like glistening fringes... In the night a hoar frost had fallen that was to snow as sleep is to death; and the pale reaped fields, the sere meadows, and silent uplands were transfigured by the first gleam of day to a mystery and glory of silver and pearl. As the light grew, nacreous tints of milky blue and rose flushed the argent pallor of the land, and when the yellow disk rolled up over the horizon's edge I travelled for some brief space in a world of intolerable splendor, where innumerable billions of frost crystals flashed back to the sun the reflection of his shining face. Even the engine-driver was moved, I fancy, by this marvellous morning vision, for though we were far from any stopping-place, there suddenly thrilled through the silence a long, keen, triumphant blast, and we trailed as we flew floating golden plumes of steam...

As I passed in my swift circle about the great ball plunging along its planetary paths, many mighty and glorious visions of the coming and passing of light were revealed to me; but none more fair than this with that radiance of youth, whose vast, sweet nature-shadow and simulacrum the dawning is... Eternally renewed, through all ages... still, with the white peace of innocence... joyous in unwasted strength and untried powers... rosy with promise and potentialities, gilding all the commonplaceness of the landscape with golden glamours and fantasies... an Eden created out of the hollow void of night, in which to rest for one dewy, enchanted moment of purity and love before the sun with his flaming sword drives us forth to the toil and heat of the day!

In developing my mental Kodak roll after returning, I found that during this period of the journey most of the views are landscapes, seeing that I was afflicted with peculiarly uninteresting fellow-travellers

---

1 Genesis 1:3
2 Small island in Aegean sea; famously the place where the Christian Bible's *Book of Revelation* was written

who made poor subjects for snap shots. Across the aisle from me was a pair of ancient little lovers who numbered some hundred or more years between them, I fancy. They had nested long since; all their fledglings were flown, and, left alone together once more, they were on their way to Los Angeles to spend a second honeymoon among the winter orange blossoms: a pretty pale afterglow of love. But though their quaint, antiquated billing and cooing was a pleasing enough thing to watch, it is notorious that even in these second bridal journeys the outsider is very much outside, and I was driven back perforce to my window.

"A perfect day," the record says... More undulant fields clothed in the yellow stubble of the gathered harvest. Here and there black loam broken for winter sowing— a square of jet set in the pale amber— and over all a faint, turquoise sky...

That night we were in Council Bluffs, Omaha, and by chance got passage on the new fast mail-train, which had been put on as an experiment in time across the continent, and was carrying but one sleeper and the General Manager's private car.

The pace was tremendous from the start... We began to climb the Great Divide.[1] Trees and shrubs grew rare and more rare, and finally vanished altogether.

Great gray plains lay all about us, covered thinly with a withered, ashen-colored plant; the bitter results of an unequal struggle for existence, and strangely resembling in miniature the gnarled, writhen cedars that cling to wind-scourged coasts. Settlements were few and far between. Scrawny horses picked up a scant living in the desolate upland meadows; and an occasional yellow cur that came out and barked at us as we went by was the only other form of animal life to be seen. From time to time we passed a dwelling, a square cabin of gray unpainted boards, always tightly closed and the dwellers always absent somewhere on business. The only distinct proof I ever saw of the human habitance of these silent, lonely homes was a tiny pair of butternut trousers fluttering on the clothesline. The minute American citizen who should have occupied these trousers was invisible, and I greatly fear they were perhaps his only pair.

---

1   The Continental Divide of the United States, consisting of a region of mountain ranges and river systems

We climbed and climbed; always at tremendous speed, and always the land growing more desolate, and wildly drear, like the cursed site of some prehistoric Sodom, sown with salt. The air shone with a luminous clearness undreamable in coast countries, and at night the stars were huge and fierce: not the soft-gleaming palpitant planets of tropic nights, but keen and scintillant as swords... There was something hideous and brutal in the doom laid upon this unhappy territory, as of a Prometheus chained on the mountain-tops; its blood dried to dust in its veins, and lifting a scarred face of gray despair to the rainless sky.

From time to time we crossed a feeble, trickling stream; but no verdure marked the course of its waters bitter and fruitless as tears. During the night our way lay through that still more desolate portion of this dry region named, with simple and expressive literalness, the Bad Lands; and here again I saw a most wonderful coming of the light. The moon, wan with the dawn, hung directly in the zenith, and on the eastern rim of the ghostly gray plain, under the quivering jewel of the morning star, burned the first vague flush of day. Slowly a dusky amethyst radiance filled the sapphire bowl of the sky, quenching the stars one by one as it rose, and when the sun showed over the world's edge the cup was brimmed, and the pale moon shone faintly in its depths, like the drowned pearl of the Egyptian queen. There was no eye but mine to see, yet in the midst of unpeopled desolation the majestic ceremonies of the sky were fulfilled with the same slow pomp and splendor as if all the worshippers of the Sun knelt in awed wonder to see the Bridegroom come forth of his chamber.

Our speed through this part of the country was terrible. Five hours away from Ogden we were two hours and a half behind the time set for our arrival there. Some three quarters of a million hung upon our arriving promptly and getting the track clear for ourselves beyond, not to mention many other important considerations that could scarcely be reckoned in figures; for a great government contract for mails would be either lost or won by morning. A certain engineer, whose name was Foley— or words to that effect— was telegraphed to meet us at the next stop. He was a gentleman of Irish extraction who labored under an entire absence of physical timidity, and who remarked with jovial determination, as he climbed into the cab, that he would "get us to Ogden—or hell— on time." Several times during that five hours' ride the betting stood ten to one on the latter goal, and Hades was hot favorite. The grade at this part of the road has a descent of 93 feet in a mile, and the track corkscrewed through gorges and cañons with but small margin between us and destruction. To these considerations Mr. Foley was cheerfully indifferent, and pulling out the throttle he let the engine have her head at the rate of sixty-five miles an hour. The train rocked like a ship at sea, and sleepers held to their berths in terror, the more nervous actually succumbing to *mal de mer.*[1] The plunge of the engine, that now and again whimpered affrightedly in the darkness, could be felt through the whole train, as one feels beneath one the fierce play of the loins of a runaway horse. From the rear car the tracks were two lines of fire in the night. The telegraph pole reeled backwards from our course and the land fled from under us with horrible nightmare weirdness. The officers of the train became alarmed and ordered speed slackened; but Mr. Foley, consulting his watch, regretted with great firmness that he could not oblige them. One man rolled in an anguish of terror on the floor; and the General Manager, engaged in a late game of whist, regarding the sufferer with sympathetic interest as he took the odd trick with the thirteenth trump, remarked that it was such episodes as this in American life that made us a nation of youthful gray-heads.

We arrived in Ogden on time.

Mr. Foley dismounted with alacrity from his cab, remarked that these night rides were prone to give a man cold, and went in pursuit of an antidote behind a swinging Venetian door on the corner, and we saw him no more.

From here the vast, desolate uplands, 8000 feet high in the keen dry air, showed no further sign of human habitation between the stations, and were ornamented only with the frequent jackrabbit, the occasional coyote, and now and then an arrangement of teepees. Indians crowded about the train at every stop; those of the female sex who were blessed with offspring permitting us to view the living contents of the corded parcels they carried on their backs in exchange for small current coin. The pappoose, I discovered, is the original Baby Bunting. He slumbers with stoical composure in a nest of rabbit skins – presumably those for which "papa went a-hunting" – that line a portable wooden

1   seasickness

cradle into which he is strapped, and from which, I am told, he rarely emerges during infancy. The girls and boys from six to sixteen I found very pretty, with smooth red skins, glittering teeth and eyes, and black Vandyked locks[1]. Those whom years had overtaken were indescribably wrinkled and parched. Old squaws squatted in the dust huddled in blankets, and were as impassive as ancient worm-eaten idols. A coin dropped into their hands brought a mumble and a glance from their rusted eyes; but indifference did not wound them, neither did the fast train or any of its passengers excite their curiosity – the vagaries of the white man were so numerous that nervous prostration would be a sure consequence of any attempt to interest themselves in his doings, and peace and composure lay only in entirely ignoring him.

All through this country the air had a delicious dry perfume, like the smell of parching vegetation, that was stimulating and wholesome as the resinous incense of pines.

The night before reaching San Francisco we found our first trees again, at a little wayside eating station, where a long row of poplars stood up stiffly in the dusk near our path, and a tiny fountain plashed with an enchanting, cool melodiousness... The air was soft and spring-like and the moist darkness pleasant with a smell as of white clover. It could not, of course, in November, have been really the sweet early flowers of the grass, yet I know nothing else that gives out the same clean, delicate perfume; nor can I guess from what that pure vernal fragrance did arise, that was like the first breath from a promised land after long wandering in a country of wilderness and drought.

Sacramento stopped us for a moment at daylight, and here we found rich, juicy verdure, watery marshes, and the first outer edges of that yellow wave from China which has broken upon the Pacific coasts. Still there were no trees. Only grassy, rounded hills, with white sea-mists trailing among them. A country much like that about Newport, but without that icy breath always in the air of the upper Atlantic coast. There was a certain genial tenderness in this atmosphere that even in the hottest day of August the eastern coast never knows.

At fifteen minutes past nine the nose of the ferry-boat from Oak-land touches the San Francisco wharf. We have crossed the continent

---

1 Style of facial hair popularized by 17th Century painter Anthony van Dyck; all facial hair is shaven except for a mustache and goatee

in four days and twenty hours— thanks to Mr. Foley— and the distance between New York and the Western metropolis is reduced by a whole day. A great achievement! There are crowds of reporters waiting to interview everybody; General Manager, engineer, conductor— even me. We splash cheerfully through the warm rain and oozing mud— the wet season began two days ago— with pleased faces that our tremendous journey is over, walking with free strides and swinging arms because of the long, cramping confinement.

To my eyes, accustomed to the soaring loftiness of New York architecture, this city seems astonishingly low. Three or four stories at the most the average is. Because of earthquake they say; but latterly these have almost entirely ceased to occur, as if the land had grown to realize that civilization would not tolerate such impulsive ways, and had gradually abandoned them shamefacedly, as being in extremely bad taste. Consequently a few of the more recent buildings have begun to climb, Babel-like, into the dripping skies.

One gets a remarkable impression of newness here such as a Londoner might on his first landing in New York. Every one tells you, "I have been here a year— six months— three months— three years." One begins to believe that no one was ever born here. All the buildings look new and fresh, and the whole atmosphere of the place is charged with a vigorous, disrespectful sort of youth.

The city, or at least the Spanish part of it, was founded in the year of the Declaration of Independence, but the American town is only forty or fifty years old. The hotel at which I stop was erected in 1875. It is a huge caravansary, built around a square and enclosing a vast asphalted court adorned with palms and ferns. There is an arcade within this court where the typical American hotel frequenter tips back his chair, reads the papers, and smokes. On the outer side of the arcade are shops of every description, so that one may purchase all the ordinary needs of life without leaving one's lodging-place.

I find here that my progress must be arrested for two days, as the arrangements for hurrying the departure of the ship have fallen through; and I do not altogether grieve, for this tremendous pace for thousands of miles across the country has told upon my nerves to an absurd degree, and I wonder, as I shiver with exhaustion and tremble with nameless, undefined apprehensions, how the coming generation that is to travel a hundred and a hundred and fifty miles an hour will bear the strain of it. Some process of adaption to a nerve-destroying environment will take place doubtless, humanity being so elastic in such matters.

Meantime, there is some space to investigate this first one of the many great cities I must pass through. The editors of the San Francisco "Examiner," who have shown me every courtesy from the moment of my arrival, invite me to luncheon at the Cliff House, which stands on the very western edge of the continent, upon one of the pillars of the Golden Gate.

There is still a soft, warm rain falling when we start. Roses climb around the porches of the residences and hang heavy-drenched blossoms amid their shining wet leaves, perfuming the damp city streets with delicious garden odors. Should I shut my eyes to the hills I mount and descend, the warmth, the humidity, and the rose odors would make me believe myself in New Orleans again... In that far distant city I might be going on just such an expedition as this to Spanish Fort on the Lakeside. It gives me a sense of nostalgia, not for the people and city I have but just left, but for an earlier home, where I would have found just such carelessly happy geniality as among these witty, good-looking men who regard the delays of a train with amiable indifference, and see their day slip from them with the carelessness of a spendthrift.

The train crawls along the edge of the harbor shut in between the grassy, treeless hills. We wind around their flanks in perilous fashion for some space, for the harbor juts deeply into the land, and as we cling to their steep sides we hear the waves dashing beneath. There is a sudden turn at last, and before us lies spread the Western Ocean! ... There is a joyous shock of astonishment in the sight... A sense of discovery, of splendid vastness, of a rich new experience seized and dominated. For one keen instant not he who stood

"Silent upon a peak in Darien"[1]

felt a more magnificent dilation of spirit than I.

---

1   John Keats, "On First Looking into Chapman's Homer" (1816)

We lunch, jovially and sumptuously, upon the sea's edge. Already the day is declining as we finish. The rain has ceased, and in the west the curtain of cloud lifts. On a balcony that overhangs the water we watch the sunset. Three great crags stand up sharply two hundred yards away— Seal Rocks— covered with grumbling, barking sea lions, the city's pets, whom the law protects. They look much like fat pigs from this distance. At the last moment the sun flames out gloriously; reddens all the heavens, and gilds a rippling road for me across the watery world I must traverse. It is a sign of promise, they tell me.

The ride home in the cable car is a curious experience. The streets are of the most astonishing steepness still, though millions have been spent in grading the hills. On each of the cars is a small open space in front where one may sit if one likes and enjoy the sensation of plunging down the most startling inclines and yet see the car stop short at perilous points to allow a traveller to leisurely dismount. The road leads past the famous Nob Hill, where the bonanza kings have their residences – huge wooden palaces of the most rococo designs. It is said that these half-dozen residences cost $9,000,000 to build. James C. Flood's house is of brown stone, the only dwelling of that material in the state, all of the stone having been imported from the East at prodigious expense. It is slightly reminiscent of the Vanderbilt house in New York, but much more florid in style. One of these palaces— the property of a bonanza relict— is of a curious lead color, which, with its overwhelmingly ornate decorations, gives it an odd resemblance to a gigantic hot-air stove.

There were beautiful public gardens, great public buildings, and many relics of the ancient Spanish domination to be seen in this charming city, but my flight was too rapid to pause for these. That night I saw the quarter known locally as China Town, peeped into some of the huge, splendid theatres and restaurants, and then, at three o'clock the next day, set sail for Japan.

Second Stage

Amid my dreams has always been a carefully elaborated and favorite one of the day upon which I should at last set out on my travels. I had thought out all the details of this episode, and what my emotions should be – a tasteful mingling of regret and exultation – as I bade my unfortunate home-staying friends adieu, and the great Cunarder[1] swung free from the docks, bearing me away to the delights and mysteries of foreign lands. Even in my childhood my sympathy for the heroes in the fairy tales was always keenest at the moment when they waved their hands in farewell and turned their faces at last towards the magical adventures that stalked about impatiently awaiting their advent in the strange countries where their havens lay. So it was a matter of active regret to me that by leaving America from the other side of the continent, this long-dreamed-of incident on the Cunard pier was forever robbed of the salt of novelty.

The White Star steamship Oceanic, of the Occidental and Oriental line— Charles H. Kempson commander— sailed from San Francisco at three o'clock Thursday afternoon of November the 21st, and I found it even under these circumstances a very exciting thing to leave one's country for the first time.

It was much as I had imagined the other picture: the cabin full of ornate flower pieces; luggage thumping down the companion-way; people running back and forth with the apparent purposelessness of ants in a hill; and the friends of the departing standing about in that helpless discomfort and uselessness that make even those whose hearts

---

1   A ship operated by the Cunard Line of Steamships

are torn by the separation long to be gone and put them out of their awkward misery.

Many of the pleasant acquaintances I had made in this short visit to San Francisco had come to bid me Godspeed, accompanied by a delegation who had got wind of my eccentric performance and came with no other credentials than a desire to gape. This was a figure not in my original picture. The whole army of martyrs to curiosity had afflicted me sorely in those two days on the Pacific coast, sending up their cards in the hotel with urgent messages, and on admission confessing with placid impudence that their sole excuse for this intrusion was a desire to look at me— presumably as a sort of inexpensive freak show. Experience demonstrated, however, the high and delightful effectiveness of an elaborate and astonished civility, that never failed to reduce their robust self-confidence to limp and writhing embarrassment in exactly three minutes, after which discovery I put the heathen to the edge of that manner and smote them hip and thigh...

It must be admitted that my emotions on the occasion of this departure were much less tastefully mingled than I had planned they should be, low spirits and loneliness being such active ingredients that they disguised all other flavors, and it is to a little incident I shall forever remember with pleasure that I did not leave America quite unmixedly miserable. At the moment when the gong had warned all visitors ashore there was handed up to me from the wharf a great nosegay of white chrysanthemums and roses, to which was attached a card inscribed "J. M. Prather," and bearing "good wishes" and "New Orleans" pencilled in the corner. A hat was lifted from a handsome gray head, and two kind dark Southern eyes gave me a smile of such friendliness and good-will that it warmed my heart like a greeting from my own people. This unknown gentleman taking the trouble to bid me a silent, fragrant farewell seems to me the most delicate and charming impulse of that much-misinterpreted and scoffed-at Southern chivalry, and should he ever see this I wish him to know how pleasant and lasting was the perfume of his flowers and kindly thought...

Perhaps this is the proper moment to speak of a feature that was to me one of the most interesting of this unusual voyage. I was a young woman, quite alone, and doing a somewhat conspicuous and eccentric thing, yet throughout the entire journey I never met with other than the most exquisite and unfailing courtesy and consideration; and if I had been a princess with a suite of half a hundred people I could have felt no safer or happier. It seems to me this speaks very highly for the civilization existing in all travelled parts of the globe, when a woman's strongest protection is the fact that she is unprotected. I owe a gratitude beyond all adequate expression for the good-will shown me everywhere. It would require many pages to catalogue the names of those who gave up their comfort to insure mine, who considered no trouble of consequence if it secured me from annoyance and disappointment, and who spared no exertion to make my journey speedy and comfortable. In every port I touched I found the kindest of welcomes, and I believe I have put a girdle round the earth of warm and generous friends whom I shall always remember with affection and gratitude. The staff of the San Francisco "Examiner," T. D. McKay, the Burlington Passenger Agent, the owners and officers of the Oceanic, Lieutenant Mitchell McDonald, the Norddeutscher Lloyd[1] people, and my fellow-passengers everywhere are among those who assisted me by every means in their power to effect my object and make my journey agreeable.

…The last wooden link with the shore is withdrawn. There is a fluttering storm of handkerchiefs— a brief space of water in the beautiful bay— and then we pass away to the west through the Gates of Gold.

America sinks out of sight, slowly— a vision of green hills in level sunshine. We are divided from it now by a long ridge of whirling foam— the bar, where we begin to rise and fall with the first pulse of the sea. Even that vanishes at last and we plunge forward lonelily on the heaving, dusky plain. The wind of the coming night is cold, and the fluttering paper prayers the Chinese passengers cast overboard to insure a safe voyage it catches and whips sharply away, like autumn leaves falling in the November night.

Not yet have the four hundred pigtails in the steerage composed themselves for the voyage. They run to and fro with queer-colored parcels of strange shapes and keep up a ceaseless, shrill, guinea-fowl chatter, very cheerful in tone. Most of them are going home to settle down upon money made from the "foreign devils," and whatever happens they can laugh.

1   German Shipping Company

Even up on the hurricane deck the chill sea wind is tainted with that clinging, pervasive odor that one comes to recognize as "the Chinese smell." No cleanliness can combat it. The ship from stem to stern is wonderfully clean, yet never in the whole voyage is one quite free from the sense of it. Pierre Loti declares it can be smelt on the Chinese coast, while the ship is still miles at sea. On analyzation it appears to be compounded of the bitter fumes of opium and the smoke of incense sticks. An object once permeated by the odor is never rid of it again, and all China reeks of these strange stifling fumes.

I smelt it first in the Chinese Quarter of San Francisco— a place that left a sinister, menacing impression upon my mind. A sense of this being the first gnawing yellow of an overwhelming flood – forced forward by the irresistible propulsion of an over-population behind. One more of those huge, blind migrations of hunger which, like a tidal wave, have obliterated flourishing peoples and races in the full flush of power and civilization, nations who have vanished as herbage vanishes before the gigantic, myriad voracity of desert locusts. Conquered by the mere dead weight of numbers that fill up interposing gulfs with countless dead, bridging all moats between food and that pitiless, relentless famine.

China has 500,000,000 of population, each unit trained by generations of bitter struggle for survival to an industry and economy almost superhuman. California has already nearly 100,000 of them; 30,000 living in San Francisco. Every westward-going steamer carries from three to four hundred home, men who have in a short time secured a competence, and are returning to enjoy it; and yet their number in America apparently suffers no diminution. Fenced out by law from California, the wave flows around this obstacle into British Columbia and trickles back, drop by drop, into the United States. We do not assimilate them as we do our other immigration. They hold to their own national dress, manners, and food. That part of San Francisco abandoned to them grows daily like a Chinese city. They gut standing houses and reconstruct the interiors to suit their needs. Outside, lanterns hang in front of doors that have Chinese signs, and above these, frail balconies are strung about the windows where jars of chrysanthemums droop their ragged blossoms over the sill. The air is thick with Oriental odors. Street stalls expose for sale vegetables and fruits unknown to us, and the tiny shops with their Chinese furnishings and inscriptions sell wares which no American seeks.

At eleven at night this transplanted city of Cathay is still all alive; the streets crowded with a moving stream of black blouses and yellow faces— every one cheerful, chattering, and wide awake. The shops stand open, and workmen continue their labors as if it were still high noon. In a basement, a few steps down from the street, gold workers toil in a little black room, seven by ten; a wheezy gas jet flares above their heads, and directly in front of each, on the work bench at which they sit, is a small bowl of cocoanut oil in which smoulder faintly a handful of thin white racines. The flame from these, with a blowpipe, softens and fuses the metals in which they work. Though the place is so narrow and squalid, the bracelets and clasps in process of manufacture – ornamented with ingeniously varied chisel marks – are of considerable value. The workers are impassively indifferent to our curiosity. They work without raising their eyes as we handle their goods, and do not even glance up as we leave, toiling on unhurriedly, though the night is half spent. Here, as everywhere, tiny corkscrews of pungent smoke curl up from a bunch of smouldering Joss sticks stuck in a little earthenware bowl of sand.

Plunging through a narrow door, we grope along a low, tortuous passage, descend to the cellar by rickety, greasy stairs, thread more back corridors, where, in little branching rooms, somnolent bundles lie motionless on shelves – sodden with poppy fumes, past greasy, hot kitchens and cackling cooks, with hissing midnight meals in preparation – and emerge at last into a crowded apartment where men with hideous masks and flaming dresses – like mediæval devils in a mystery play – stand idly about waiting for a cue, and others, radiant and befeathered as tropical birds, pass to the stage by the two doors.

A hideous din of banging, scraping, and clashing of brass. Above all a shrill monotonous chant in a penetrating falsetto. It is the greenroom and wings of the Dom Quai Yuen – The Elegant Flower-House – where the gems of the classic drama of China are enacted, and where the actors lodge, eat, and smoke their opium.

The performance began at four in the afternoon, and has gone on without intermission ever since. It will end at twelve.

Rapid changes of costume— stiff with gold needlework— are taking place. Faces are being painted— those of the fiends with Oriental ingenuity of hideousness— huge beards are assumed, and gorgeous head-dresses with flags and long pheasant feathers waving above them. We go through the left door and sit on the stage, as if it were the time of Queen Bess[1] and this was one of Mr. William Shakespeare's new plays.

The play goes on, undisturbed by our presence, the actors carefully stepping to one side as they pass us.

The auditorium is packed tight as a sardine box with standing Chinamen who listen as long as they find it amusing and then go away. Up in the gallery two or three sheep-faced Chinese women lend a somewhat indifferent attention.

The heat is frightful... There are no windows and but one door, and the smell is overpowering. Not a stench of unwashed bodies, as in a low-class Caucasian crowd, but this same strangling mixture of opium and incense. By contrast even the ill-smelling streets are delightful, and we escape.

The detective, who bears himself with amiable, scornful courage in this resort of "Highbinders,"[2] leads the way through fetid, crime-stained alleys. A loud warning note sounds from somewhere near us, and in an instant the street swarms with men passing composedly with their hands under their blouses. The detective turns into a low room with a double nail-studded door. A table covered with a strip of matting and two benches are the only furniture. The owner is calmly smoking a cigarette, apparently engaged in some remote and subtle ratiocinative process. Ten seconds ago, in this room and fifty others, the game of fan-tan was in furious progress. That one note emptied them all.

We mount stairs to a dingy Joss-house,[3] where more incense sticks burn before a trinity of calm-eyed idols— the God of the Sombre Heavens, the God of the Southern Seas, and the God of Happy Wealth – and stroll through the rooms of a restaurant beautiful with carvings and silk hangings, Kakemono and marble and ebony furniture.

---

1   Elizabeth I of England
2   Member of a Chinese secret society
3   Chinese temple

But the night wanes and our heads are giddy with this clinging, sickening odor. We will go back to the hotel.

It is the smell of the Chinese sailors and passengers that wakes the memories of the strange sights and sounds.

The night is cold. Top-gallant sails are being set to catch the rising evening wind, and the cries of the pig-tailed yellow seamen are shrill and raucous, like the interjectional and acrimonious talk of cats on a back fence.

It is time to go below and prepare for the first night at sea.

For the next four days my only memory of the Pacific Ocean is of a foaming flood of emerald that roars past my port-hole, making a dull green twilight within. I see only this and the slats of the upper berth. There are six of these slats. Of this I am unwaveringly sure— though I am not usually accurate about figures— because I counted them several thousand times. It was the only mental process of which I was capable during the long nights while I lay and listened to the loud combat of the thundering squadrons outside, whose white plumes flashed into sight again with the first gray gleam of day— the battle still raging. Every plank in the ship creaked and groaned, and shrieked without once pausing to take breath, and I regarded with contemptuous indifference the frantic tobogganing of my most treasured possessions all over the stateroom. What were the fleeting things of this world to one to whose unexampled sufferings death must soon put a period? It was comforting to think that one's last will and testament was made, but hateful the contemplation of burial at sea. It was such an unnecessarily tragical end to this ridiculous wild-goose-chase.

The fifth day the boiling pot of the sea subsided, and I began to take beef tea[1] and resolution to live. Other women were also beginning to straggle back to life on deck— pale, wan, and with neglected hair tied up in lace scarfs. They lay in steamer-chairs swathed in rugs, and were indifferent about their appearance and to the charms of conversation. The week was nearly done before the whole ship's company assembled at table, and we began to take note of our fellow-voyagers in this water caravansary.

It was a cosmopolitan crew— Norwegians, Russians, English, French, Japanese, Americans, Germans, Hungarians, and even one

1   Broth made from beef bones, a typical home remedy for sickness

Manx-man— our chief-engineer, with a pleasant "out-country" flavor to his speech, and full of tales of a profoundly esoteric humor – a kindly, mellow nature, like one of William Black's old Highland lairds.

There is the Englishman who has made his fortune in China and retired, and is bringing a new-made wife out, by way of America, to see the East, where he had lived so long— an angular English girl, containing the potential British matron, who knits gray stockings and keeps herself carefully aloof from acquaintances that might be detrimental in the future.

The typical American girl is with us, travelling alone— greyhound-waisted, tiny of foot, clad with tailor-made neatness, and armed with an amateur photographer's outfit. She is on her way to visit the American Minister to Japan.

And a couple from Georgia, who have lived twenty years in Los Angeles, but have lost nothing of their genial old-fashioned Georgia ways and looks, and still speak with a soft Southern drawl.

We have a full cargo of missionaries— fifteen in all— mostly young women, and, on this occasion, all Presbyterians. There is much missionary travel back and forth on this line, for the work of proselytization in China and Japan goes briskly on. Among them is a young doctor, who has just taken her degree, and is going to the East to save both souls and bodies. She wears "reform" clothes, and has a strong, well-cut face, from which the heavy hair is brushed smoothly back. She regards the ten years' exile into which she is entering as merely the apprenticeship of her professional career, and is likely to consider the physical welfare of her patients of more importance than the acceptance of her creed. She is the plain, wholesome product of Northwestern life and a Northwestern female college— speaking the speech of that region with a broad and blurring R... Her future is simple and pleasant to guess at.

One is less sure of the handsome, slim girl of twenty with deep-set gray eyes, and the delicate pointed fingers of what the palmists call "the psychic hand," indicating undue spiritual intensity of nature. In a spasm of the romantic exaltation to which young women of her age are subject, she has condemned herself to a decade of lonely exile in a remote Japanese town; but a pair of enchanting dimples in her fresh young cheeks war with the maiden severity of her earnest eyes, and she is not indifferent to a young girl's natural joys, though she mentions them loftily as things in the remote past appealing to her – now forever put away. It would be pretty and amusing, as a girl's exalté fancies are sometimes, were not the sacrifice of her best young years to indifferent heathen not so real and so melancholy to think on. One is tempted to pray that some Cymon may come to rescue this Christian Iphigenia[1] from her squalid little Oriental altar before the knife of distaste and ennui shall have murdered her youth and charm.

The sea is becoming very blue.

The emerald fades as we pass into these vast liquid fields, and the blue deepens and deepens until one finds no words to express, no simile to convey, the intensity of its burning azure. Sapphires would be pale and cold beside this sea— palpitating with wave shadows deep as violets, yet not purple, and with no touch of any color to mar its perfect hue. It flames with unspeakable, many-faceted splendor, under a sky that is wan by contrast with its profundity of tint, and the very foam that curls away from our wake is blue as the blue shadows in snow. The cutter-like prow of our ship flings up two delicate plumes of pearl, and the sunlight shining through these has wrought upon the blue floor beneath us a rainbow arch that encircles our onward path, moves with our moving, and shimmers upon the waving flood as the iris shimmers upon a peacock's breast...

It is here enormously deep. The longest plummet line ever let into the sea went down here, and only found bottom at the depth of 4000 fathoms. If one should choose this place to be cured of the wound of living he could never reach the firm earth beneath. He would hang forever in these soundless, icy depths, moving scarcely at all with the slow, obscure flux of the deep-sea tides, surrounded by strange, formless, protoplasmic life, blind, senseless, and inert— the germs from which through billions of years he himself had risen— working out here in these blue solitudes of silence the mysteries of generation and upward growth. He would never perish or be devoured or reabsorbed like his fellows, but age after age would lie enclosed as in a frozen blue gem, with burial more splendid and secure than the Pharaohs... The voyage is a lonely one. In all these many thousand miles we never see a sail or any shore. There is no sea life about us, save of the sword-winged birds

1   Reference to Fredric Leighton's painting, *Cymon and Iphigenia* (1884)

that follow us from San Francisco to Japan without sign of fatigue, wheeling easily after us as we plunge onward at the rate of three hundred and fifty miles a day, and having quite the appearance of loafing along and waiting for us to catch up. It fills one with a sort of despair to get up every morning and see the same sea, the same horizon, the same birds— nothing to mark our progress except the figures marked each day at noon on the map hanging over the companion-way.

Our small, circumscribed world daily grows in importance in our estimation. We know intimately the characters, tastes, and histories of our companions. We take each other's photographs, and exchange warm professions of friendship; we advise each other about the future, and confide the incidents of the past. We play draughts[1] and quoits [2]and cards; we get together in corners and criticise the missionaries and are criticised by them— and all the while go steadily westward and westward, driven by wind and steam... With all our brown sails spread, we fleet through the moonlight with stately courtesyings. Calm mornings dawn behind us. We sail under the vast arches of rainbows that rise out of the water but half a mile away from the ship and span the whole heavens; and at evening the sun falls into the sea, straight before us, amid unimaginable flames and glories, where for an hour we rise and fall on the heaving bosom of the ocean in a great dream-world of jewelled splendor of sapphire and gold, of purple and pearl...

This lonely vessel swarms with life. Down in the steerage are over four hundred yellow people... All sorts and conditions of Chinamen going home with their earnings. Many are merchants who have a merchant's pass, which enables them to return to America when their business across the water is finished. One old gentleman with an iron-gray pigtail is a "Forty-niner." He came to California during the gold fever, and is now going home to die in China, having thriftily calculated that it costs less to cross the waters alive than it does in a coffin. He was rich in those early days, but, as he explains in fluent and profane American, fan-tan, poker, euchre, and horse races have reduced his store to an immodest competence. However, as he nears the Chinese shore he feels he can afford to wear a magnificent and lurid pair of brocaded trousers, of

---

1   Checkers
2   Ring-toss

the sort popular in China when he left, and still – after forty years – of the very latest fashion.

Down in these Chinese quarters, placed where he can catch the best of the healing salt breezes, is a young fellow of six-and-twenty, who lies motionless all day, with crossed hands and half-closed eyes. These hands and the sunken face are the color of old wax, as impassive as if indeed they were cut from some such substance.

It is common among the emigrants to America to fall sick with a consumption and to struggle back in this way to die at home. He seems afraid to breath or move, lest he should waste the failing oil or snuff out the dying flame ere he reaches his yearned-for home— the Flowery Kingdom— the Celestial Empire!

On the after-deck fan-tan rages all day long; also an intricate game of chess, or dominoes, when a less dangerous amusement is desired. Forward there is a space for women, where five or six retroussé-eyed females find a temporary home. They are gentle, mild-faced little creatures, who are quick to give smile for smile and answer English amiabilities with what appears to be equally amiable Chinese. All the sailors are Chinamen, and are popular with the commanders. They are obedient, not given to strikes at inconvenient moments, and are un-der the control of a boatswain, one of their countrymen with a keen, shrewd face and an air of unquestioned authority. He hires them and pays them their wages, and the owners reckon with him alone. He is a person of consequence and wealth, and owns much real estate in San Francisco, sufficient proof that the Chinese, as the white Jack Tar,[1] is the victim of fraud and oppression.

These ships, like those of the merchant Antonio, voyage to the East for cargoes of tea, silk, and spices. There are three lines between China and America; two, the Pacific Mail and the Oriental and Occiden-tal— controlled by the Central Pacific Railway magnates, Huntington, Crocker, and Stanford— have their termini in the United States, and the Canadian Mail sails from Vancouver. They carry out to China re-turning subjects of the yellow emperor, passengers for the East, flour, Connecticut clocks, hats, shoes, and such select assortments of Yankee notions as are required by the Barbarian.

---

1   Sailor

Returning, they fetch hundreds of bales of raw silk, worth $700 apiece, which must be rushed across the continent immediately upon arrival, and have left the ship and are on their way across the country to the Eastern mills before the passengers have landed. The usual cargo is from 1200 to 1300 bales, and in June the tea trade begins, 1700 to 2700 tons in every ship— the whole of the Formosa crop, some 6,000,000 tons, comes to us. The English will not drink the light, perfumed Oolong. They demand something coarser and stronger. Spices, pepper, and tapioca come from Singapore, and gambier in great quantities for coloring American beer, with thousands of bales of gunnysacks from Calcutta for American wheat, and, from Manila, hemp and jute.

At last there comes a day when one rises in the morning and the sailors, pointing to the horizon, say, "That is Japan," and one cries with cheerful excitement, "Yes! yes!" though there is nothing but same monotonous sea and sky visible to the unpractised eye.

The missionaries all land here, and are full of emotion at arriving at the scene of their labors to save immortal souls. The Chinese steerage clatter more noisily than ever, pleased to behold this outlying portal of their home. The Japanese poet Kachi, returning from travels in America, where he has been arranging for translations of his works into English, lifts his head again. He is a grave, mysterious-eyed person, who has not spoken to any one during the voyage, and has usually had his face— his dark, smooth, mask-like face— hidden behind a French novel.

This face is lit now with a fine patriotic glow as a delicate gray cloud grows up along the edge of the water and slowly a vast cone-like cumulus, a lofty rosy cloud, takes shape and form, gathers clearness of outline, deepens its hue of pink and pearl, melts softly into the gray beneath, soars sharply into the blue above, and reveals— Fujiyama ... the divine mountain!

Having seen it, one no longer marvels that it dominates the Japanese imagination; that every fan, screen, and jar, every piece of lacquer and porcelain, bears somewhere its majestic, its exquisite outline. Twelve thousand three hundred and sixty-five feet high,[1] it rises up alone and unmarred by surrounding peaks; alone in fair calm beauty— the highest mountain in all the islands. In the old Aino tongue—

1   The actual height is 12, 388 feet.

the Ainos whom the warlike Japanese conquered and drove north-ward—"Fuji" signified "Mother of Fire," and the Japanese added the word "yama," their general term for all mountains. For more than two hundred years the Mother of Fire has been clad in snows and has made no sign. Traces of terrible ancient rages lie along her ravaged sides; but her passions are all stilled, peace and purity crown her; and he who hath seen Fuji-yama's fair head lifted out of the blue sea and flushed with the dream of the coming day layeth his hand upon his mouth and is silent, but the memory of it passeth not away while he lives.

Third Stage

AND IT CAME TO PASS that on the morning of the 8th day of December we rose up and perceived that we had come unto Fan-land... to the Islands of Porcelain... to Shikishima— the Country of Chrysanthemums. The place across whose sky the storks always fly by day, and the ravens by night— where cherry-branches with pink-and-white blossoms grow out of nothing at all to decorate the foreground, and where ladies wear their eyes looped up in the corners, and gowns in which it is so impossible that any two-legged female should walk that they pass their lives smiling and motionless upon screen and jars...

Sailing so long due west, we had at last reached the East. The real East, not east of anywhere, but the East... the birthplace of Man, and of his Religions... of Poetry and Porcelains, of Tradition, and of Architecture. And I who had come to it from the country of common-sense, of steam-ploughs and newspaper enterprise, bowed my head reverently in the portal of this great Temple of the World, and fell upon my knees, awed by its mysterious age and vastness... My heart within me was stirred, and I was led to great recklessness in the use of capital letters.

There lies here, by the gates of the East, a land, as we discovered, stranger and more wonderful even than we had dreamed. Captain Kempson had steered us in sixteen days from the coast of America to where a mountain of pink pearl rose out of the sea; and when the gray clouds about its base resolved themselves into land, we found they were the green hills of fairyland! It is revealed to those who live long enough and who go up and down the earth, and to and fro upon the face of it, that man has never conceived an ideal that is not somewhere a reality. There are women living as beautiful as any of the marble Venuses;

26

there are even men as pure and high-minded as Galahad; there are
Edens in existence— perchance, somewhere, there is something nearly
resembling Paradise— and certainly the enchanting fairy dreams of
our childhood, ravished from us by the cruel misrepresentation of our
elders, have an actual existence, yet more fantastic and delicious than
our baby minds could ever have imagined, in these islands lying hard
by the coast of China... Let no one scoffingly set this down as a figure
of speech. All who have every set foot on these shores bear the same
testimony to the elfin witchery of Nippon— the land of the rising
sun. There may be something suggestive, in this name, of that eternal
tie between youth and the dawn, because certainly here the people
are still children, and possess all a child's sweetness, simplicity, and
imaginativeness... I spent, alas! less than two days in these fairy islands;
but all ballad literature declares with great positiveness (see Thomas
the Rhymer, the ballad of May-Janet, Mary of Caldon-Low, and other
notorious examples) that, having spent even the briefest moment in
the Land of the Fays engenders an unquenchable yearning that must
some day, some hour, bring one back again – and with this I comfort
my heart...

   We double a headland, pass a slim white pharos,[1] and we make
our way up the long bay to Yokohama. The town has been in existence
only since 1859, when Japan opened a few ports to foreign trade, but
already it is a place of size and importance; for what the Japanese did,
they did thoroughly. They jettied the harbor, built ample wharves and
go-downs, and bade their own people confine themselves to the inner
town across the canal, and not encroach upon the Europeans.

   The queerest craft come to meet us in the bay— light-winged
junks with gray and russet sails, so carelessly and crazily built that were
the sea to but give them a playful slap she would crush them in an
instant to kindling-wood. Their feebleness insures her gentleness, it
would seem, for they spread their great butterfly wings and skim along
without fear, going far afield for the fishing. Many large ships lie at
anchor in the harbor— American men-of-war, English, French, and
German merchant vessels, and a few neat Japanese coasters. I am told
the Japanese were childishly impatient of the foreign tutelage necessary
to acquire knowledge of steam navigation, and in haste to try the ex-

1   Lighthouses

periment of running a boat themselves. Starting off with a native crew for the first time, all went well until it was necessary to stop, and this they suddenly discovered they had forgotten how to do. Great was the panic, and she was driving fast on shore, when one bethought him to put the helm hard down; and then they steamed round and round in a circle for hours until steam was exhausted, and the boat stopped of her own volition... After which they went to school again for a bit and learned steam navigation in all its branches.

A cloud of sampans[1] descend upon us as we anchor – craft as crazy as the junks – made of three unpainted boards lightly fastened together, with a sharp prow and wide, high stern, across which the standing boatman lays a long oar, and waggles it carelessly in the water, attaining thereby an astonishing speed. Like a certain famous epitaph, it is "simple but sufficient."[2]

These boatmen are the vanguard of elves from Elfland— small, lithe creatures with good-looking yellow countenances, bearing no resemblance to the flat-faced Chinese, and with thick, shining black locks, through which is twisted a blue fillet. Their dress is of dark blue cotton; sometimes the gown-shape called a kimono, and worn by both sexes; but for the most part a costume much like that worn in England in the time of Henry II – cloth hose to the waist, a short jerkin, and loose sleeveless coat reaching to the hips. These blue coats have on the back a great white circle surrounding decorative Japanese characters which set forth the owner's occupation, so that he who runs may read. The intention is business-like, but utilitarianism in Japan is inseparable from the picturesque, and these portable advertisements only add a new charm to the wearer's delightful queerness. There are boys of ten or twelve in some of the boats with the men— quaint little brats with varying patterns shaved on the tops of their heads, entering into the contest to secure part of the carrying trade with the stern and enthusiastic vigor known only to the small boy of all countries.

I attach myself for the time being to a party of agreeable Americans. One of them, a pretty brown-eyed girl named Madge, finds everything as dear and astonishing a delight as do I; but the Lady— the Other Lady— and the Lay-Brother have been here before, and, knowing the

---

1   A small, East Asian style of boat
2   Arthur W. Pink, *The Attributes of God*

greater joys still in store for us, are impatient and superior. The Gentleman from Germany— always pleased in the pleasure of others— is indulgently sympathetic. We— Madge and I— secretly desire to be ferried over to the pier by one of these elfish ferrymen; but the others are so lofty that we meekly submit to allow a commonplace steamlaunch to set us on shore, making the journey with the missionaries, who have much exaltation and baggage.

I move in a joyous dream. Can this be I?... I, to whom Japan had seemed as fair and vague as heaven— a place to which only the excessively virtuous and fortunate ever went?... And, lo! I, in all the fullness of earthly imperfection, am permitted to see it!

More mediæval folk in blue stand about on the stone pier and welcome us with friendly smiles, and we charter their jinrikishas to take us to the hotel. Now, the jinrikisha[1] is exactly the vehicle in which one would expect to ride in this land of fairy children— large perambulators that hold one person comfortably; but instead of being trundled from behind by a white-capped nursemaid, one of the Henry II gentlemen, who wears also straw sandals and an enormous blue mushroom hat on his head, ensconces himself between the little shafts in front and prances noiselessly away with it. He has legs as light and muscular as a thoroughbred horse, and can spin along with the 'rikisha at the rate of five miles an hour. He can, with few intervals for rest, keep this up all day; he will charge you seventy-five cents for the whole; he will not be winded at all, and will be in a gay and charming temper when the day is done...

Our way lies along the Bund, a broad, handsome street on the water-front, with a fringe of slim pine-trees strange of outline as are those one is familiar with upon fans. Other jinrikishas are scampering about. Tonsured doll-babies in flowered gowns, such as one buys at home in the Oriental shops, are walking about here alive, and flying queer-shaped kites, with a sort of calm unconscious elfishness befitting dwellers in fairyland. Two little Japanese ladies with pink cheeks, and black hair clasped with jade pins, toddle by on wooden pattens that clack pleasantly on the pavement. Their kimonos are of gay crape, and their sashes tied behind like bright-tinted wings. Every one— even the

---

1   A small, two-wheeled carriage pulled by either an animal or one or two people

funny little gendarme[1] who stands outside of his sentry-box like a toy soldier— gives us back smile for smile.

The Grand Hotel is at the upper end of the Bund, and here another specimen of the Moyen-âge in his stocking feet shows us into beautiful rooms facing the water— rooms with steam-heat and electric bells!... The darkness closes down swiftly, but charming things are still to be seen from our veranda. The air is crisp and keen; gay cries and clinking pattens tinkle in melodious confusion from the street below. The 'rikishas have swinging from their shafts now crimped pink and white paper-lanterns, and flit by in the dark like fire-flies. A broad yellow moon rises up from the other side of the water and turns the bay to wrinkled gold, against which the ships and junks show delicately black, as if drawn with a pen; and a few clear black lines of cloud are etched across the moon's path...

After dinner we are lucky enough to fall into the hands of Lieutenant McDonald. He is a paymaster in the American Navy, and has been here two years. He knows the place well, and offers to be our guide to-night through the native town. In the flowery hotel-court we find our 'rikishas standing in a row in the moonlight, each with one of the pretty lanterns swinging; and we too flit away behind our sandalled steeds. Only the whir of our wheels and our calls and laughter sound through the city's quiet, moon-washed ways. Here in the European town the houses of two stories of stone stand flush with the narrow asphalt-paved street. A tiny foot-path runs under the shadow of their tiled caves; but as these are paved with little cobblestones, and the roadway is smooth and clean as a table, no one by any chance ever walks in the foot-paths. Occasionally we meet a figure enveloped in dark, shapeless drapery, or a grave, bland Chinese merchant goes by on his soundless cork soles, but this is the business quarter, and people have gone to their homes on the Bund, or upon the Bluff, where consuls and foreigners of importance reside.

We skim around corners with a shrill ki-yi! of warning; debouch into a great square upon which churches and public buildings face; cross a broad canal where acres of sampans are huddled for the night, and find on the other side Shichiu, the native town. Hancho-dori lies before us, the wide main thoroughfare from which spring hundreds of

1   An armed guard, a term usually only used in French-speaking areas

narrow branches, all swarming with a frolicsome, chattering crowd tin-kling about in pattens, their multitudinous tapping making a vibrant musical undertone to the sound of the many voices...

The houses, delicate little match-boxes of thin, unpainted wood, fifteen or twenty feet high, and divided into two stories, crowd close together, and give upon the street. The fronts of these houses— indeed, the greater part of the walls all around, are sashes of many tiny panes glazed with white, semi-transparent paper, through which the inner light shines as from a lantern; and the shop fronts are mere curtains of bamboo, rolled up during business hours, and let down when the shop is closed for the night.

Business is not nearly over yet. The Japanese are as little inclined to early bed as the Chinese, it seems, and the tide of trade runs strong... From all the eaves swing soft bubbles of tinted light— lanterns of many shapes and sizes. The shops are lit and busy, and contain every need, from crabs to curios, that Japanese flesh is heir to. Here and there clus-ter flocks of light, portable booths, each also with a swaying lantern, where steaming tea is sold in thimble-cups; where saki may be drunk hot and hot, poured from long-necked porcelain bottles, or trays of queer, toothsome-looking sweetmeats are to be had for coins of infin-itesimal value. Along the street lie heaps of fresh vegetables— making pretty bouquets of color, all clean and ready for the pot— or fruits of many sorts massed with skill and beauty;... little red oranges in bam-boo nets, set about with their own green leaves; plums, pomaloes, and fruits whose names we do not know. Everything, everywhere, is radi-antly clean, dainty, and inviting. All the folks, too, are gay and voluble. The children play about unchidden; and one might imagine it, if not corrected, some Festival of Lanterns, the place is so joyous, bright-tint-ed, and fantastic under the smiling, benignant moon...

We are on our way to the theatre— one of the humbler sort, where acrobats do their feats for a few cents, where stage and auditorium are on a level, and both merely platforms. A little gallery to one side is reserved for the moon-eyed babies with whimsically shaved heads; but they come down occasionally and rollic about as they wish, quite unre-proved. They are never harsh with children in this fair country, and in return the children display a courteous tolerance of the foibles of their elders that is extremely soothing. A group of tumblers on the stage are going through some supple contortions to the sound of a shrill little pipe and a blattering wooden drum, playing out of time with one another. The whole front of the theatre, a curtain of matting, is rolled up at intervals and, when the feat in progress is at its most thrilling climax, is let fall. This artful proceeding stimulates the interest of the passers-by to such poignancy that they succumb in platoons to the pangs of curiosity, and so crowd the little platform that we depart hastily...

More moon and lanterns, more laughter and flutter, more clacking of sandals, and then a Japanese Madame Tussaud's, with pleasing little horrors in wax at the entrance as earnest of more of the same cheerful entertainment within. Here is better music, that, during a naïve pantomime of Japanese ghosts, plays what negroes call a "lonesome tune," in a soft minor key. This does not hold us long, for farther up the street is a large and fashionable playhouse, where we may see the best talent of Nippon. At the box-office are piles of flat sticks, six inches long and two wide, painted with numbers in the native character, which, inquiry reveals, are shoe checks for the many sandals hanging on rows of pegs by the door; for here, as in every other house in Japan, one enters in stocking-feet. In consideration of our being benighted foreigners, we are allowed to retain our shoes...

The interior is large and lofty. The common folk occupy the level floor of the pit, marked into squares, where family parties sit on small wadded rugs, and are quite at home, bringing their little charcoal braziers to warm their fingers, furnish lights for their tiny pipes, and keep the teapot steaming. The galleries on two sides are divided into matting-lined boxes, one of which they furnish with chairs, seeing that we display small skill in sitting on our heels. We enter during an entr'acte; and before the stage, which is not deep, but lofty, sways lightly in the draught a gay crape curtain. The men in the pit are smoking or curled up in their rugs snatching a nap, while the women drink tea and gossip, and the children romp all over the house. High up on either side of the stage comes from a latticed box the sound of the samsien[1] and other stringed instruments that make a soft, plaintive, and pleasing music. The play has been going on for three weeks and is to end tonight. A gong sounds, the children are recalled, the men wake, and the

---

1   Alternative spelling of *shamisen*: a small, 3-stringed instrument, similar to a banjo

curtain being pulled aside shows the front of a Japanese house. Two maids appear from a side door and wait respectfully on their hands and knees for the entrance of their mistress, a man very skillfully painted and gorgeously arrayed, but somewhat too masculine to satisfactorily represent the babyish roundness of the real thing. This lady has affairs of great pith and moment to convey to the maids, who make timidly respectful suggestions, which evidently carry small comfort, for the lady retires depressedly. Her lord, followed by his attendants, next appears— an extremely well-bred and aristocratic-looking person in the daimio dress with the two swords; and one judges by his manner that he can add nothing to the cheerfulness of the situation. While matters are at this stage of melancholy, a great clash of music startles the audience, the curtain is drawn aside from a little room on the opposite side of the house, and a magnificent personage appears, who paces with an awe-inspiring strut along the little raised pathway that leads from this room to the stage. The daimio[1] hastens with his attendants to meet him. It is the great shogun himself, stern of mien, and with fierce, orgulous brows; a very impressive figure, notwithstanding he wears black velvet trousers a yard and a half too long for him, and is accompanied by a train-bearer who skips about and disposes this superfluous length in graceful folds whenever his master comes to a standstill... He is the embodiment of the sterner side of the Japanese character— the aristocratic spirit that kept alive a proud feudalism long after Europe had forgotten it; the haughty courage that bid a gentleman expiate his offences only by his own hand; the spirit that has allowed no conqueror to ever set foot on Japanese soil, and still makes these people the bravest and freest race in Asia...

This tremendous personage makes short work of the handsome daimio, and stalks away after pronouncing some decree to which the noble bows his head in calm acquiescence... Madame and the maids are still more unhappy... The shogun appears to have suggested the advisability of the "happy despatch," and the lady fails to appreciate this little attention on the part of her sovereign. An aged and garrulous mendicant next enters, and one guesses at once that this is the element of comedy which is to relieve the gloom of the situation, and probably the humble deus ex machinâ who will arrest the tragedy. His acting is

1   Alternative spelling of *daimyo*: a Japanese feudal baron

extremely clever, and for myself I should like to see how it all turns out; but the smile of the Gentleman from Germany is growing wan, and the Lay-brother, who has no chair, is becoming distinctly cross, and so we go home.

The shops are shut by this time, and we see some curious little domestic episodes shadowed on the paper window-sashes, when householders thoughtlessly pass between them and the lamp. The European town is flooded with a high tide of moonlight, and we are, it seems, the only ones who wake sweeping in a long, swift line through the streets in our silent fairy carriages with the rosy lantern swinging...

A nipping and an eager air blows among the rose-trees in the court next morning when Madge and I start out for early shopping. Lieutenant McDonald, magnificent in brown cords and laced Russia-leather riding-boots, offers us his pony carriage, but we scoff at anything less foreign than a jinrikisha, and set off together for Benton-dori, the fashionable shopping-street of Shichiu. In spite of the fall in the thermometer, the spirits of the public in general appear in no way chilled. The bare feet in straw sandals look red and uncomfortable, but the owners of them merely acquire great plumpness of appearance by adding three or four more cotton-wadded kimonos to their costume, tuck their chilly fingers away in their ample sleeves, and laugh at the passing discomfort. Everything looks ridiculously tiny by day, and deliciously absurd. One has a feeling that it is all a game that one is playing to amuse the children. We sit on the edge of the little platform that forms the floor of the shop, and, in the baby talk that is called pigeon-English,[1] bargain with the amiable shopkeeper seated on his own heels and within easy reach of all his goods. Just so one used to play "keep store" in the nursery when one sold one's toys for astonishing sums to wealthy playmates whose purses were bursting with scraps of torn envelopes— fiat money of arbitrary value. We have been instructed not to pay more than half that is asked, but the prices are so delightfully low that we give them joyfully, and without haggling. We wander from shop to shop, received with an air of affectionate friendliness everywhere; we warm our fingers at many different braziers, and might drink little thimble-cups of tea at every hospitable place of business were we so minded. The really valu-

---

1   Misspelling of *pidgin* English: a simplified version of a language, usually used for communication between two different languages

able bric-à-brac is costly here as elsewhere; but many charming things in common use among the people, pretty proofs of their universal love of beauty, are to be picked up for a mere trifle.

In the silk-shops we find the very poetry of fabrics: crapes like milky opals, with the pale iris hues of rainbows; crapes with the faint purple and rose of clear sunset skies, embroidered with wheeling flights of white storks. Out of a sweet-smelling box comes a mass of shining stuff that the low-voiced fourteenth-century-looking shopkeeper calls by three musical syllables, which, translated, signify the Garments of the Dawn. Its threads shimmer like the crystals of dry snow, and amid its folds the whiteness blushes to rose, deepens to gold, or pales to blue, while through it here and there runs a sort of impalpable cloudiness like a morning mist. He shows us Moon-cloths, duskily azure with silver gleams; crapes, pearl-white and rich with needlework in patterns of delicate bamboo fronds or loose-petalled chrysanthemum-blossoms, fairy garments all, woven of rainbows and moonbeams!

We are in the train going to Tokyo. We have lingered too long in the enchanted wardrobes, Madge and I, and are in disgrace with the others for our tardiness, which has nearly lost them the train, but the world is too much to our liking to-day for even this to depress us, and we feel that the Gentleman from Germany is secretly on our side. It is a funny train, as absurdly toy-like and doll-housey as is everything else in this country; and our destinies are committed to-day into the hands of a sweet-mannered gentleman in a gray kimono and an American hat, who is to guide us amid the beauties of his country's capital... Delicious little pictures run past our car windows, astonishing us with the sudden revelation of what nonsense the Occident has talked about the conventionality of Japanese art, when, in truth, it is the most exquisite fidelity to the nature the artist has seen about him. The world the Japanese artist has painted has been the world just as it exists in his own country, and, moreover, he has in his art caught and expressed with perfect and subtle veracity its atmosphere of gay grotesquerie— of delicate fantasticality— its crisp and fragile fairy likeness— the soul of things about him that has so far escaped the brush of every foreign artist endeavoring to portray the outward forms of things Japanese...

The charm of all we see from our car— the Tokaido (the great imperial highway that intersects the whole empire), the queer little farm-houses and railway stations, and even the water-soaked pad-dy-fields, reaped of their rice— lies in the exquisite, faultless cleanli-ness and propriety of it all. Nothing is out of place; nothing requires allowance and forgiveness; ... all is beautifully posed and arranged as if sitting to have itself instantaneously photographed; and the Other Lady, recognizing this attitude of expectancy, the click of her camera is heard in the land...

Arrived at Tokyo, we go to the residence of the American minister, who is very agreeably housed, and where we find— as in all private dwellings throughout the East— a most astonishing profusion of flow-ery plants blooming and bourgeoning in every corner of the mansion. We tell the American girl with the camera and the small feet good-bye, for she is remaining here as a guest, and we see the minister's carriage drive up, accompanied with two out-runners in gorgeous native liveries of orange and blue. These out-runners accompany all folk of impor-tance in Japan, and keep pace with the horses without fatigue. A fine, picturesque bit of mediæval swagger they make...

We take our tiffin[1] in a little latticed glove-box of a tea-house, the polished daintiness of whose interior will not permit of our wearing our shoes; and a grotesque spectacle they make— those American shoes, standing in a row just inside the entrance while we tiptoe awk-wardly and shamefacedly in our stocking-feet up the stairs. A mild dif-fused light through the paper panes illuminates our tiny upper cham-ber, whose only furnishings are sweet-smelling mattings, a kakamono hanging on the wall, and a tall jar full of red-berried branches in the corner. We are served by a moon-faced little maid in a flowered gown, who bows at each entry and draws in her breath to signify what a priv-ilege it is to breathe the same air with us, ... one of the customs of a national courtesy so thorough and far-reaching that even the domestic animals are civilly addressed as Mr. Cat and Mr. Dog... She brings us braziers to warm our fingers and wadded rugs to sit upon, tailorwise, and serves us delicious tea, sugarless and straw-colored, in tiny cups without handles, and bowls of rice across which are laid crisp, freshly broiled eels— a delightful dish that we eat with polished black chop-sticks.

---

1   A light midday meal (British)

The 'rikishas race away with us quite to the other side of town – past great forts and fosses, past the mikado's palaces and gardens, to the famous temples at Shiba. The road is smooth and broad and overshadowed by pines. A superb gilded and lacquered gateway admits us to the temple grounds, and here the guide goes in search of a shaven-headed priest who will show us his treasures. Immediately before us stands a lovely red temple, rich with gold and carvings and lacquered figures, and with a marble-paved veranda polished as onyx; but we cannot wait to examine it. We go to the left and climb the hill by stone steps strewn with crimson petals of the camellia blossoms... At the end of an avenue of tall gray stone lanterns— where lights shine during the great religious festivals— stands the tomb of Ieymitsu, the son of Ieyasu, the great shogun who usurped supreme authority and reduced the mikado to the position of a primate. But the little finger of Ieymitsu was thicker than his father's loins. He consolidated the feudal system, and chivalry under his rule achieved its noblest development; Japanese arms were feared and respected abroad and at home; and under the sun of his kingly favor Japanese art blossomed into its supreme, consummate flower. To-day the curios of his period are worth their weight in gold, and all the knightly traditions of the land cluster about his name and reign.

Laying down a life of power, he yearned for an immortality of beauty— to be magnificent and impressive even in death; and, choosing this spot, he spent millions in glorifying his last resting-place. He had a nice taste in tombs, had this splendid old Japanese. The hill is clothed in pines, through which the light winds go softly sighing. The westering sun shines slantingly along the green arcades and makes golden shadows across the path we have come. The mild-moving air has stolen red blossoms from the glossy-leaved camellia-trees and shred them upon the hoary gray lanterns and mossy stairs... Never monarch slept among sweeter verdure, space, and calm... The tomb has, as have all these shrines and temples, walls of a deep rich red, whose clear color three centuries have not dimmed... Above is a broad frieze of gorgeous carving— dragons, birds, lotus, and chrysanthemums tangled in fantastic intricacies, and all lacquered and gilded with such honest pains that Time's teeth cannot gnaw through the color or his breath tarnish the gold. Above the frieze leans the green and gray tiled roof, with its fretted ridges and airy, upturned gables, of a fine lightness and unmatched grace of outline... The interior is octagon-sided and mosaic-paved, and up from the centre, where the great shogun lies, curls the cup of a giant stone lotus, whose calyx is the jewelled shrine, springing to the roof which rests on a ring of polished columns, and each of these in turn on a base of lotus leaves. Everywhere, from pavement, shrine, and wall, shines the shogun's golden crest of three lotus leaves meeting at the stems... Space does not avail to tell of the splendors of this tomb, ... the plating of gold and silver bronze; the myriad-tinted lacquers, hard and polished as gems; the untarnished gilding, the inlaying of precious stones, and, most wonderful of all, the grace and gorgeousness of the myriad delicate fantasies wrought out by art to soothe the king's last sleep.

"Et ego in Arcadia – 'I too have been in fairyland!'" I cry to the lay-brother as we stroll away in the mild sunshine and down the flower-strewn stairway. He had warned me of the exceeding great loveliness of the place, and, having seen it, I am fain to declare that I forgive fate in advance for any future trick, because of this one day of unmarred delight.

We race across the city again in our 'rikishas to the great park of Uyeno, to see the sun go down behind Fujiyama ... to look out across the city's vast hive with its million or more of folk whose myriad lights begin to twinkle in the violet dusk... We worship a moment before a gigantic, calm-lidded stone Buddha set on a little hill, amid a thicket of roses.

Then the railroad again, ... a broad, yellow moon shining on the ever-present Fujiyama, ... regretful farewells to the charming Americans and Lieutenant McDonald, and then the visit to fairyland is over... I must pass on in my swift course, and be ready for new sights and friends.

FOURTH STAGE

HONG KONG! ... I like the name of my next port. It has a fine clangorous significance, like two slow loud notes of some great brazen-lunged bell... Hong – Kong!

We have one more glimpse of Fujiyama the next morning as Japan sinks out of sight... During the day the young Chinaman with the pallid waxen hands dies. He has struggled hard to keep the flame burning until he sees his own land, but the crisp breath of the Japanese coast puffs it suddenly out. A canvas screen is hung across one corner of the steerage deck, and the doctor goes back and forth from behind it... They will carry him back to his country, though he will not be glad or aware. But the sea knows she is being defrauded of her rights, and wakes and rages. She comes in the nights and beats thunderously with her great fists upon our doors. She leaps to look over our bulwarks for her hidden victim; she roars with wrath and will not be appeased. For two days we steam in the face of the northwest gale she has raised, and for three the ship plunges like a spurred horse. I find that bodily I am proof now against seasickness, but my temper has a violent attack of mal de mer. It makes me bitterly cross to go leaping and plunging about the ship, not to be able to keep my seat, and to gradually collect my soup and entrées in my lap; so I retire to bed, wedge myself in tight with pillows, and go steadily through every word the ship's library affords on the subject of Japan. I am refreshed and cheered to find that the writer of each book fails, as signally as I shall fail, to convey any adequate idea of the fairy charms of the Land of Chrysanthemums... Shall one then paint a dragonfly with a whitewash brush? ...

Nevertheless, I gather from these books much confirmatory of my own swiftly gathered impression. The very faults of the Japanese are such as are misdemeanors in adults but quite forgivable in children. They are hopelessly immodest, with the unconscious shamelessness of babies, and they fib imaginatively with an infant's inability to discern the relative value of truth and falsehood. They are brave with the headlong courage of the child who is ignorant of the meaning of danger, and in matters of honor they have youth's reckless passionate exaltation. They are unfailingly sweet-tempered and courteous. Their artistic conscientiousness ascends into the realm of morality. They are frugal and temperate; they detest all ugliness, dirt, and squalor; they are unique; they are delightful— they are Japanese!

On Sunday, the 15th, we reach Hong Kong. The sea turns to a cool profound emerald, and we descry again on the horizon the bamboo wings of the fishing and coasting junks. These sails are somewhat larger and deeper of hue than those of Japan, and still more resemble the fans of giant yellow and russet butterflies.

More treeless mountains rise out of the green waters. They are broken and rugged; of volcanic origin; and where the scant herbage fails their naked sides show tawny as a lion's hide. It is one of the three beautiful harbors of the world, the water winding deeply inland between the hills, and flowing around island mountains ringed with girdles of foam. At one o'clock we are in the broad antechamber of the port, known as the Lyee-Moon, and are signalled from the lofty peak to the inhabitants of the town lying at its foot. At two o'clock we drop anchor in the roadstead amid a great host of shipping of all character and nations – twenty-three days out from San Francisco. The White Star people had instructed Captain Kempson to make all due haste for my sake, and it is one of the swiftest voyages ever known at this season of the year, when the winds are contrary, coming to the west. We were sixteen days to Japan, where we remained thirty-six hours, and five days from Yokohama to Hong Kong.

The island of Hong Kong is a cluster of lofty abrupt hills with scanty vegetation, seized by England in 1842 after a struggle with China. At that time the town was an insignificant fishing village, but the value of the site was great commercially and strategically. It is a convenient and safe harbor for the squadron detailed to watch and menace the Russian navy in the Pacific; and the English have elevated the village into a flourishing city and made it the fourth shipping port of the world. The harbor is navigable for the largest merchant vessels and men-of-war in existence, and is perfectly sheltered and easy of access.

As in Japan, sampans swarm about us as soon as we are made fast to the buoy, but they are far less picturesque than were those. Each sampan wears a bamboo hood in the stern, and here the owner houses his wife and rears his family. A brood of babies is in each one of these little hutches, and while the pigtailed subject of the Celestial Emperor stands and rows in the bow, his helpmeet sculls in the stern with a long oar that serves as a tiller. The Chinese woman of the working class, I find, decided centuries ago the question still in its stormy infancy with us – of the divided skirt. She clothes herself in a pair of wide black trousers, a loose tunic, jade earrings and cork-soled shoes, and is ready for all the emergencies of life. Should they take the form of marriage with a sampan owner, she will but rarely set her foot on shore again, but will, in common with something like 20,000 of the "water population" of Hong Kong, work, sleep, eat, bear her children, rear them, and die in this crazy little boat.

I am very regretful at leaving the Oceanic, where I have received so much kindness; but "hateful is the dark blue ocean" after more than three weeks of it, and delightful the thought of even three precious days on land. I am to stay with personal friends in Hong Kong in order that I may see something of domestic life in the East; and I am taken ashore in their private steam launch. Chairs and bearers are waiting for us on the dock— comfortable fauteuils of bamboo, trimmed with silver and supported by long bamboo poles. This is even more amusing than the 'rikishas. There are four Chinamen for each chair, dressed in my friend's livery— loose trousers and tunic of white cotton bordered with rose color. Their feet are bare and their queues are gathered into Psyche knots, on the back of their heads, like the hair of the shop girls in America.

They lift the poles to their shoulders and start off in a swift swinging trot. We pass across the narrow strip of level land that lies on the water's edge— the business quarter of the city built handsomely and solidly of native stone— and begin to mount the broad steep ways that lead to the residence quarter. These are cool and shadowy with great trees, with the clattering feathered spears of the tall bamboos, with gigantic ferns, and prodigious satiny leaves of tropical lilies. The streets are paved with asphalt and have no sidewalks; here and there they resolve themselves into broad flights of shallow steps up which the bearers carry us with perfect ease... The verdure is magnificent; the town is submerged in it, and flowers are everywhere. On every wall stand rows of earthen jars full of greenery and blossom— rows on rows of them in the courtyards— more rows on both ends of every flight of steps, and on all balcony railings. Every nook and corner that will hold a jar is filled with bloom, and the rarest orchids are strewn carelessly about, industriously producing flowers, in delicious provincial ignorance of their own value and of what they might exact in the way of expensive attention.

We meet the most astonishing varieties of the human race. All sorts and conditions of Chinamen— elegant dandies in exquisitely pale-tinted brocades; grave merchants and compradors, richly but soberly clad; neat amahs with the tiny deformed Chinese feet, sitting at the street corners, taking in sewing by the day; street sellers of tea, shrimp, fruit, sweetmeats, and rice; women working side by side with the men, mending the streets, ... horrible old women, weazened and wrinkled beyond all imagining, all the femininity shrivelled out of them, their only head-covering a bit of black cloth across their seamed and humble foreheads, and the last pathetic spark of the female instinct for adornment displaying itself in the big jade and silver rings in their ears.

From windows shaded by light bamboo blinds look out coarse olive faces— heavy and dull of eye, repulsively sensual. These are Portuguese; descendants of the hardy sailors who explored and ruled these southern seas before the English supplanted them. They have bred in with the natives everywhere and have grown an indolent mongrel race... Plump and prosperous-looking gentlemen go by in European dress and with tight-fitting purple satin coal-hods on their heads. Their complexions are dark and their features – dug out of a mat of astonishingly thick beards – are aggravatedly Hebraic in their cast. They are Parsees, and look uncommonly like the lost tribes – exhibiting also, I am told, the same eminent abilities in business probably possessed by those much-sought-for Hebrew truants.

At the corner stands a haughty jewel-eyed prince of immense stature— straight and lithe as a palm— in whose high-featured bronze
countenance are unfathomable potentialities of pride and passion...
He wears a soldier's dress and sword, and a huge scarlet turban of the
most intricate convolutions. I cry out with astonishment at the sight of
this superb creature.

"Is it an emperor?" I demand, in breathless admiration.

"An emperor! Poof! it's only a Sikh policeman. There are hundreds
about the place quite as splendid as he."

When the Arabs who had seen Europeans only in trousers fled
before the magnificent onslaught of the kilted Highlanders at Tel-el-
Kebir, they exclaimed in amazement:

"If these are the Scotch women, what must the men be!" so,
though a bit dashed, I say to myself, "If these are the Sikh policemen,
what must their princes be?" and secretly resolve to go some day and
discover.

It gives me my first real impression of the power of England, who
tames these mountain lions and sets them to do her police duty. It
would seem incredible that this rosy commonplace Tommy Atkins who
comes swaggering down the street in his scarlet coat can be the weap-
on that tamed the fine creature in the turban... What is it makes this
cheerfully vulgar Anglo-Saxon the lord of the Hindoo? ... Physically he
is not the Sikh's superior, and in profound and passionate sentiment, if
one may judge by the countenance, the Hindoo is infinitely above the
Briton. Nor is the latter greater in courage or dignity, for these Indians
made a noble resistance to English encroachment, and after submission
were enrolled in the army of the conquerors as their bravest and most
loyal native troops... What is the secret? ... Is it more beef and mutton
perhaps – or more of submission to orders and power of self-discipline?

Here comes one of the conquerors of India, a kilted Highlander,
swinging down the road in his plaided petticoats, with six inches of
bare stalwart pink legs showing, and a fine hearty self-confidence in his
mien that signifies his utter disbelief in the power of anything human
to conquer him.

We leave this olla-podrida[1] of nations behind, and mount into a
broad street curved around the flank of the hill. On the upper side of

1   Spanish stew made from meats (often pork) and a variety of beans

it is the heavy wall of the Portuguese convent, once painted a lovely light blue, and now freaked and stained a thousand charming tints by time and weather. Creepers bearing great yellow flower disks trail across it; trees shadow it, and the convent's massive outlines loom from behind... A beautiful work is done inside in teaching Chinese girls the sweet decencies of life and pretty feminine arts. Opposite is my friend's house— two stories of stone surrounded by great verandas. The coolies run down a curving flight of steps and deposit us at the door.

These Hong Kong houses have admirable interiors. A lofty hall divides this one, terminating on a rear veranda, with a wide view of the precipitous white city, buried in verdure, sloping down to the flashing emerald of the bay, that is ringed with tawny hills. The hall is filled with more potted plants, and massive furniture of Indian ebony and marble. To the left is a great drawing-room, fifty feet long and eighteen high, with a dozen windows. Here are more palms and ferns, rich European fittings, and Eastern bric-à-brac. Scattered about are photographs of all the Hohenzollerns,[1] for my friends are Germans. We rest awhile in the cool green gloom of this apartment, and drink tea brought by a tall yellow gentleman in silk trousers, a black satin cap, and a crisp rustling blue gown reaching nearly to his ankles. My bedchamber is another huge shadowy place, with a dressing-room and bath as large as the ordinary drawing-room at home, furnished with old mahogany and silver fittings brought from Germany two generations ago. Its airy, unencumbered spaces remind me of the fine old bedchambers in the plantation houses at home in the South... Here I am awakened in the morning by another pigtailed gentleman, who brings me my tea, prepares my bath, and arranges all things ready for my toilet. Female servants in Hong Kong are rare; and after the first surprise is over these clean, grave male-maids seem perfectly efficient and convenable servitors. Our meals are stately functions— adorned, of course, with profuse greenery and flowers— with fine wines and delicate food exquisitely prepared... A sumptuous Eastern life that flows on with cool and unhasting repose and gravity. I was never in a German household before, and find here many pretty unfamiliar customs— one of them a nice fashion of repeating upon rising from the table a German phrase which expresses mutual good-will and affection, a sort of grace

1   Family dynasty of Prussia, the German empire and Romania

of friendshipafter meat. There is a careful sweet civility too in their intercourse with one another, very pleasant to share.

In all our expeditions about the place we are luxuriously carried by our coolies, who apparently put forth no special effort or haste, but with whom a rapid walker with no burden is unable to keep pace. The streets are a panorama of unending interest. 'Rikishas are employed occasionally in the level part of the town, but the general mode of travelling in the steeper streets is by chairs, the distinctive livery of private bearers consisting of the color of the border of their white garments. Stout, haughty, red-faced Englishmen go by in these chairs, and occasionally a covered one is met, with bamboo blinds, in which sits an equally fat and haughty mandarin. Coolies run about at a dog-trot bearing immense burdens swung at the two ends of a pole carried on their naked muscular yellow shoulders. Pretty round-faced children, dressed exactly like their elders, play in the doorways and exchange smiles with the passer-by. There is a general public amiability— without the gay and gracious vivacity of Japan— in all save the lowest class of laborers. These toil terribly and incessantly for infinitesimal sums, and by the most minute economies manage to exist— to continue these labors and privations. They are old in youth, parched, callous, and dully indifferent. Incapable of further disappointment, they exist with the stolid patience of those who expect only stones and serpents, having abandoned all hopes of bread and fish...

The town is growing and prosperous. The shops, hotels, clubs, and counting-houses are handsome stone buildings with deep arcade-like verandas surrounded by pointed arches. The banks and public buildings are imposing and massive, and the place is noisy with the sound of mason's tools. The harbor for 200 yards in front of the Praya (the broad water street) is shallow, and preparations are being made to fill it up and give Hong Kong the benefit of this extra width of level land. The same was done some years ago at Kow-Loon, on the opposite side of the harbor, where England owns a strip of the mainland. On this reclaimed land fine wharves lined with godowns (warehouses) have been built, and huge dry-docks and shipyards established where shipbuilding goes industriously on and the largest vessels afloat can put in for repairs. The export trade in cotton, tea, silk, spices, and rice is enormous, and the place develops year by year considerable manufacturing industries.

Though three great lines of trans-Pacific steamers ply between Hong Kong and America, there is only one resident of that nationality in the city besides the consul. The English, Germans, Parsees, and Chinamen conduct its business. The strategic importance of Hong Kong is so great that four or five war ships are always in its harbor or cruise in the neighborhood, and two full regiments are kept in garrison. At the time of my visit one of these regiments was of Highlanders who wear in this hot climate white jackets and helmets with their kilts. They are being put through a rapid and vigorous drill one morning when we pass the parade ground, and the pipes are shrilly skirling— music to stir the heart in which runs the smallest drop of Scotch blood. Not even the Sikh policemen stand first in my affections at this moment, as, to that wild keen sound, the solid ranks of brawny red-haired Caledonians trot by, with their petticoats fluttering about their bare knees and their bayonets set in a glittering hedge... Oh, braw sight! ... Oh, bonny lads! ... Scotland forever!

The climate of Hong Kong at this season is of Eden. Airs of Paradise wave through the splendid tropical foliage. The sun is pleasantly hot at midday, and the mornings and evenings are dewily cool. Coolies do their work naked to the waist, but ordinary European garments are comfortable. From every point is seen either the light flashing from green waters, or the red and yellow hills outlined against a turquoise sky. My friends are loath that I should lose a single pleasure, and we are out all day long in this adorable weather. One of our paths lies through the green twilight of the Botanical Gardens, filled with such vegetation as I have always regarded with a doubting eye in the picture of the Asiatic half of the geographies. We pass under the tremulous lacey shadows of ferns twenty feet high, through trellises weighted with ponderous vines that blow a myriad perfumed purple trumpets up to the golden noon, and emerge upon sunny spaces where fountains are sprinkling silver rain upon banks of crimson and orange flowers. The flaxen-haired, muslin-clad English children play here, cared for by prim trousered Chinese amahs; and we meet pretty blue-eyed German ladies in their chairs taking this road home.

Another expedition leads to the top of the peak, whose head is 2000 feet above the water and up whose side the town climbs year by year. Our way— at an angle of forty-five degrees— is by a tram dragged up the mountain by means of an endless chain. This peak is the city's summer resort and pleasuring-ground. Handsome bungalows cling to its steep sides— built in the Italian style, of warm cream-white stone. There is ten degrees difference in temperature between the summit and the town, and a summer hotel is in process of construction at the top... We can see from here how the water flows between the hills, and how the harbor broadens to bays and narrows to straits between the island mountains. Only at Rio Janeiro and Sydney, they tell me, is there a harbor whose beauty compares to this. The man in charge of the windy signal station comes out and explains to us the various ways in which the town is warned of the coming of vessels, and also introduces us to an extremely low-spirited and discontented-looking lady with battered features who turns her back on us and stares in unwinking disgust out to sea. She was once the gay and gilded figure-head of the Princess Charlotte, wrecked in these waters long since, and plainly resents what she looks upon as her fall in life, and the banal jocosity of those who rescued her— bobbing detachedly about in a sheltered cove— and brought her up here to assist a low signal officer!

Our chairs have come up another way, and we are to be carried down the long winding road that sinks by slow stages to the town. During the first stage we are in full sunlight, passing under the walls of the white palace-like bungalows with smooth-shaven tennis-courts where ruddy-cheeked, spare-loined young Englishmen toss the bass to fair-haired, light-footed English girls. Then the road— the earth here is a thousand beautiful shades of buff and rose— winds about to the east, and we pass into the shadows. A tiny Greek church with a sparsely populated graveyard clings to the declivity above us, and from far below comes the faint cool sound of waters foaming round the foot of the hills.

The sun has set; only the utmost heights are gilded now, and the twilight deepens on our path. We swing around the hills— in and out, and down, down, with smooth, easy motion— to the regular pad, pad, pad of the bearers› feet. Here and there in the dusk we discern the scarlet turbans of Sikh warders, standing motionless as bronze statues. Below in the harbor the lights of the town, the ships, and the flitting sampans sparkle through the faint evening mist like multitudinous fireflies. The town climbs the hill to meet us, and we pass into the still heavier gloom of trees. A great pure calm reigns where we sink into this cool flood of darkness; ... half-naked figures go by noiselessly on unshod feet... I know all this; I remember it well... Somewhere— once— I passed through just such shadowy ways in the warm nights... This silent peace of darkness after long hours of burning light is quite familiar to me. I try to recall where it was— but it was a long, long, time ago and I have forgotten the name of the place and the people who lived there... I only remember that I used to pass under the great trees, ... that some wonderful secret delight waited for me beyond them. Alas! That was very long ago; to night only an excellent dinner attends my coming...

> "In Xanadu did Kubla Khan
> A stately pleasure dome decree—"[1]

Kubla Khan did come to tiffin one day— a handsome dark gentleman of forty years or so, with very white teeth and eyes like black velvet. He wore extremely well-fitting London clothes, and in his soft, slow voice he signified that on the morrow he would take us to see the pleasure dome— not yet entirely complete... Kubla Khan was his name in Xanadu of course, but in Hong Kong, for the sake of convenience and brevity, he was called Catchik Chater. Also for convenience and brevity he gave it out that he was a British subject, resident in China, born in India, and with a certain mixture of Greek and Armenian blood in his veins; naturally in Xanadu his rank and pedigree were far more complicated... It had been his fancy to come to Hong Kong twenty years before, neglecting to bring with him any drafts on his treasury, and in the interim he had collected something like a million pounds it was said. It was he who had made the long water-front at Kow-Loon, rescuing it from the sea, and had covered it with great godowns filled with merchandise of the East, and it was he who was proposing the same feat on the opposite side of the harbor. He had interested himself more or less in the banks, the shipyards and manufactures of various sorts, and he now felt prepared to erect in China a repetition of the Xanadu pleasure dome. He took us first to see his docks and godowns, resounding with the loud clangors of trade, and then through the grassy Kow-Loon plains, by a wide red road shadowed with banana-trees, to this lordly

---

1   Samuel Taylor Coleridge, "Kubla Khan" (1816)

pavilion set on the crest of many flowering terraces— its pale-yellow outlines cut cameo-like against the burning blue of the equatorial sky. To the right is the naked side of a hill all deep-tinted buff warmed with red, and everywhere else a sea of satin-leaved tropical foliage.

The centre of the pavilion is a great banqueting-hall with domed roof thirty feet above the tessellated pavement. The walls are frescoed in the same deep cream color of the exterior, touched here and there with blue and rose and gold. Twenty lofty arched doors give on the veranda, from whence beyond the roses of the terrace one sees the glitter of the green waters of the harbor. At each end of the banqueting-hall opens a drawing-room set with mirrors and lined with divans. Beneath are tiled bath-rooms, needed in this hot climate after using the tennis-courts and bowling-alleys. Here Kubla Khan's guests come— come by twenties and fifties— and feast splendidly on high days and holidays and on hot star-lit tropical nights. It is like the sumptuous fancy of some splendid Roman noble, pro-consul of an Eastern province. The pavilion for the moment is in the hands of workmen, so we may not dine there; but we do dine with the Khan in his town house, eating through many courses, drinking many costly wines, and served by a phalanx of tall Celestials in rustling blue gowns.

Another day we go to the shops and turn over costly examples of Chinese art— coming home through the many-colored ways of the native town;— steep streets that climb laboriously up and down stairs, and so narrow that there is hardly room for our chairs to pass through the multitudes who swarm there. Sixteen hundred residents to the acre they average in this part of the town, buzzing and humming like the unreckonable myriads insects bred from the fecund slime of a marsh. Two thirds of their life is passed out of doors in the streets, and all seem to be patiently and continuously busy. Children are as the flies in number and activity. The place smells violently; smells of opium, of the dried ducks and fish hanging exposed for sale in the sun, of frying pork and sausages, and of the many strange repulsive-looking meals being cooked on hissing braziers in the streets and in doorways. There is no lack of color. The shops are faced with a broad fretwork richly gilded, and the long perpendicular signs are ornamentally lettered with large black characters. Every house is lime-washed some strong tint, and the whole leaves upon the eye the color-impression one gets from Chinese

porcelains – of sharp green, gold, crimson, and blue; all vigorous, defi-
nite, and mingled with grotesque tastefulness.

My plan had been to sail from Hong Kong on the Nord-
deutscher-Lloyd ship Preussen, but a Peninsular and Oriental steamer
sails three days earlier; I am advised to go in her as far as Ceylon, and
I do. So on the morning of the 18th of December I find myself on the
deck of the Thames, surrounded by the charming friends and acquaintances of this Hong Kong episode, who have come to give me a final
proof of their goodness, and wish me speed on my journey.

This boat is as polyglot as the land I have just left, and swarms with
queer people. The sailors are Lascars,[1] clad in close trousers and tunic of
blue cotton check and red turbans. Many of the Parsees in their purple
coal-hods come aboard to bid farewell to a parting friend. One of the
Highlanders is going home and his comrades have brought the pipes
to give him a last tune. Grief and Scotch whiskey move them finally to
"play a spring and dance it round" in spite of the heat, which brings
the sweat pouring down their faces. Sampans cluster about with pretty
little Chinese dogs, bamboo steamer chairs, and canary birds for sale,
driving a few final bargains.

The bell warns them all away. I wave good-bye to my friends and
to the beautiful city with the keenest regret.

The fifth stage of my journey has begun under the shadow of the
Union Jack.

---

1   Southeast Asian sailor or malitia man

FIFTH STAGE

Hong Kong vanishes in a haze of sunlight. I am desperately tired— worn out with delights. My head swims with a glorious confusion of tropic splendors, and there is no room or capacity in it for more impressions just now. I will go below...

It is a beautiful ship; like a fine yacht in its spacious commodiousness. Here and there hang canary cages thrilling with song. Narcissus bulbs in bowls are ablow with fluttering white flowers, and everywhere are deep-colored jars full of palms and ferns. The space assigned to me is a large, pleasant white room, from which a great square lifts up outward on the water-side, leaving me on intimate terms with the milky, jade-tinted sea. Beneath this window is a broad divan, and here, laved in tepid sea winds and soothed by rippling whispers against the ship's side, I sleep— the langorous, voluptuous sleep of the tropics; ... sink softly into that dim warm flood where one lies drenched, submerged in unconsciousness; a flood that ebbs slowly, slowly— bearing with it all fatigue and satiety— and leaves me on the shores of life again in a pale lilac dusk glimmering with great stars...

Yea, verily, life is good in this magnificent equatorial world! Again I am a great sponge, absorbing beauty and delight with every pore. Every day brings new marvels and new joys. I go to bed exhaustedly happy and wake up expectantly smiling. Everything pleases, everything amuses me; most of all perhaps the strong British atmosphere in which one finds one's self on board a P. and O. steamer. I am— with the exception of a charming little old lady from Boston, who after two years of travel in the East has suffered no diminution of her respect for the Common and Phillips Brooks— the only woman on the passenger list; so the British atmosphere has a pronounced masculine flavor; but despite even this limitation it is interesting.

The men, from captain to cook, are fine creatures. Their physical vigor is superb— such muscles! such crisply curled hair! such clear ruddy skins, white teeth, and turquoise eyes. They are flat-backed and lean-loined; they carry their huge shoulders with a lordly swagger; they possess a divine faith in themselves and in England; and they have such an astonishing collection of accents! No two of them speak alike: the burly bearded giant three places off from me at table speaks with a broad Scotch drawl; the handsome, natty little fourth officer with the black eyes and shy red face who sits opposite, in white duck from head to heel, has a bit of a Yorkshire burr on the tip of his tongue; the Ceylon tea-planter talks like a New-Yorker, and there are fully a dozen variations more between his accent and that of the tall young blond, whose fashionable Eton and Oxford inflections leave one speechless with awe and admiration of their magnificent eccentricities.

Even the menu is of daily interest, for here I become for the first time familiar with food upon which the folk of the English novels are fed. I learn to know and appreciate the Bath bun and the Scotch scone. I make the greatly-to-be-prized acquaintance of the English meat pie, including Mr. Weller's favorite "weal and 'ammer," and I recognize touching manifestations of British loyalty in the sweets christened impartially with appellations of royalty: Victoria jelly-roll, Alexandra wafers, and Beatrice tarts. Waterloo pudding is one of our favorite desserts, and other British triumphs and glories adorn the bill of fare from time to time.

Sunday the Lascar crew, who have contented themselves all the week with garments of blue cotton check and red turbans, suddenly bloom and burgeon garden-wise. We are lounging in our bamboo chairs on the wide decks; the awning flutters lazily in the breeze; and we, swimming between two worlds of burning blue, are endeavoring by supreme indolence to recover from the fatigues of morning service, when this startlingly variegated vision bursts upon us: All the brown feet are bare, but the brown nether limbs are clad airily in Swiss muslin trousers, over which falls to the knee a tunic of the same material striped with fine lines of gold, silver, or scarlet thread and girdled with a vivid-hued sash, this again partly covered with a loose silk waistcoat—

pink, green, or blue— glittering with spangles. Brimless hats of red and yellow straw, like inverted flat-bottomed baskets, are wrapped with many scarlet folds, and the boatswains add one more touch of splendor in their great wrought-silver buttons and yards of silver chain, from which hangs suspended the whistle of their office. I am at first inclined to suspect them of having looted the wardrobe of an odalisque, but am assured it is only the muster for the usual Sunday-morning inspection and their accustomed costume for such occasions. A brief but imposing ceremony, this. The officers exchange their white jackets for blue coats. The doctor solemnly confers with the captain, and those in imperfect hygienic condition stand on one foot in apologetic embarrassment, as they catch the piercing and reproachful glance of their command-er, who passes ceremoniously down the line accompanied by the en-tire staff, acknowledging with condescending salute the row of brown hands lifted to the brown brows.

The boatswain sounds his whistle, the ranks are broken, and the affair is over.

Every one goes and gets something to drink as a freshener after so much excitement and the officers change back into white jackets.

As the little fawn-eyed punkah-wallah (to put it in American, the boy who pulls the hanging fan over the table) passes me, I snatch off his turban and find his round brown head shaved smooth as my palm, ex-cept for the one lock over the brow by which Mahomet is to catch him up to heaven. He finds this liberty only an amusing condescension on my part, and smiles indulgently and shyly, following me about always afterwards with little mute services and attentions— so sweet-natured are these Eastern folk.

We sail through the blue days on a level keel. The sea does not even breathe; but it quivers in the terrible splendors of the noon with undreamable peacock radiances.

The sky arches to a dome of intolerable vastness, filled with a blinding light. Hardly can its glories be borne, even in the shadow of the wide awning where one lies half the day in Indian lounging-chairs, warmed to the very heart and soaked through and through with color and light.

There are no pageants of sunsets. The burning ball, undimmed by any cloud, falls swiftly and is quenched in the ocean, and after an in-

stant of crepuscular violet the prodigious tide of light vanishes abruptly, like some vast conflagration blown out suddenly, and as suddenly
succeeded by

> "The night of ebon blackness,
> Laced with lusters of starry clusters."[1]

Then the constellations hang in the awful vault of darkness like enormous gleaming lamps trembling in suspension. And from the swart
deep beneath whirl up myriads of great ghostly jewels, glittering with
unearthly fires and trailing a broad waving path of spectral silver along
the black waters in our wake.

Every hour brings us nearer the equator, and on the morning of
the 23d of December we sight Singapore, seventy miles only from the
centre of heat. The waters of the harbor are curiously banded in broad
lines of brilliant violet, green, and blue, each quite distinct and with no
fusions of color. Against the skyline everywhere are the feathery heads
of palms, and the tremendous riot of verdure upon all the hills is of a
vivid, dazzling green. The vegetation is enormous, rampant, violent... It
stands round about the place like an army with banners, ready to rush
in at any breach and destroy. It contests every inch of space with man,
and, aided by incessant heat and moisture, constantly wrests from him
his conquests and buries them in a fury of iridescence. Seven hundred
years has this City of the Lions stood, but the never-ending battle with
tropic nature's lust for disintegration has left it with no monuments of
its great age, no venerable buildings to testify to its antiquity. In the
twelfth century Singapore was the capital of the Malayan empire, but
in 1824 the British purchased it from the sultan of Jahore, scarcely
more than a heap of ruins.

Only those who travel to these Eastern ports can form any adequate conception of the ability which has directed English conquest in
the Orient. When they bullied the Malayan sultan into selling Singapore, they were apparently acquiring a ruinous and unimportant territory. To-day this port is the entrepôt of Asian commerce, a coaling
station for vessels of all countries, a deep, safe harbor for England's own
ships and men-of-war, and a point from which she can command both

1   "Grishma, or the Season of Heat," from the Ritu Sanhara of Kalidasa
(translated by Edwin Arnold)

seas. The inhabitants of her Straits Settlements number considerably more than half a million, and the exports and imports are each in value something like £10,000,000 yearly. The United States alone buys there every twelvemonth goods worth more than $4,000,000.

It is very hot. The tall blond, who is grandson of one of the world-famous conquerors of the East, arrays himself in snowy silk and linen and dons a Terrai hat with a floating scarf; but even in this attire moisture sparkles on his rosy skin, and his yellow curls cling damply to his brow. The Ceylon tea-planter, twenty years resident in the tropics, is garbed in the ordinary costume of civilization, and apparently suffers no discomfort. Accompanied by these two and the lady from Boston, I go ashore.

Queer little square carriages, made for the most part of Venetian blinds, wait for us, drawn by disconsolate ponies the size of sheep. Conveyance in the East is a constant source of unhappiness to me. I was deprecatory with the jinrikisha men in Japan, I humbled myself before the chair-bearers of Hong Kong, and now I go and make an elaborate apology to this wretched little beast before I can reconcile it to my conscience to climb into the gharry, or let him drag me about at a gallop.

The earth beneath us is a deep red, the trees are brightly green; to the right lies a rainbow sea, and overhead a sky of burning blue. The town is every color— blinding white, azure, green, red, yellow; the houses heavy squares of lime-washed brick, mostly without windows. Interiors are gloomily cool, and more than enough of the huge fierce glare of day enters through the open door. We pass swiftly through the business part of the town, and beyond to the broad red water-road where the houses face the sea.

One is suddenly aware that the sensory nerves awake in this heat to marvellous acuteness. The eye seems to expand its iris to great size and be capable of receiving undreamed possibilities of luminosity and hue. The skin grows exquisitely sensitive to the slightest touch— the faintest movement of the air. Numberless fine under-currents of sound reach the ear, and the sense of smell is so strong that the perfumes of fruit and flowers at a great distance are penetrating as if held in the hand. One smells everything: ... delicious hot scents of vegetation, ... the steaming of the earth, ... and the faint acrid odors of the many sweating bodies of workers in the sun...

The water-road is full of folk. Tall Hindoos go by leading little cream-white bulls with humped necks, who drag rude carts full of merchandise or fruits— pineapples, mangoes, and cocoanuts. English officials spin past in dog-carts with bare-footed muslin-clad grooms up behind, and wealthy unctuous Chinese merchants bowl about in 'rikishas. Nearly all foot-passengers are half or three-quarters naked. It is an open-air museum of superb bronzes, who, when they condescend to clothe themselves at all, drape in statuesque folds about their brown limbs and bodies a few yards of white or crimson cloth, which adorns rather than conceals. One gasps for breath as there suddenly emerges from a side street what appears to be a fat old lady coming from the bath, her gray hair knotted up carelessly and a towel as her only costume. In reality there is no cause for alarm; it is a dignified elderly Malay merchant in conventional business attire. Every one has long hair and wears it twisted up at the nape of the neck; this, with the absence of beards and the general indeterminateness of attire, makes it difficult to distinguish sexes. The lower class of work people are black, shining, and polished as Indian idols. At work they wear only a breechcloth, but when evening comes they catch up a square of creamy transparent stuff, and by a twist or two of the wrist fold it beautifully and loosely about themselves, and with erect heads tread silently away through the dusk— slender, proud, and mysterious-eyed. The Malays are of an exquisite bronze, gleaming in the sun like burnished gold. They have full silken inky hair, very white teeth, and dress much in draperies of dull-red cotton, which makes them objects delicious to contemplate. Mingled with all these is the ubiquitous Chinaman in a pair of short loose blue breeches, his handsome muscular body shining as yellow satin.

We reach the hotel at last, its gloom, its cloistered arcades and great dark rooms pleasant enough as a refuge from the sun. The dining-room, a great vaulted hall through the centre of the building, is level with the earth, paved with stone and without doors, opening upon the veranda through three archways. Without windows, one can scarcely distinguish anything at first entrance from the glare outside; but presently we find the place full of tables of green and growing plants, and two huge punkahs waving slowly overhead, making a cooling breeze. We are served by Hindoos in garments and turbans of white muslin, who have slender melancholy brown faces, and eyes that shine through wonderful lashes with the soft gleamings of black jewels. I can scarcely eat my tiffin for delight in the enchanting pathetic beauty, the passionate grace and sadness, of the face of the lad who brings me butter in a lordly dish, the yellow rolls laid upon banana leaves, and serves me curry with a spoon made of a big pink shell.

Every one is in lily white from head to heel, like a bride or a debutante— white duck trousers and fatigue jacket, white helmet, and white shoes.

This is the dress of two young subalterns[1] with heads like canary birds, and the sappy red of English beef still in their cheeks, just out from home for their first experience of Eastern service. They are full of energy, interest, and enthusiasm; they order beer and beef, and mop their hot faces from time to time, listening meanwhile with profound respect to the words of their superior officer, who condescends to tiffin with them and to give them good advice. His dress is similar to theirs, save for the gold straps on his shoulders, but all the succulent English flesh has been burned off of him long ago, and left him lean, tawny, and dry. He quenches his thirst with a little iced brandy and soda, eats sparingly of curry and fruit, and seems not to feel the heat much He has no enthusiasms, he has no interests except duty and the service, and he does not think any brown or yellow person in the least pretty or pleasant. His advice to the youngsters, while valuable, is saturninely patronizing and full of disillusionment, and one can see it falls somewhat coldly upon their youthful ardor.

Mine is a huge dim apartment with a stone floor opening directly upon the lawn and into the dining-room, and has only slight jalousies for doors; but no one peers or intrudes. The bed is an iron frame; the single hard mattress is spread with a sheet, and there are no covers at all. Even the pillow is of straw. My bath-room, a lofty flagged chamber, opens into this one, and contains a big earthenware jar which the coolies fill for me three times a day, and into which I plunge to rid me of the burning heat.

That night I have the most terrible adventure. Immediately I get into bed and blow out the candle, I hear what sounds like some great

1   British army officer below the rank of captain

animal stalking about. I am cold enough now – icy, in fact... What can it be? ...

They tell me tigers come over from the mainland and carry off on an average one person a day... This is probably a tiger. He could easily push open those blind doors and walk in! ... He is coming towards the bed with heavy stealthy rustlings. There is not even a sheet to draw up over me. The room is hot, utterly black and still, save for the sound of those feet and the loud banging of my heart against my ribs.

The hotel seems to be dead, so horribly silent it is. Has the tiger eaten every one else already?

The darkness is of no use; he can see all the better for that; so I will strike a match and at least perish in the light.

As the blue flame on the wick's tip broadens I meet the gaze of a frightfully large, calm gray rat who is examining my shoes and stockings with care. He regards me with only very faint interest, and goes on with his explorations through all my possessions. He climbs the dressing-table and smells critically at my hat and gloves... This is almost as bad as the tiger, but as I have no intention of attacking this terrible beast and my notice appears to bore him, I blow out the candle and go to sleep, leaving him to continue those heavy rustlings which so alarmed me.

We secure an open carriage with two fine bronzes in muslin and turbans on the box, and go for a drive. The blond takes us first to call at a great white airy stone bungalow, set on a hill where resides the chief of police, another English officer clad in white and as brown and lean as are all who have seen long service here. He gives a command in Malay to his khitmagar, and we are served with tea in the Chinese fashion. No other English official can equal him in his knowledge of the Malay tongue and character, and for this reason he is sent to conduct negotiations with the sultan of Jahore whenever that potentate grows restless. None of his own suite understand what he says while there, but he always comes back with the desired concessions from the monarch and may therefore be supposed to speak the language convincingly and with eloquence... He has learned in his score of years in the East great gentleness of voice and manner, but underneath it is felt at once the iron texture of this man whom the natives regard with undisguised respect and fear.

From his gates the road turns towards the botanical gardens, a great park where wide red ways wind through shaven lawns and under enormous blossoming trees. Every plant one knows as exotic is here quite at home – the giant pads of the Victoria regia pave the moats with circles of emerald, and the lotus lifts its rose-flushed cups from glassy pools where swans float in shadow. We leave the carriage and pace through the translucent green twilight of the orchid houses built of wire gauze, the plants needing no protection here, where for six thousand years or so the thermometer has been ranging between seventy-five and ninety-five degrees of heat. The place is full of strange unfamiliar perfumes and grotesque blossoms, ghostly white, pallidly purple, and writhen into fantasticalities of scarlet. Our carriage waits for us in the shade of a blooming tree, and, returning, we find it sprinkled with small golden trumpets poignantly sweet.

On the way home we pass the governor's palace with its wonderful palms and bamboos, and it is upon this road that we come suddenly upon a race of brown goddesses— Klings they are called— transplanted here from Pondicherry, the fragment of India still retained by France.

We pass one alone, then two, then several more going singly along the wide road shaded by enormous trees.

They are very tall, with round slender limbs... Their garments— a long scarf of thin white wrapped firmly about the hips, drawn lightly over the bosom and crossing the back from shoulder to waist— but half conceal beneath the semi-transparent drapery the fine outline of breast and hip, clear and firm as ancient statues, and warmly brown with a curious faint bloom—almost as of a grape— upon the skin. As they go forward, lightly and fleetly, on their slim bare feet they have the proud, upstanding grace of palms, and with a strange sinuous motion make all their heavy anklets and bangles tinkle like little bells and a wave of fluent movement stir their garments from throat to heel. The ripples of their hair, drawn back from the broad brown brows and knotted in silken abundance at the nape, glitter like polished jet, and the fine, haughty, dark features lit with little points of gold— tiny studs set in the high nostrils and the upper rims of the little ears.

As we pass, they raise languid great eyes of unfathomable blackness with a gaze half mystical, half sensual, that stirs the heart with a vague sudden pain of yearning and sadness... It is a race famous throughout India for the astonishing beauty of its women; but as they will not allow themselves to be photographed, I can get no record of their loveliness.

Half-past four! The ship is about to sail. We have wandered through the shops and museums, and have returned once more to our old quarters. Tiny canoes cluster about the vessel, full of beautiful shells of which one can buy a boat-load for a dollar. Other canoes hold small Malays ranging from three to seven years of age, all naked save for the merest rag of a breechcloth, all pretty as little bronze curios, and all shouting in shrill chorus for coins. A few shillings changed into the native currency procures a surprising number of small pieces of money, which we fling into the clear water. They plunge over after these with little splashings like frogs, and wiggle down swiftly to the bottom, growing strange and wavering of outline and ghostly green as they sink. They are wonderfully quick to seize the glinting coin before it touches the sands below, and come up wet, shining, and showing their white teeth. We play at this game until the whistle blows, and then sail away, leaving the blond waving his handkerchief to us from the shore.

An hour later we are still steaming near the palm-fringed coast. There is a sudden cry and struggle forward— a naked yellow body with manacled hands shoots outward from the ship's side and disappears in a boiling circle of foam. A Chinese prisoner, being transported to Penang, has knocked down his guards and taken to the water. The engines are reversed and a life-buoy thrown overboard, but he does not appear. After what seems a great lapse of time, a head shows a long distance away and moves rapidly towards the shore. Evidently he has slipped his handcuffs and can swim. A boat is lowered full of Lascars very much excited, commanded by the third officer, a ruddy young fellow— calm and dominant. They pursue the head, but it has covered more than half the distance, some two miles, between us and the shore before it is over-taken. There is some doubling back and forth, an oar is raised in menace, and the fugitive submits to be pulled into the boat. I am standing by the gangway when he returns. He is a fine, well-built young fellow. His crime is forgery, and he is to be turned over to the native authorities against whom he has offended. Their punishments are terrible: prisoners receive no food, and must depend upon the memories and mercies of the charitable.

One of the Lascars holds him by the queue as he mounts the steps. He is wet and chilled, and has a face of stolid despair.

They take him forward, and I see him no more.

It is Christmas Day— still very hot; and off to our right are to be seen from time to time the bold purple outlines of the coasts of Sumatra. The ship is decorated with much variegated bunting, and the servants assume an air of languid festivity; but most of us suffer from plaintive reminiscences of home and nostalgia. There is a splendid plum-cake for dinner, with a Santa Claus atop, huddled in sugar furs despite the burning heat. We pull Christmas crackers, as in the holidays at home, and from their contents I am loaded with paste jewels and profusely provided with poetry in brief segments and of an enthusiastically amatory nature.

Penang. —Its peaks shoot sharply up into the blue air 2000 feet, wrapped in a tangle of prodigious verdure to their very tops, enormous palm forests fringing all the shore. The ship anchors some distance from the docks, and will remain but a few hours. We are ferried to land in crazy sampans, the only alternative from out-rigger canoes— a narrow trough set on a round log and kept upright by a smaller floating log connected with the boat by bent poles. Only a native, a tight-rope walker, or a bicyclist would trust himself to these.

The same crowd of Hindoos, Malays, and Chinese.

Little girls of twelve or thirteen stand about with their own children in their arms. They have been wives for a year or two. Very pretty they are, miniature women fully formed; the babies fat and brown and nearly as large as the mothers.

A gharry and another pitiful little horse take us towards the gardens and the famous waterfall. The road skirts the town and intersects lagoons, where Malay houses of cocoanut thatch stand upon piles like ancient lake dwellings. They live over this stagnant water by preference, and apparently suffer no harm. Farther on, where the ground rises, are the huge stone bungalows of English officials and rich Chinese merchants, the entrance to the grounds of the latter adorned with ornate doors and guarded by carved monsters, curiously colored.

We overtake a Chinese funeral winding towards the cemetery, all the mourners clad in white. The coffin, of unpainted wood, is so heavy and so large that twenty pall-bearers are required to carry it. It is a most cheerful cortége. No one seems in the least downcast or dispirited by this bereavement— death is accepted by that race with the same stolid philosophy as are the checkered incidents of life.

The road turns and sweeps into the palm forest. Innumerable slender, silver-gray columns soar to an astonishing height— a hundred feet or more— bearing at the top a wide feathery crown where the big globes of the cocoanuts hang, green and gold.

Up there, in the tops of the palms, flows a dazzling flood of light, and as the faint warm wind waves the huge drooping fans we catch flashes of flaming blue; but below we are in shadow and cannot feel the wind's breath. A profound green twilight reigns here, with something, I know not what, of holy sadness and awe amid these silent gray aisles— delicate, lofty, still— such as might move the heart in an ancient minister's calm pillared silences...

Our guide, a brown lad of ten, stands on the carriage-step clinging to the door, and chatters fluently in tangled and intricate English, of which he is obviously inordinately vain. At the garden entrance he makes us dismount, vehicles not being allowed inside, and leads us along the broad, beautifully tended paths. The garden lies between two very lofty cone-shaped peaks and is as well kept and full of tropical blossoms and verdure as are all the others we have seen. The boy stops to show me in the grass tiny fronds of the sensitive-plant, that shudder away from his rude little finger with a voluntary movement startling to see in a plant.

We hear the rushing speech of waters calling loudly in the hills, but see nothing save the mountain's garments of opulent verdure. A path zigzags sharply upward through the trees and vine labyrinth, and by this the boy leads the way with the speed and agility of a goat. We pant along in his wake, barely keeping him in sight.

It is frightfully hot in here among the trees. The atmosphere is a steam bath, and the moisture pours down our faces as we spring from stone to stone and corkscrew back and forth, deafened by the vociferations of the fall, but catching no glimpse of it. Exhausted, gasping, streaming with perspiration, we finally emerge upon a plateau high on the peak's side and are suddenly laved in that warm wind that stirred the palm fronds... At our feet is a wide, quivering green pool, crossed by a frail bridge; from far above leaps down to us a flood of glittering silver that dashes the emerald pool into powdery foam, races away under the bridge, and springs again with a shout into the thickets below. We lose sight of it amid the leaves, but can hear its voice as it leaps from ledge to ledge down to the valley and is silenced at last in the river.

A tiny shrine built here at the side of this first pool is tended by a thin melancholy-eyed young priest, who lives alone at this great height, his only companions the ceaseless bruit of the waters and the little black elephant-headed god in the shrine. He bears a spot of dried clay upon his forehead— a token of humility. At his morning devotions he dips his hand in the water, then in the dust, touches it upon his brow, and wears this sign of submission all day. I lay a piece of money upon the altar, and in return am given a handful of pale, perfumed pink bells that grow upon the mountain-side, and are the only sacrifice offered to the little black god. The priest will have me remove my hat and decorate my hair with the flowers in the fashion in which his country-women wear them, and is pleased when I comply.

Back again through the steaming woods and the palm aisles; then the ship once more, and our faces are turned towards Ceylon.

Sixth Stage

It is a five days' run from Penang to the island of Ceylon; the shop's company has dwindled to a handful, and time hangs heavily upon us. We are reduced, for lack of other occupations, to an undue interest in the ship's menagerie.

The pretty little fifth officer has a monkey— a surreptitious monkey, not allowed to members of the staff— and at such time as the stern seniors are on duty we amuse ourselves fearfully and secretly with his antics.

A tiny Methuselah-faced simian, regarding all his human cousins with loathing suspicion, but to be placated with raisins. A small shivering, chattering captive, dancing to amuse his jailers, with a grin of hate on his sorrowful weazened countenance. At other times, while the powers that be look on, the Fifth and I sport ostentatiously with two gorgeous and permissible cockatoos, whom we find, like most things permissible, dull and uninteresting.

The consul to Bangkok— a slim, brown gentleman with a soft, languid voice and tiny feet— is carrying home a family of Siamese cats; white, with tawny legs and fierce blue eyes; uncanny beasts with tigerish ways. They live in the fo'castle in company with an impulsive Chinese puppy of slobberingly affectionate disposition; and their prowling, long-legged behavior gets upon his nerves most terribly. He is too manly a little person to hurt them, and his only refuge is an elaborate pretence of not seeing; even when they rub against his nose he gazes abstractedly off into space and firmly refuses to be aware of their existence.

The doctor has two families of felines— one a respectable tortoise-shell British matron, absorbed with the cares of a profuse maternity, and the other a splendid Persian lady, madly jealous of the division in her owner's affections. He purchased her from a native on the wharves at Bombay— smelling of violet powder and with a gold thread around her neck— a theft from some zenana,[1] and wild with several days' starvation and bad treatment. She has not, however, forgotten the ways of her odalisque mistress, and is greedy, luxurious, indolent, and bad-tempered. If the doctor dares, after touching the kittens, to caress her without having previously washed his hands, her keen nose detects his perfidy; she flies into a fury, claws, spits, rages, and finally rushes up into the rigging to sulk until he grovels with apologies and holds out seductive visions of dinner.

It is eight o'clock in the morning. The ship is anchored off the coast of Ceylon.

We arrived late last night; sailing into the harbor by the light of great tropical stars and the planet gleams of a pharos shining from the tall clock-tower of Colombo. Already many ships lie in the narrow roadstead, and it requires the fine art of navigation to slip our boat's huge bulk into her berth between two of these and make her fast to her own particular buoy. The pilot came aboard just outside, and it is his firm hand that jams her nose up to within three hairs' breadth of the vessel in front, holds her there with a grip of iron, and with cautious screw-revolutions swings her into line with her heels in the very face of the Australian mail-ship— arrived a few hours earlier.

Then the entire passenger list— on deck for the last half-hour, aiding the pilot by holding its breath— sighs relievedly and joyously, and goes below in a body to recuperate on brandy and soda.

I linger a moment in the darkness to smell the fragrance of the night, moved by the vast flowings of a warm sweet wind. Seafarers of other days told of these perfumes of the Spice Island filling their sails far out at sea, but the coal smoke of the modern ship deadens the nostril of the modern traveller, and fills his heart with naughty doubts of the veracity of the Ancient Mariner.[2] Natheless there are in

---

1   Section of a house meant for the seclusion of women
2   Reference to Samuel Taylor Coleridge's "Rime of the Ancient Mariner" (1834)

the mountain forests of Ceylon strange, treeless, lake-like expanses of aromatic lemon grass from which the winds come heavy with intoxicating scents... I fancy I can detect faint delicious savors in the air, and that night – sleeping with open port-holes— I dream of perfumes.

I am up early to have the first possible view of an island so like to Paradise that Adam was first banished to this place that he might not feel too sharply in the beginning his loss and the contrast.

Upon Adam's Peak— a soaring pinnacle seven thousand feet high, of which we caught a glimpse yesterday while still far at sea— stood the father of men and wept his lost Eden, for which even Ceylon might not console him; the bitter rain of this immeasurable grief trickling down the mountain-side into the rocks, the rivers, the sea, and the sands, where it is found to-day as clear shining gems and pearls like tears. It was upon this peak that, having clothed himself in the skins of beasts, he shred abroad to the winds the first green garments that hid his primal nakedness, and these, scattered far and wide by the breeze, sprang up in spice plants— so ambrosial a potency had even the leaves of the trees in Paradise.

Very like in the early morning looks this island of jewels, of flowers, and palms to the long-lost heavenly gardens. It floats upon a smooth, nacreous waste of waters, under a sky of pale warm violet, veiled in a dawn-mist faint and mysterious as dreams. Beyond the massive break-water of our straitened harbor curve the rims of white beaches frilled with foam, where palms lean over to look at themselves in a sea of green mother-of-pearl. Inland the purple distances rise into lofty outlines deliciously softened and rounded by their enormous garment of verdure. The prospect is very pleasing. One is prepared to condone any possible vileness of the inhabitants.

It is very hot. The thermometer even at this hour (it is the last day of December) registers 80°; but it is less oppressive than at Singapore, where one seemed to be breathing tepid water rather than air.

A long wharf juts out into the harbor with a custom-house at its landward end. We pause here to exchange some civilities concerning the weather, and pass on with our luggage unmolested, so soothing and plentiful a lack of curiosity have these officials in British ports.

The soil is red— bright red— the color of ground cinnabar. Not "liver-colored," as the earth seemed to the ancient Northmen, but deep-tinted as if soaked with dragon's blood, of which antiquity believed cinnabar to be made. A broad street, fringed with grass and tulip-trees, goes inland, and on either side are massive white buildings with arched and pillared arcades... The vividness of color here is astounding— brilliant, intense, like the colors of precious stones. We doubt the evidence of our senses— doubt the earth can be so red, the sea and sky so blue... It is a miracle wrought by the ineffable luminosity of the Eastern day! One's very flesh tingles with an ecstasy of pleasure in this giant effulgence of color, as might a musician's who should hear the prodigious vibrations of some undreamably colossal harp.

The Grand Oriental Hotel lies to the right of this road, near the water; big and glaringly white without, cool and shadowy within. Ships from India, China, and Australia have just arrived, and the place is crowded. The clack of many heels rings on the stone floor of the arcade, which opens upon an inner flowery court, where also look out the windows of the sleeping-rooms above, veiled by delicate transparent straw mattings— waving softly in and out in the little hot breezes, giving treacherous glimpses now and again of a pretty dishevelled head and tumbled white draperies... The arcade is full of British folk— Australians and Anglo-Indians, passing to and fro to the dining-room, to the stairs, to the front entrance. Handsome, as an Anglo-Saxon crowd of the well-to-do is apt to be— tall, florid men in crisp white linen and white Indian helmets; tall, slim, well-poised girls in white muslin, with a delicious fruit-like pink in their cheeks, brought there by the heat, which curls their blond hair in damp rings about their brows and white necks. And tall, imposing British matrons, with something of the haughtiness of old Rome in their bearing— the mothers and wives of conquerors.

Our rooms are at the end of a long corridor, looking on the street. They are carpetless and uncurtained, their dim twilight being sifted from the burning glare without through green mattings hung at the windows. Before my door sits my own particular servant, detailed to wait upon this bedroom. Similar servants are stationed along the corridor in front of their respective charges. This attendant seems never to go away, for at whatever hour I need him he is there. Even at night he does not desert his post, unrolling a rug and sleeping where he sat all day... A curious creature— of a sex not easily to be determined. Mildbrowed and woman-eyed, with long, rippling black hair knotted at the back and kept smooth with a tortoise-shell band comb, the brown femininities of his face disappear at the chin in a short close-curled black beard. He is full-chested as a budding girl, but clothes himself to the waist in shirt, coat, and waistcoat, the slender male hips being wrapped in a white skirt that falls to the ankles.

He is, however, an eminently agreeable person. The gentle and confiding affection of his manner leaves speechless with joyful amazement the humbled victim of the harsh and haughty tyranny of the American servant-girl. He not only executes orders with noiseless despatch, but receives them with a little reverence of the slim fingers to the brow, and a look in his lustrous eyes of such sweet eagerness to serve that my heart is melted within me. I find myself asking for hot water with the coo of a sucking dove; I demand butter at table in the mild tones of a wind-harp, and converse with the guide in a manner I might naturally assume to a beloved younger sister. This atmosphere of loving-kindness is that of Paradise. It expands the heart with unreflecting happiness, and makes man, even servant-man, my brother. Discreetly I refrain from too close examination, lest this refreshing mirage resolve on nearer view to blank and desert indifference, and for these two days I choose to live in a sunshine of reciprocal amenities.

It is the sacred and beautiful hour of tiffin. The dining-room is as white, cool, and nobly plain as a Greek temple; long and very lofty—reaching to the roof— the second story opening upon it in an arched and balustraded clere-story. Two punkahs[1] of gold-colored stuff wave above us. On one side we look upon the arcaded court, and through the heavy-arched veranda upon the hot gorgeousness of color outside. Bowls of tropical flowers are set on each table, and under the salt-cellars and spoons at the corners are laid large leaves of curious lace-like pattern, freaked with splashes of red and yellow. More of the fawn-eyed men with long hair serve us, and the assemblage gathered here for the moment is a remarkable one. Near the door sits a good-looking young man, accompanying a party of blond girls in smart frocks. It is Wordsworth's grandson, and the owner of Rydal Mount. At the table next him is a stern, lean soldier with a melancholy face— the Lord Chelms-

---

1   (Indian) cloth fan hung from the ceiling, moved by pulling on hanging cords

ford in whose African campaign the Prince Imperial was killed and the English suffered a hideous butchery, surprised by the savages. On the other side of the room is a young man with a heavy blond countenance— Dom Leopoldo Agostino and half a dozen things more, who has just met here, in his voyage round the world in a Brazilian warship, the news of his grandfather Dom Pedro's dethronement and exile. The captain of the ship dares not continue the cruise in the face of peremptory cables from the new government, and the young man is suddenly marooned here, with all his luggage and attendants, under the protection of the British lion, who has always a friendly paw for *les rois en exil.*[1] Near us is a man with a bulging orehead and a badly-fitting frock-coat of black broadcloth— a noted mesmerist from America, with a little Texan wife fantastically gowned; she, poor soul, having a picturesque instinct, but no technique. Beyond him is a man of middle age, with a fine, saturnine countenance, lean and bold as the head of Cæsar, and an air of great distinction. It is Sir William Robinson, an Irishman, a well-known composer, and a colonial governor. Beside him sits Sir Henry Wrenfordsly, a colonial chief-justice. At their table is Lady Broome, a tall, handsome woman with a noble outline of brow and head. Under the title of Lady Barker, she is the author of many well-known and delightful books on life in the Antipodes. Sir Napier Broome is also tall and handsome, and is on his way home from an Australian governorship.

In the arcade that faces on the street are native shops— tiny cells full of basket-work, wrought brass, laces, jewels; carvings in ivory, ebony, and tortoise-shell; India shawls and silks, Cingalese silver-work, and such small trinkets and souvenirs best calculated to lure the shy rupee from its lair in the traveller's pocket. Most of these shops are kept by Moormen— large, yellow, unpleasant-looking persons in freckled calico petticoats, heads shaven quite clean and covered with a little red basket too small for the purpose. They inspire carking disgust and suspicion by their craven oiliness; their wares for the most part not worth a tenth of the sums asked.

Jewels are to be had at astonishing rates— cat's-eyes and moonstones being sold carelessly by the handful. The arcade is full of itinerant merchants who carry their stock of precious stones – sometimes

1   French: "kings in exile"

quite valuable— tied up in a dingy rag, disposing of them by methods of barter quite unique. Twenty times the proper value is demanded, and poignant outcries of bitter astonishment greet the unbelievably meagre offer of the Sahib, who should be as father and as mother to the merchant, but who proffers him only an insult. The rag is tied up in wounded amazement half a dozen times before a compromise suggests itself. Innocent joy dawns on the vender's countenance— chance shall settle it. Will the Sahib toss to decide whether he shall give for this beautiful cat's-eye two pounds or five? The original sum asked having been twenty, the Sahib sees signs of relenting, and consents to try the turn of the coin. The toss is fairly conducted, and whether he wins or loses the importunate merchant appears content, as in any case he makes a profit. This warfare of barter being as the breath of his nostrils, he is reduced to the verge of tears by the heartless conduct of those who pay him his price without protest or haggling. He himself is given to discomposing coups de commerce— offering a bit of tortoise-shell carving for five pounds, and accepting the five shillings proffered in derision with breath-snatching alacrity.

A snake-charmer is squatting in the dust before the hotel, perform-ing feats of juggling: playfully depositing an egg in one ear, and in a moment picking it, with a sweet smile of surprise, out of the other— or seeming to do it.

Tossing into the air a cocoanut, which obviously he has no present use for, as it remains up there out of sight for a time while he goes on with his other tricks, until we are suddenly aware of its lying beside him, and cannot recall whether it was there from the first or not.

—Rubbing his egg between open, outstretched palms until they meet and the egg is rubbed away to nothing at all, and restoring it to existence by rotary movements of his palms in the opposite direction.

Simple feats that are surprising, because he is quite naked save for a turban and a loin-cloth, and has no aids to his art but the brown cot-ton bag in which he carries his few properties, and a small flat basket where a cobra is coiled. But his hands are marvellously deft and supple – the hands of an old race, slim, pliant, well modelled, and exquisitely dexterous.

—He takes off the cover of the snake basket, the reptile within lying sullenly sluggish until a rap over the head induces him to lift himself angrily, puff out his throat, and make ready to strike. But his master is playing a low, monotonous tune on a tiny bamboo flute, with his eyes fastened upon the snake's eyes, and swaying his nude body slowly from side to side.

The serpent stirs restlessly, and flickers his wicked, thin red tongue; but the sleepy tune drones on and on, and the brown body moves to and fro— to and fro. Presently the serpent begins to wave softly, following the movements of the man's body and with his eyes fixed on the man's eyes, and so in time sinks slowly in a languid heap of relaxed folds... The music grows fainter, fainter; dies away to a breath— a whisper—ceases. The man hangs the helpless inert serpent— drunk with the insistent low whine of the flute— about his bare neck and breast, and comes forward to beg a rupee for his pains.

We— the Lady from Boston, her son, the Ceylon tea-planter, and myself— hire a guide and carriage and go for a drive. Through the town, past the tall clock-tower whose flashing light showed our path last night; past the banks and the haunts of the money-changers— "shroffs" with fat, yellow, hook-nosed faces, clad in crisp white buttoned with gold, and with great circles of thin gold wire in their ears and black-and-gold head-dresses on their smooth-shaven crowns.— Past the beautiful sickle-shaped beach of Galle Face, and then inland along the shadowy dank roads under the heavy green vault of the multitudinous palms— cocoanut palms (forty millions of these, the guide says), Palmyra palms, from which the heady palm-wine is made; Kitul palms that yield sugar and sago; talipot palms, upon whose papyrus-like leaves were inscribed the sacred writings—Mahawanso— five hundred years before Christ, and preserved twenty-two centuries at Wihares; and the areca palm, that gives the nuts the natives chew with their betel leaves. We pass banyan-trees with roots like huge pythons coiling through the grass, and down-dropped stems from the far-spreading branches, making dim, leafy cloisters. Breadfruit-trees, monster ferns, pools full of lotus plants, and orchids growing almost as freely as weeds.

The guide, a gentlemanly person in a skirt, has the usual mane of rippling hair bound in a sleek knot at the nape, and at my request he untwists this and lets it fall far below his waist in silky black waves— restoring it in a moment by a quick turn of the wrist to its former neat compactness. He has never seen a hair-pin, and the gift of one of mine childishly delights and amuses him. He thrusts it in and out of his hair, and finally fastens it upon a string of queer charms and fetiches worn in his bosom.

He wraps for me a bit of areca nut with a paste of wet lime in a leaf of the betel pepper, and bids me chew it. Instantly my mouth is full of a liquid red as blood, and tongue and lips are shrivelled with a sharp aromatic astringent resembling cloves. I hasten to spit it out, but all day my lips are still hot and acrid from the brief experiment. The entire population of Ceylon are wedded to the betel habit, save the servants of Europeans who object to the unpleasant vampire red of the stained mouth and corroded teeth. It harms no more than tobacco, and the natives prefer it even to food. From time to time along the road we come upon old women sitting upon the earth with little stores of nuts, lime, and betel leaves spread before them for the refreshment of the wayfarer.

"Mem Sahib," says the guide, touching his brow with his fingers, and giving me one of those smiling black glances— "you are my father and my mother. Will you that we go to the cinnamon gardens?" ... And on the way he feeds upon ripe mangoes that have a reddish custard-like pulp, sweetly musky in flavor.

From among the cinnamon bushes growing without order in the white sand, and breathing faint odors in the steaming heat, starts out a lean, naked lad begging for alms. He is not to be shaken off, following in a leaping dance with flying hair and a white-toothed smile, clapping his elbows against his ribs with a noise like castanets, and rattling his bones together loudly and merrily as though a skeleton pranced after us through the dust; so that we are fain to end the exhibition of his unique powers with a few coins.

In the museum that stands in the cinnamon gardens we find Eden's serpents – the reverse side of this painted island paradise. The dull, venomous cobra in his spotted cowl; clammy, strangling folds of long pythons; twenty-foot sharks with horrid semi-circular hedges of teeth— the wolves of these pearl-sown seas— and endless stinging, biting, poisoning creatures wrought into wanton bizarreries by nature in some mood of cynical humorousness. Here are also the uncouthly hideous masks of the old devil dancers; great gold ornaments, splendid robes, and the ingeniously murderous weapons of this mild-mannered race, who count in their history twenty-six kings done treacherously to death. In other rooms are the stuffed skins of beautiful birds, huge mammals, and collections of rich-colored butterflies and moths— all very hardly defended from the ravenous tropical disintegration, as fierce and implacable as the productiveness is profuse. It is a nature that devours her own children; creating with a furious fecundity, and consuming all her creations with insatiable, relentless voracity.

A long road among palms. Palm-thatched huts, with idle brown folk, half naked, dreaming in the heat. A door in a ruinous wall— shaven-headed priests in yellow robes— then a dim temple, with tall gods whose heads reach stiffly up to the roof.

Penetrating jasmine odors from altars heaped with stemless pink blossoms, and the Lord Buddha reclining on his elbow, drowsing in the hot semi-darkness among the stifling scents. He is forty feet long, painted a coarse vivid crimson and yellow, but his flat wooden face is fixed in the same passive, low-lidded calm that we saw upon it when he sat on his lotus among the Japanese roses, or listened in his tiny mountain shrine at Penang to loud voices of the waters. A Nirvana peace, undisturbed by passions or pity ... dreaming eternal dreams in the hot, perfumed gloom. About the walls are painted in archaic frescoes the pains and toils of his fifty incarnations of Buddhahood, through which he attained at last to this immortal peace. Vishnu and Siva are the tall gods that stand by the doorway, for to these he gives room and shares with them his altar flowers.

A swarm closes about us as we emerge, crying for alms, and not to be ignored or beaten off. They have roused themselves from their lethargy in the simmering gloom of the palm-shaded huts, and throng clamorous and insistent for the charity the Lord Buddha has enjoined, impeding our footsteps and clinging to the carriage. Old women hold out the little soft hands of the dimpled naked babies they carry on their hip. They themselves are hideous, repulsive hags— mere wrinkled, disgusting rags of humanity, with red-stained, toothless mouths; and this at forty years. The young women are plump and pretty, with a discontented knot in their brows, and hopeless, peevish mouths— femininity being a perplexing and bitter burden in the East. Small brown imps, naked as Adam, save for a heavy silver necklace hung about their fat, little stomachs, cling to our knees and use their fine eyes with a coquette's conscious power, smilingly seducing the coin out of our pockets.

It is the last night of the old year, and the dining-hall has been converted into a ballroom. The men, all in white, with gay sashes about their middle, are circling languidly with pretty English girls in their arms. A high, warm wind whirls through the veranda and flutters the draperies of the lookers-on.

The woman from Texas, in a fearful and wonderful costume, that casts a slight but comprehensive glance at the modes of three centuries and muddles them all, is tossing her powdered head and flirting shrilly with the soft-voiced governor with the Cæsar face. A handsome ruddy old soldier with gray hair is moodily mounting guard over his three lank-elbowed partnerless daughters, whose plump and pleasing mamma is frolicking jovially about, clasped to the bosom of all Ceylon's military ornaments. Wordsworth's grandson, who looks as if designed to an order by Du Maurier,[1] is waltzing, lazily graceful, with one of the smartly gowned blond girls...

Faint rhythmic breathings of the music come to my chamber window. The night is hot and silent— full of musky perfumes, of vague ghostly stirrings, of "old unhappy far-off things," that move one with poignant mysterious memories of the dense tropical darkness, with its silent, flitting figures— full of the glimmering, bewildered phantoms of passions and pains that perished centuries ago.

Morning!— The new year is coming in a beautiful green dawn. A chrysoberyl sky, translucent golden green, a misty green sea, and an ocean of feathery green plumes tossing noiselessly, as with a great silent joy, in the morning wind.

I have sprung out of bed to receive a letter— my first one from home. A few lines, scrawled on the other side of the world, that I lean from the window to read in the faint early light. How beautiful they make the new year seem!— Whatever this coming year will contain of grief and rebuffs, at least it has begun with one good moment, and for that it is well to be grateful...

---

1   Daphne du Maurier, English author and playwright famous for her romantic novels

SEVENTH STAGE

AT CEYLON the Australian mail-ship Britannia waits for us. She is one of the enormous Peninsular and Oriental vessels built in the Jubilee year, and is on her way home to England.

Here again farewells: to the dear little old lady from Boston and to my kind and charming friend the Ceylon tea-planter, who has placed me under an endless debt of gratitude by his many courtesies. It is four o'clock in the afternoon of the 1st of January when we swing out of the harbor and direct our course towards Africa.

The height of luxury is achieved on these Peninsular and Oriental steamships. No steerage travel being provided for, space is not stinted to first-class passengers, and saloons, decks, and bedrooms are ample and handsome. The ship's company, Australians on their way home to England, have made themselves thoroughly at home for the six weeks' cruise. Their rooms they have hung with photographs and drapery and bits of bric-à-brac, and on deck each one has a long bamboo lounging-chair, a little table, and a tea-service for that beautiful ceremony of five-o'clock tea— all being made possible by the fact that the sea is smooth as glass and the decks level as a drawing-room floor. Courtesies are exchanged in the form of invitations to this afternoon tea. Three times a week the band plays for dancing on deck; tableaux, private theatricals, and fancy balls fill the evenings, and in the afternoons the after-part of the ship is lively with games of cricket.

The principal personage on board is Miss Ethel Roma Detmold, aged two and a half years, and familiarity known as Baby Detmold. There are other infants aboard, but merely "the common or garden" baby, not to be mentioned with this blue-and-gold girl child who sparkles out upon us a morning vision in a white frock and an enigmatic smile. The entire male force of the ship is her slave, and trailing about after her, humbly suing for favors she is most chary in granting, she possessing already the secret of power over her kind in an airy, joyous indifference to any one's attentions and services, which we therefore— with the curious perversity of human nature— persist in thrusting upon her.

All women are not borne free and equal... There is some subtle force in this tiny turquoise-eyed coquette which will secure for her without effort, her life through, devotion other women may not win with endless sacrifices or oceans of tears. Even the cook's pet chicken, who flies from every one else, allows himself to be hauled about by one leg or squeezed violently to her youthful bosom, and, far from protesting, looks foolishly flattered by the notice of this imperious cherub. Always above and below us it is intensely blue, hot, and calm. Flights of film-winged fishes rise from our path and flit away like flocks of sea-sparrows. Sometimes a whale blows up a column of shining spray and leaves a green wake to show his hidden path. But nothing marks the passing of the hours save the coming and going of light.

When the azure blossom of the day dies in irised splendors, rosy clouds float up over the horizon's edge like wandering fairy islands drifting at will in a golden world— vanishing when the moon appears.

Magical white nights of ineffable stillness and purity fade into the blaze of daffodil dawns... Time goes by in lotus dreams that have no memory of a past or reckoning of a future till we wake suddenly, and find anchor cast in the gulf of Aden.

Red barren masses of stone, broken and jagged like

"An old lion's cheek teeth"[1]

An astonishing aridity everywhere, all the more startling by contrast with the fierce verdure of the lands we have last seen.

Not a drop of rain has fallen here in three years, and no green thing lives in the place. Even the tawny hills rot and fall to dust in the terrible desiccation. The earth is an impalpable dun powder that no roots could

---

1   Robert Browning, "An Epistle Containing the Strange Medical Experience of Karshish, the Arab Physician"

grasp; the rocks are seamed, cracked, and withered to the heart;— the dust and bones of a dead land.

As a coaling station and harbor from which war-ships may guard the entrance of the Red Sea, Aden is valuable; and therefore, like Hong Kong, Singapore, Penang, Ceylon— like everything much worth having in this part of the world— it is an English possession. There are wharves of heavy masonry; the governor's residence, a verandaed bungalow shut in with green persiennes, standing on a little eminence some distance back from the water; and one narrow street of heavy white stone houses with flat roofs, fringing the shore.

A carriage is hired to convey us to the Tanks— the only bit of sight-seeing to be done at Aden.

These Tanks are of unknown antiquity and are variously attributed to Solomon, the Queen of Sheba, the Arabs, and— as a last guess— to the Phœnicians.

Historians, when in doubt, always accuse the Phœnicians.

In this rainless region, where water falls only at intervals of years, it was necessary to collect and preserve it all, and some one built among the hills huge stone basins with capacity of hundreds of thousands of gallons. These basins are quite perfect still, though the name of the faithful builder thereof has long ago perished.

The road winds upward from the sea to a barrier of rocks, and pierces them with a black echoing pass two hundred feet high and fifteen wide, where the English fortifications lie— a place to be held by twenty men against an army.

Here we find Tommy Atkins again, still clad in white linen from top to toe and still rosily swaggering.

On the other side of the wall of hills is the town, a motley assemblage of more flat-topped stone dwellings, all lime-washed as white as snow. In the midst is a well where women in flowing drapery, with tall jars, draw water as if posing for Bible illustrations; and a camel market in which fifty or more of the brown, ungainly beasts have been relieved of their burdens and lain down for the night— doubled into uncomfortable heaps and bubbling and moaning with querulous discontent.

We rattle through the silent, dusty town and find beyond it a garden where a dozen feeble trees have by constant watering been induced to grow as high as our heads, but appear discouraged and drooping and ready to give up the effort at any moment. Behind these are the irregular bowls of masonry set in the clefts at the foot of the rocks, and stretching enormous thirsty mouths open to the arid hills and rainless sky. They are terraced down the sides— steps by which the retreating water can be followed— but happily the place is independent of them now— with a condensing-engine and the inexhaustible supply of the sea...

Night is coming on. There is a crystalline luminosity in this dray air that the vanished sun leaves faintly golden-green. Every fold and crevice of the red rock wall over-flows with intense violet shadows that still are full of light. There is no evening mistiness of vision; the little flat white town, the shore, the turbaned figures moving to and fro in the streets, the ships afloat on the glassy sea, the tawny outline of the rocks— all standing out with keen clearness through the deepening of the twilight.

So might have looked some Syrian evening of long ago; and, as if to answer the thought, there slowly lifts itself above the crest of the hills, in the green dusk, a huge white planet— the Star in the East! ...

The dusk has vanished when we reach the wharf—

"At one stride comes the dark,"[1]

and suddenly, in an instant, innumerable glittering hosts rush into the heavens with a wild, astonishing splendor, startling as the blare of trumpets ... unimaginable myriads, unreckonable millions.

And as our oars dip, the water answers with equal multitudes of wan sea-stars that whirl and wimple through the flood.

Later, when the silver fire of a full moon, by whose light one can read and see colors, has swallowed up this glittering pageant, we go again to the Tanks, passing on the route a loaded train of camels lurching away to the desert through the black shadows of the pass, and, stepping beside them, lean, swarthy Arabs, draped statelily in white— such a caravan as might have gone down into Egypt to buy corn from Pharoah four thousand years ago— nothing in the interval changed in any way.

---

1   Samuel Taylor Coleridge, "The Rime of the Ancient Mariner" (1834).

Our footsteps and our voices echo in hollow whispers from the empty Tanks and the mysterious shadows of the hills, though we walk lightly and speak softly, awed by the vast calm radiance of the African night.

Other than this it is very silent in this dead and desert spot; not a leaf to rustle, not an insect to cry— and even the sea has no speech.

The world grows dreamlike and unreal in the white silence.

We should feel no surprise to come suddenly among the rocks upon a gaunt Hebrew with wild eyes, clothed in skins, and wrestling in the desert with the old unsolvable riddles of existence— a prophet whose scorching words should wither away in one terrible instant all the falsities and frivolities of our lives, leaving us gaping aghast in the awful visage of Truth.

Nor should we start to hear the thin, high voice of a wandering lad with the shadow of a crown above his brow, who should come chanting psalms of longing for green pastures and still waters.

It is a night and a place for such things as these.

The town, beyond which shines the silver sea, is white as pearls in the moonlight, with here and there a yellow gleam from a lamp through an open door. The population is gathered in the square playing dominoes and games of chance at little tables and drinking coffee— liquor being forbidden to these Mohometans.— Bearded Arabs with delicate features and grave, sad eyes, who fold their white bornouses[1] about them with a wonderful effect of dignity; and more jovial and half-naked negroes of every tint and race— from Zanzibar, the Soudan, Abyssinia. The Soudanese are fine, stalwart animals— fighting-men, all— stripped to the waist, shining like polished ebony, with beardless mouths full of ivory teeth, and long wool combed straight out and vividly red – made so by being plastered down for a week under a coat of lime. Egypt and England know well how these men fight; yet when I lean forward and take into my hand the little case of camel-skin containing verses from the Koran, hanging on the muscular black breast of one of these gigantic Africans, he laughs the same mellow, amiable laugh I should hear from a negro at home on the plantation, did I show a like familiarity and interest.

1 Alternative spelling of *burnoose*: a long cloak with a hood, originating in Western Africa

Our way home lies through a reverberant tunnel beneath the fort, where we meet more camels still with that same lounging stride, still with that air of evangelical superiority to a wicked world, and still making, with closed mouths, those suppressed moans of wounded feeling.

The port is fast asleep. In the distance a man-of-war is slowly steaming out of the harbor on its way to the lower coast to over-awe the Portuguese making futile protests against English domination in the neighborhood of Delagoa Bay.

Quite in a moment it seems, it is tomorrow— our last day in the tropics— and I go up on deck before the sun has risen, into the delicious moist warmth of the equatorial morning.

A man— a young man— is lounging in one of the bamboo chairs in a négligé of India silk— drinking a tiny cup of coffee and enjoying the early freshness. No one else is visible.

I hesitate a moment, conscious of the dishevelment of locks beneath the lace scarf tied under my chin, but think better of the hesitation and remain. I may never see this again, this world, where one is really for the first time

"Lord of the sense five,"[1]

—where the light of night and of day have a new meaning; where one is drenched and steeped in color and perfume; where the husk of callous dulness falls away and every sense replies to impressions with a keenness as of new-born faculties.

The young man's silky black head is ruffled too, and his yellow eyes still sleepy as he comes and leans over the rail. He is holding a little black pipe in a slim olive hand that is tipped with deep-tinted onyx-like nails, and with it he points to the first canoe putting out from shore. It is a long brown boat, very narrow, and filled with oranges heaped up in the centre.— It is cutting a delicate furrow along the pearly lilac of the glass-like sea.

A faint gray mist, scarcely more than a film, lies along the shore. Above it the red rocks stand up sharply against the white sky, which the coming sun is changing to gold.

---

1   Alfred Lord Tennyson, "The Palace of Art" (1832, revised 1842)

The young man turns and smiles, showing a row of white teeth through lips as red as pomegranate flowers. He is English, but takes on here certain warm tones of color like a Spaniard.

Every moment I have spent in the tropics is to me just as vivid as this. I see everything. Not a beauty, not a touch of color, escapes me. Every moment of the day means intense delight, beauty, life... And now, after six months, not a line has faded or grown dim. I can live back in it in every emotion, every impression, as though not an hour divided me from it... It is well to have thus once really lived.

The deck swarms with native merchants selling ostrich feathers, grass mats and baskets from Zanzibar; ornaments of shells, boxes of Turkish Delight, embroideries, photographs, and a three-months-old lion cub in a wooden cage.

The Bombay mail, for which we waited, has arrived, and new passengers come ashore with mountains of luggage. Among them is a man with a heavy, smooth, pink face, an overhanging upper lip and long white hair. It is Bradlaugh, the famous atheist, who fought the whole House of Commons, and forced it to admit him without taking the oath. He proves to be a jovial person, with an astounding ingenuity in misplacing h's, and an amusing little way of confiding small details concerning himself with an air of expecting you to snatch out a notebook and jot them down as one who should later make an article for one of the reviews, "Some Confidential Talks with Charles Bradlaugh, M.P." He is returning from India, where he has been attending a congress of natives agitating for representative government. His colleague, Sir William Wedderburn, returns with him— a Scotch baronet, a gentle enthusiast and theoretical radical, whose heart is overflowing with vague tenderness for all mankind.

There is some stir among us because Mr. Stanley has just arrived on the coast from the interior of Africa, and there is talk of his going home in our ship; but the government sends down a special convoy to take him to Egypt, and we steam away without him.

A cold west wind meets us in the Red Sea; the passengers get out their furs, and there is no more lounging on deck— one must walk briskly or sit in the sun wrapped in rugs.

I wake one night missing the throbbings of the screw, and find that we are going at a snail's pace in smooth water. The moon is very dim behind the clouds, and from the port-hole it would appear that we are sailing across endless expanses of sand: nothing else is to be seen. Morning shows a narrow ditch in a desert, half full of green water— so narrow and so shallow apparently that nothing would convince us our great ship could pass through save the actual proof of its doing so.

At one of the wider parts made for this purpose we pass a French troop-ship which dips her colors and sends a ringing cheer from the throats of the red-trousered soldiers on their way to Tonquin.

Later a dead Arab floats by in the green water, but is regarded with indifference as a common episode, and merely suggestive of an imprudent quarrel overnight.

Nothing is to be seen save stones and sand to the very horizon.

A dim and lurid sunset ends the day, and when night comes we are anchored off the town of Port Said— a wretched little place, dusty, dirty, and flaring with cheap vice— all the flotsam of four nations whirling about in an eddy of coarse pleasures. The shopkeepers are wolfish-looking, and bargain vociferously. Almost every other door opens into a gambling-hell and concert-hall. One of these gambling-places boasts an opera. At the tables stand amid the crowd two handsome young Germans— blond, but with none of the ruddy warmth of the English blond; pale and flaxen, with deep-blue eyes and haughty of manner. Not nice faces; high-bred, but cold and brutal. They are officers from Prince Henry of Prussia's ship, the Irene, lying now in the harbor.

In the concert-hall, "Traviata" is being sung by a fourth-rate French troupe, and the audience sit about at little tables, drinking, and eating ices. I ask for something native— Turkish— to drink, and they bring me a stuff that to all the evidences of sight, taste, and smell cries out that it is a mixture of paregoric and water, and one sip contents me. We are glad to go away.

The Mediterranean is cold and not smooth, but here there comes upon one a sense of historical association.

In India nature is so tremendous she swallows up all memory of man; in Aden one remembers only the Bible; but nearing Greece the past takes shape and meaning, and history begins to have a new vividness and significance. Here man has been "lord of the visible earth;" has dominated and adorned her. She has been but the stage and background against which he played out the tragedies and comedies of humanity.

One morning at sunrise the stewardess taps at the door:

"The first officer's compliments, miss, and will you please get up and look out of the scuttle."

I wrap myself in my kimono— treasure-trove from Japan— and thrust head and shoulders through the wide port-hole. Directly before me is Candia— abrupt mountains rising sharply from the sea and crowned with snow. Among them are trailing clouds looping long scarfs of mist from peak to peak; at their feet Homer's "wine-dark sea," furrowed by a thousand keels: ... Greek galleys, Roman triremes, fighting vessels from Carthage, merchant and battle ships from Venice, Genoa, and Turkey; the fleets of Spain; men-o'-war with the English lions at the peak; and, lastly, the world's peaceful commerce, sailing serenely over the bones and rotting hulls that lie below.

The sun comes up gloriously out of the sea, deepening it to a winy purple in its light. Suddenly the mountain-tops take fire; the snow flushes softly, deepens rosily in hue, grows crimson with splendor; the sleeping mists begin to stir and heave, to lighten into gold, to float and rise into the warming blue above. Once more the splendors of a new day— such a sunrise as Cervantes may have seen; as glad Greek eyes may have witnessed bowing in prayer to the sun-god; as the galley-slave may have watched dully as a signal for new labors, and admirals gazed upon with tightening lip, not knowing whether the new sun should look upon defeat or victory, glory or death.

Then the dressing-gong clangs noisily through the ship and the colors pale into the common day.

Next morning, the 16th of January, we are fast to the docks at Brindisi, and but one more stage of the journey remains to be made.

Last Stage

It is a vividly bright day in January, 1890— the 16th. There is a tingling crispness in the air as if it were early autumn— a slight frostiness that chills the skin, but does not penetrate the veins. Rather the deep breaths of this keen, pure sea ozone make the blood pulse with a swift, delicious warmth, like a plunge into cold water.

We are anchored at Brindisi— the ancient Brundusium of the Romans— a town more than twenty-five centuries old, but which does not by any means look its age. It does not appear particularly attractive either from the wharves, and I am more than ever certain— as I always have been certain – that I could never agree with the haughty provincial who preferred to be first in Brundusium rather than second in Rome. Indeed, all efforts now are bent on being first out of Brundusium, as the train leaves within the hour. The Britannia goes on and around to Portsmouth, but the English government runs a train down through France and Italy to meet the P. and O. steamers, and thus gain five days in the arrival of the Indian and Australian mails. This mail train carries one passenger coach for the benefit of personages from the colonies who may be in haste to reach home; and if there are not a sufficient number of these distinguished servants of the empire to fill the car, more ordinary travellers can occupy the vacant berths by cabling ahead and securing them. I have taken this precaution at Ceylon, and find there will be no difficulty in the matter, provided I can get my luggage through the customs in time.

It is almost impossible to get anything done. The whole ship is in an uproar. Mails and luggage are being disembarked. Many passengers are leaving for a tour through Italy before finally returning to England, fearful of the winter fogs and of the influenza raging there. Italians, with cocked hats and imperial importance of manner, are bullying every one and getting things into a hopeless tangle. My luggage is finally marked as passed; a porter is hired to transport it; I go off to attend to the visé of tickets, despatching of cables, and other minor matters, and arrive ten minutes before the advertised departure of the train.

No luggage! I fling out of the car, rush back again to the ship, and discover the missing possessions in the hands of a pig-headed Italian who insists they have not been properly examined, and demands the keys.

Various necessary additions to my wardrobe during the voyage have so enlarged the contents of my little box that only careful packing and the emphatic sitting down upon it of the stewardess and myself have induced it to shut at all. Now this amiable official insists, despite the fact that it goes under seal and bond straight through to England, upon opening it and strewing my garments about the deck.

I hope I did not forget the dignity a gentlewoman should preserve under the most trying of circumstances, but I fancy that my tones, while low, were concentrated, and that the little American I used was "frequent and fluent and free," for the man turned pale and wavered.

I snatched up my belongings, flung them in pell-mell, jumped upon the box, snapped to the hasp, and ran off with a porter towards the train, blank despair in my heart. Happily, Italian trains are not bound down by narrow interpretations of time-tables, and I do succeed in catching it, with the luggage and some few tattered remnants of a once nice temper.

It is very destructive of the mental equilibrium to lose the temper so thoroughly, especially if one is out of practice, and it is fully an hour before the exceeding beauty of the country through which we are passing begins to have its soothing effect and to make me fain to forgive the Italians because of Italy! On our right is the Adriatic, blue as lapis-lazuli and gay with flocking sails. Here and there lie little snow-white towns along its shores, and between are the gray olive orchards, that have something strangely human in their gnarled grotesqueness. Even in flying by one sees flashes of fantastic gargoyle-like resemblances to persons one has known, caricatured into impossible contortions, as if by some mediæval humorousness. It is not difficult to comprehend how people who lived among olive groves developed dryad superstitions and created legends of flying women transformed into trees.

The English government pays the Italian government a large subsidy for this train and the swift passage of the mails, but the ubiquitous person who attends to all our needs— is porter, guard, steward, cook, and brakeman in one— has his own ideas on the subject of haste, and acts accordingly. When we reach a town where he has friends he goes out, quietly winds us up like a Waterbury watch, dismounts, and is received with affectionate enthusiasm by a little crowd on the platform. He inquires solicitously after each one's kin unto the fourth and fifth generation, gives his careful attention to all the local gossip, and retails the news he has been gathering all along the line. When he can no longer hear or tell some new thing he remembers our existence, climbs once more upon his perch, lets us run down with a sudden whir, and we go on our way. At mealtimes he retires into a tiny den amidships, and from a space but little larger than a match-box produces delightful soups and salads, excellent coffee, well-cooked game, baskets of twisted Italian bread; wine and oranges. At night he arranges our sleeping-berths, and I think would perform barber duties and assist with our toilets if called upon to do so. He is a fatigued and blasé personage who looks as if chronically deprived of his due allowance of sleep, and he evidently regards the travelling public as a helpless, nervous creature always in a peevishly ridiculous hurry.

We begin to climb into the mountains, and it grows very cold. Oddly-angled vineyards hang precariously to the steep sides of the heights, propped into place by dams of stone that keep the soil from sliding down hill. Queer villages are tucked into clefts, with streets that are merely narrow stairs. Now and again we flash by the bold outlines of a ruined castle crowning a crag: the site always chosen with so much discretion that one wonders not only how enemies ever got in, but how the owners themselves ever emerged— unless they fell out.

A film of snow appears here and there, and the cold intensifies. Suddenly we catch a glimpse of white heights outlined against the blue – we are among the Alps, and the Mount Cenis tunnel is not far away.

A space of darkness, of thundering, clattering echoes— and then France!

Everything is quite different all at once. A fine new fortress commands the tunnel; the station is better built, larger, and in better repair than those we have seen in Italy. The customs officer, a well-set-up and good-looking Frenchman in a smart uniform, inquires politely if we have anything to declare, and when we answer in the negative sets his heels together, gives a profound salutation, and vexes us no more.

Everywhere is an air of greater prosperity, thrift, and alertness. The train does not stop to admit of gossiping, and goes at added speed.

Telegrams have been following me along the route concerning the possibility of catching a ship at Havre. The train is rather behind time, and unless the Transatlantique will consent to delay her departure for an hour or two, it will be useless to attempt to cover the space between Villeneuve, Paris, and Havre before to-morrow at seven. There is hope, however, that she will wait, and Friday night, some two hours after midnight, the guard rouses me to deliver a telegram which says I must be ready at four to change cars for Paris. This means leaving my box – it is under seal for London— and crossing the ocean with the few belongings in a travelling-bag. I rise and dress quietly, scribble a few notes of farewell to such of my fellow passengers as have been especially courteous, and am all ready when we halt at Villeneuve. A young Frenchman, agent for Cook's tourist bureau in Paris, has come to meet me, but brings the discouraging intelligence that the ship has refused to wait and that there is no chance of catching her. It is not until reaching America that I discover this is a mistake and that the Transatlantique waited several hours, not only in the harbor, but when the tide made it necessary to cross the bar, lingering outside for another half-hour in hopes I might still come, for the French captain was interested in my endeavor, and had received official permission for the delay.

This change subjected me to inconvenience and to suffering, from the effects of which it took much time to entirely recover. For then began a most trying experience, from the strain of which not even the most vigorous constitution could escape unharmed. The cause of this false information was never satisfactorily ascertained. It, however, succeeded in lengthening the voyage four days.

It is too late— half-past four— to return to bed, so I throw myself on the couch and wait for day. A faint rime clouds the window when dawn breaks, but a breath dispels it, and outside are lovely Corot-like visions— pale, shadowy, gray— worth the lost sleep to have seen. Here and there a thin plume of smoke curls up against the dull frosty sky from the chimney of a thatched, lime-washed cottage set amid barns and stacks.

As the day grows peasants such as Millet pictures come out of the cottages and follow the road, carrying fagots or baskets of potatoes and turnips.

Two legs and a pair of sabots appear under a perambulating heap of hay.

A big dog drags a small cart full of milk-cans, and a woman with a cap and tucked-up skirts trudges along beside, blowing on her fingers to warm them.

All this, just as did Italy, seems very familiar. I know it quite well from pictures and books. It gives one the sensation— reversed— awakened by reading a realistic novel in which all the little details of daily life are minutely and accurately reproduced.

It is ten o'clock when we reach Calais, and the Dover boat has gone, so there is time for a bath and breakfast— luckily, as I shall not have another meal for forty-eight hours; but of this I have no prevision.

The Channel is gray and stormy when we start, and a gout of rain splashes now and then upon the deck. Fat old French gentlemen spread themselves out in chaises longues and make all necessary preparations for sea-sickness. The English turn up the collars of their long coats, thrust their hands in the pockets, and stride along the rolling deck. Later the sun struggles through the clouds and turns the gloom to a stormy gray-green and shifting silver— and there looms slowly through the mists the white cliffs of England!

For me this keen windy sea is thick with phantom sails: ... the high-beaked galleys of the Conqueror, the silken wings of the White Ship, Henry's fleet carrying victorious armies into France, Drake's and Raleigh's prows, galleons from the East, certain small sailing craft going swiftly and furtively by dusk, carrying fugitive monarchs— the myriad wings of a nation of sea-birds, spread for pleasure or for prey...

Starting two months ago from a vast continent which the English race have made their own, where the English tongue, English laws, customs, and manners reign from sea to sea, in my whole course around the globe I have heard that same tongue, seen the same laws and manners, found the same race. Have had proof with my own eyes of the splendor of their empire, of their power, their wealth, of their dominance and orgulousness, of their superb armies, their undreamable commerce, their magnificent possessions, their own unrivalled physical beauty and force— and lo! now at last I find from a tiny island ringed with gray seas has sprung this race of kings. It fills my soul with a passion of pride that I, too, am an Anglo-Saxon. In my veins, too, runs that virile tide that pulses through the heart of this Lord of the Earth— the blood of this clean, fair, noble English race! ...

It is worth a journey round the world to see—

"This royal throne of kings, this sceptred isle,
This earth of majesty, this seat of Mars,
This other Eden, demi-paradise;
This fortress built by nature for herself
Against infestion and the hand of war.
This happy breed of men, this little world;
This precious stone set in a silver sea;
This blessed plot of earth, this realm, this England,
This nurse, this teeming womb of royal kings,
Feared by their breed and famous by their birth,
Renownèd for their deeds so far from home,
For Christian service and true chivalry,
This land of such dear souls, this dear, dear land –
England, bound in with the triumphant sea!"[1]

— and I understand now the meaning of this trumpet-cry of love and pride from the greatest of earth's poets— an Englishman.

Dover— and one sets foot at last on the mother soil. (We are, by the way, the only people who call our land a mother.)

... the blue boudoir of a first-class carriage— then English landscapes under the level rays of a setting sun.

Certain characteristics here are very reminiscent of Japan. The neatness and completeness of everything; the due allowance of trees dispersed in ornamental fashion; nature so thoroughly tamed and domesticated; the picturesque railway stations, and a certain moist soft-

---

1   William Shakespeare, *Richard II* (1597)

ness in the air. But where everything there is light, fragile, and fantastic, here it is solid, compact, and durable.

Like the English sea, the English land swarms with phantoms— the folk of history, of romance, of poetry and fiction. They troop along the roads, prick across the fields, look over the hedges, and peer from every window. I hear the clang of their armor, see the waving of their banners; their voices ring in the frosty winter air, their horses' hoof-beats sound along the paths. Without regard to time or period, to re-ality or non-reality, they come in hosts to welcome me— to say, "And so you, too, have come to join us. We have waked to greet you. We are the ghosts of England's past!"

Even the folk of the contemporary fiction have not failed to be present. I see the sunk fence by the coppice where Angelina always bids Edwin an eternal farewell in the last chapter of the second volume, and they are there doing it now. There rides Captain Cavendish in his red coat, home from the hunting-field, and on his way to the handsome old country-house yonder where he will squeeze Mrs. Fitzroy's fingers under the teacup he passes her and thus lay the foundation for for-ty-two chapters of jealously, hatred, and all uncharitableness.

Darkness falls. A dull glare is reflected from the heavens that speaks the presence of a great gas-lit city. A myriad sparks twinkle in the dis-tance— the "Lights o' London!"

Miles and miles and miles of houses. A huge, shadowy half-globe looming against the sky— the dome of St. Paul's.

... towers and delicate spires, and lights shining through many lance-like windows— Parliament Houses, where lords and commons sit in debate.

... long gleams quivering serpent-like across a wavering black flood— we have passed over the Thames, and here is Charing Cross.

Clatter, hurry, and confusion— every one giving different sugges-tions and directions. I had meant to remain overnight in London and take the North-German Lloyd steamer at Southampton the next day, but here the news meets me that this ship has been suddenly withdrawn and will not sail till late in the week. My one chance is the night mail to Holyhead and to catch the Bothnia, which touches at Queenstown next morning. This train leaves in an hour and a half. I have not slept since two o'clock the night before, nor eaten since breakfast, and my courage is nearly at an end. One of my fellow-travellers, who has been most kind to me all the way from Ceylon, comes to my rescue and assumes all responsibilities. I am sent off to the hotel to dine in company with two kind and charming fellow-voyagers, Sir William Lewis and his daughter, while he arranges my difficulties. I am far too tired and disturbed, however, to eat, and can only crumble my bread and taste my wine. At half-past eight my friend appears and carries me off to the Euston station. He has snatched his dinner, got rid of the dust of travel, and into evening clothes. He has brought rugs and cushions that I may have some rest during the night, a little cake in case I grow hungry, and heaps of books and papers. My foot-warmer is filled with hot water, the guard is induced to give me his best care and attention, and then I go away alone again, somewhat comforted by the chivalrous goodness of the travelling man to the uncared-for woman.

I fall asleep from fatigue, am shaken by horrible dreams, and start awake with a cry. The train is thundering through a wild storm. I try to read, but the words dance up and down the page. The guard comes now and then to see if I need anything, and deep in the night I reach Holyhead. Gathering up my multitudinous belongings, I run through the rain and sleet to the little vessel quivering and straining at the pier. The night is a wild one, the wind in our teeth, and the journey rough and very tedious. The cold and tempestuous day has dawned before we touch Kingstown and are hurried— wretched for lack of sleep and the means of making a fresh toilet— into the train for Dublin. The Irish capital is still unawake when I rattle across it from station to station this Sunday morning, and immediately I am off again at full speed through a land swept with flying mists and showers— a beautiful land, green even in January.

Later I see ruddy-cheeked peasants going along the roads to church— a type I am familiar with in America. I gaze contemplatively at these sturdy young men, and wonder how soon they will be New York aldermen and mayors of Chicago; how soon those rosy girls, in their queer, bunchy, provincial gowns, will be leaders of society in Washington and dressed by Worth.

I am growing frightfully hungry, having eaten nothing since yesterday morning in Calais. There is the spice cake, but with no liquid save a little brandy in a flask, I soon choke upon the cake and abandon it. The train is behind time, owing to the late arrival of the Channel boat, and stops only for the briefest moments. At noon we reach Queenstown, having curved around a fair space of water and past the beautiful city of Cork. The ship has not yet arrived, but will doubtless be here in a few moments, the bad weather having delayed her; and my luggage is all hurried down to the tender, where I should be sent, too, did I not wail with hunger. The Queen's Hotel is not far from the station, but the evil luck which has pursued me for the last two days ordains that the kitchen of this hostelry should be undergoing repairs at this particular moment, and no food is to be had. By dint of perseverance, in frantic protest and reckless objurgation, I finally secure a cup of rather cold and bitter tea and a bit of dingy bread that looks as if it had been used to scrub the floor with before being presented to me as a substitute for breakfast. I am warned to hold myself in readiness for an instantaneous summons to the tender, for when the steamer is signalled there is no time to waste. So hastily I make such toilet as is possible with my dressing-bag aboard the tender, and sit alone in the waiting-room attendant on the summons.

Hour after hour goes by, but no summons comes. I dare not move lest the call come during my absence, and sit there hopeless, helpless, overwhelmed with hunger, lack of sleep, and fatigue. At six o'clock my patience is at end, and I am clamorously demanding more food, when they bring the long-expected notice. The ship has been signaled, and the tender must be off.

It rains in torrents, mingled with sleet, and the wind blows a tempest. The tender puts out from shore and is whirled about like an eggshell. The wind drives us back, and over and over again we essay the passage before we can make head against the wild weather. It is two hours and a half later when we get alongside the ship, and I am chilled to the bone, sick and dizzy for want of food and sleep, and climb stumblingly across the narrow, slippery, plunging path that leads from one ship to the other. No sooner have I set foot on the glassy deck than the push of an impatient passenger sends me with a smashing fall into the scuppers, where I gather bruises that last a week. A compassionate stewardess comes to the rescue and puts me to bed— speechless and on the verge of tears.

The weather is terrible— a season long to be remembered for the January storms of the north Atlantic. The waves toss our ship back and forth among them like a football. Even were I not too miserable to move, the plunging of the vessel would make it impossible to keep one's feet. The ship laboriously climbs a howling green mountain, pauses irresolute a moment on the crest, and then toboggans madly down the farther side, her screw out of water, and kicking both heels madly in the air to the utter dislocation of one's every tooth and joint. Down, down she goes, as if boring for bottom, and when it is perfectly certain that she can never by any chance right herself, she comes nose upmost with a jerk, shakes off the water, and attack a new mountain, to repeat the same performance on the farther side.

Two thirds of the passengers are very seasick, and I quite as wretched and prostrate from my late painful experiences as if still subject to the malady. It is the third or fourth day out, and I am beginning to take heart of grace and to long to leave my stuffy little cabin. The ship is rolling frightfully still, and while revolving in my mind an attempt to rise, a sudden lurch sends the heavy jug full of water flying out of its basin into the berth, where it smashes into twenty pieces upon my face and chest, and drenches me with icy water. The doors of the gangway are left open lest they freeze together, and therefore a bitter wind sweeps through the cabin, so that when hauled from my dripping bed, and it is discovered that the key of my box, where are the only dry changes of garment, is mislaid, I am stabbed through and through my wet and clinging clothes by this terrible cold. Thus suppressed again for another three days, it is only towards the end of the week— the storm being abated— that I am able once more to stand on my feet. It is a most amiable and friendly little company that finally assembles in the cabin; the recent woes we have all passed through having made us sympathetic and considerate. We even get up in time a concert for the seamen's orphans, and play shuffle-board on the still uncertain deck for prizes. But this crossing of the zone of storms has greatly delayed us, and it is late in the evening of the eleventh day when we take our pilot aboard. The morning of the twelfth day is cold, but evidently has some thought of clearing, and the sea is less rough.

A rim of opaque film grows on the horizon that the emigrants on the forward deck regard with eager interest and hope. The passengers stand about in furs, pinched and shivering; their noses red, but their eyes full of pleased anticipation. Any land would be dear and desirable after near a fortnight of this cold and frantic sea— but when it is one's own— !

The film thickens and darkens, and suddenly resolves itself into Coney Island, where, as we swiftly near the shore, the plaintive reproachful eyes of the great wooden elephant are turned upon us as if to deprecate our late coming.

The water has smoothed itself into a bay, and a huge gray woman, holding an uplifted torch, awaits our coming; the emigrants regard her wonderingly— the symbol of liberty held aloft, and a benignant countenance turned towards all the outer world. We are by the shores of Staten Island. A pretty English girl who has braved the winter storms to follow her new husband to a foreign country remarks surprisedly that all this looks much like England— evidently having expected log-cabins and a country town. But I have no time to be amused at her ignorance— I am saying joyously to myself

> "Is this the hill, is this the kirk,
> Is this mine ain countrée?"[1]

Suddenly a great flood of familiarity washes away the memory of the strange lands and people I have seen and blots out all sense of time that has elapsed since I last saw all this. I know how everything— the streets, the houses, the passers-by— are looking at this moment. It is as if I had turned away my head for an instant, and now looked back again. My duties, my cares, my interests, which had grown dim and shadowy in these last two months, suddenly take on sharp outlines and become alive and real once more. I feel as if I had but sailed down the bay for an hour, and was now returning.

The ship slides into dock. I can see the glad faces of my friends upon the pier. My journey is done. I have been around the world in seventy-six days.

THE END.

---

1   Samuel Taylor Coleridge's "Rime of the Ancient Mariner" (1834)

AROUND THE WORLD IN SEVENTY-TWO DAYS

Nellie Bly

CHAPTER I.
A Proposal to Girdle the Earth.

WHAT GAVE ME the idea?

It is sometimes difficult to tell exactly what gives birth to an idea. Ideas are the chief stock in trade of newspaper writers and generally they are the scarcest stock in market, but they do come occasionally.

This idea came to me one Sunday. I had spent a greater part of the day and half the night vainly trying to fasten on some idea for a newspaper article. It was my custom to think up ideas on Sunday and lay them before my editor for his approval or disapproval on Monday. But ideas did not come that day and three o'clock in the morning found me weary and with an aching head tossing about in my bed. At last tired and provoked at my slowness in finding a subject, something for the week's work, I thought fretfully:

"I wish I was at the other end of the earth!"

"And why not?" the thought came: "I need a vacation; why not take a trip around the world?"

It is easy to see how one thought followed another. The idea of a trip around the world pleased me and I added: "If I could do it as quickly as Phileas Fogg did, I should go."

Then I wondered if it were possible to do the trip eighty days and afterwards I went easily off to sleep with the determination to know before I saw my bed again if Phileas Fogg's record could be broken.

I went to a steamship company's office that day and made a selection of timetables. Anxiously, I sat down and went over them and if I had found the elixir of life I should not have felt better than I did when

I conceived a hope that a tour of the world might be made in even less than eighty days.

I approached my editor rather timidly on the subject. I was afraid that he would think the idea too wild and visionary.

"Have you any ideas?" he asked, as I sat down by his desk.

"One," I answered quietly.

He sat toying with his pens, waiting for me to continue, so I blurted out:

"I want to go around the world!"

"Well?" he said, inquiringly looking up with a faint smile in his kind eyes.

"I want to go around in eighty days or less. I think I can beat Phileas Fogg's record. May I try it?"

To my dismay he told me that in the office they had thought of this same idea before and the intention was to send a man. However he offered me the consolation that he would favor my going, and then we went to talk with the business manager about it.

"It is impossible for you to do it," was the terrible verdict. "In the first place you are a woman and would need a protector, and even if it were possible for you to travel alone you would need to carry so much baggage that it would detain you in making rapid changes. Besides you speak nothing but English, so there is no use talking about it; no one but a man can do this."

"Very well," I said angrily, "Start the man, and I'll start the same day for some other newspaper and beat him."

"I believe you would," he said slowly. I would not say that this had any influence on their decision, but I do know that before we parted I was made happy by the promise that if any one was commissioned to make the trip, I should be that one.

After I had made my arrangements to go, other important projects for gathering news came up, and this rather visionary idea was put aside for a while.

One cold, wet evening, a year after this discussion, I received a little note asking me to come to the office at once. A summons, late in the afternoon, was such an unusual thing to me that I was to be excused if I spent all my time on the way to the office wondering what I was to be scolded for.

I went in and sat down beside the editor waiting for him to speak. He looked up from the paper on which he was writing and asked quietly: "Can you start around the world day after tomorrow?"

"I can start this minute," I answered, quickly trying to stop the rapid beating of my heart.

"We did think of starting you on the City of Paris tomorrow morning, so as to give you ample time to catch the mail train out of London. There is a chance if the Augusta Victoria, which sails the morning afterwards, has rough weather of your failing to connect with the mail train."

"I will take my chances on the Augusta Victoria, and save one extra day," I said.

The next morning I went to Ghormley, the fashionable dressmaker, to order a dress. It was after eleven o'clock when I got there and it took but very few moments to tell him what I wanted.

I always have a comfortable feeling that nothing is impossible if one applies a certain amount of energy in the right direction. When I want things done, which is always at the last moment, and I am met with such an answer: "It's too late. I hardly think it can be done;" I simply say:

"Nonsense! If you want to do it, you can do it. The question is, do you want to do it?"

I have never met the man or woman yet who was not aroused by that answer into doing their very best.

If we want good work from others or wish to accomplish anything ourselves, it will never do to harbor a doubt as to the result of an enterprise.

So, when I went to Ghormley's, I said to him: "I want a dress by this evening."

"Very well," he answered as unconcernedly as if it were an everyday thing for a young woman to order a gown on a few hours' notice.

"I want a dress that will stand constant wear for three months," I added, and then let the responsibility rest on him.

Bringing out several different materials, he threw them in artistic folds over a small table, studying the effect in a pier glass[1] before which he stood.

---

1   Large mirror, usually placed between windows to fill up wall space

He did not become nervous or hurried. All the time that he was trying the different effects of the materials, he kept up a lively and half-humorous conversation. In a few moments he had selected a plain blue broadcloth and a quiet plaid camel's—hair as the most durable and suitable combination for a traveling gown.

Before I left, probably one o'clock, I had my first fitting. When I returned at five o'clock for a second fitting, the dress was finished. I considered this promptness and speed a good omen and quite in keeping with the project.

After leaving Ghormley's, I went to a shop and ordered an ulster.[1] Then going to another dressmaker's, I ordered a lighter dress to carry with me to be worn in the land where I would find summer.

I bought one hand-bag with the determination to confine my baggage to its limit.

That night there was nothing to do but write to my few friends a line of farewell and to pack the hand-bag.

Packing that bag was the most difficult undertaking of my life; there was so much to go into such little space.

I got everything in at last except the extra dress. Then the question resolved itself into this: I must either add a parcel to my baggage or go around the world in and with one dress. I always hated parcels so I sacrificed the dress, but I brought out a last summer's silk bodice and after considerable squeezing managed to crush it into the hand—bag.

I think that I went away one of the most superstitious of girls. My editor had told me the day before the trip had been decided upon of an inauspicious dream he had had. It seemed that I came to him and told him I was going to run a race. Doubting my ability as a runner, he thought he turned his back so that he should not witness the race. He heard the band play, as it does on such occasions, and heard the applause that greeted the finish. Then I came to him with my eyes filled with tears and said: "I have lost the race."

"I can translate that dream," I said, when he finished; "I will start to secure some news and some one else will beat me."

When I was told the next day that I was to go around the world I felt a prophetic awe steal over me. I feared that Time would win the race and that I should not make the tour in eighty days or less.

1   Victorian daytime overcoat with cape and sleeves

Nor was my health good when I was told to go around the world in the shortest time possible at that season of the year. For almost a year I had been a daily sufferer from headache, and only the week previous I had consulted a number of eminent physicians fearing that my health was becoming impaired by too constant application to work. I had been doing newspaper work for almost three years, during which time I had not enjoyed one day's vacation. It is not surprising then that I looked on this trip as a most delightful and much needed rest.

The evening before I started I went to the office and was given £200 in English gold and Bank of England notes. The gold I carried in my pocket. The Bank of England notes were placed in a chamois-skin [1]bag which I tied around my neck. Besides this, I took some American gold and paper money to use at different ports as a test to see if American money was known outside of America.

Down in the bottom of my hand-bag was a special passport, number 247, signed by James G. Blaine, Secretary of State. Someone suggested that a revolver would be a good companion piece for the passport, but I had such a strong belief in the world's greeting me as I greeted it that I refused to arm myself. I knew if my conduct was proper I should always find men ready to protect me, let them be Americans, English, French, German or anything else.

It is quite possible to buy tickets in New York for the entire trip, but I thought that I might be compelled to change my route at almost any point, so the only transportation I had provided on leaving New York was my ticket to London.

When I went to the office to say good-bye, I found that no itinerary had been made of my contemplated trip and there was some doubt as to whether the mail train, which I expected to take to Brindisi, left London every Friday night. Nor did we know whether the week of my expected arrival in London was the one in which it connected with the ship for India or the ship for China. In fact when I arrived at Brindisi and found the ship was bound for Australia, I was the most surprised girl in the world.

I followed a man who had been sent to a steamship company's office to try to make out a schedule and help them arrange one as best

1   A soft leather made from a a European mountain goat, commonly known modernly as sheepskin

they could on this side of the water. How near it came to being correct can be seen later on.

I have been asked very often since my return how many changes of clothing I took in my solitary hand-bag. Some have thought I took but one; others think I carried silk which occupies but little space, and others have asked if I did not buy what I needed at the different ports.

One never knows the capacity of an ordinary hand—satchel until dire necessity compels the exercise of all one's ingenuity to reduce every thing to the smallest possible compass. In mine I was able to pack two traveling caps, three veils, a pair of slippers, a complete outfit of toilet articles, ink-stand, pens, pencils, and copy-paper, pins, needles and thread, a dressing gown, a tennis blazer, a small flask and a drinking cup, several complete changes of underwear, a liberal supply of handkerchiefs and fresh ruchings, and most bulky and uncompromising of all, a jar of cold cream to keep my face from chapping in the varied climates I should encounter.

That jar of cold cream was the bane of my existence. It seemed to take up more room than everything else in the bag and was always getting into just the place that would keep me from closing the satchel. Over my arm I carried a silk waterproof, the only provision I made against rainy weather. After-experience showed me that I had taken too much rather than too little baggage. At every port where I stopped at I could have bought anything from a ready-made dress down, except possibly at Aden, and as I did not visit the shops there I cannot speak from knowledge.

The possibilities of having any laundry work done during my rapid progress was one which had troubled me a good deal before starting. I had equipped myself on the theory that only once or twice in my journey would I be able to secure the services of a laundress. I knew that on the railways it would be impossible, but the longest railroad travel was the two days spent between London and Brindisi, and the four days between San Francisco and New York. On the Atlantic steamers they do no washing. On the Peninsular and Oriental steamers—which everyone calls the P. & O. boats— between Brindisi and China, the quartermaster turns out each day a wash that would astonish the largest laundry in America. Even if no laundry work was done on the ships, there are at all of the ports where they stop plenty of experts waiting to show what Orientals can do in the washing line. Six hours is ample time for them to perform their labors and when they make a promise to have work done in a certain time, they are prompt to the minute. Probably it is because they have no use for clothes themselves, but appreciate at its full value the money they are to receive for their labor. Their charges, compared with laundry prices in New York, are wonderfully low.

So much for my preparations. It will be seen that if one is traveling simply for the sake of traveling and not for the purpose of impressing one's fellow passengers, the problem of baggage becomes a very simple one. On one occasion— in Hong Kong, where I was asked to an official dinner— I regretted not having an evening dress with me, but the loss of that dinner was a very small matter when compared with the responsibilities and worries I escaped by not having a lot of trunks and boxes to look after.

CHAPTER II.
THE START.

ON THURSDAY, November 14, 1889, at 9.40.30 o'clock, I started on my tour around the world.

Those who think that night is the best part of the day and that morning was made for sleep know how uncomfortable they feel when for some reason they have to get up with— well, with the milkman.

I turned over several times before I decided to quit my bed. I wondered sleepily why a bed feels so much more luxurious, and a stolen nap that threatens the loss of a train is so much more sweet, than those hours of sleep that are free from duty's call. I half promised myself that on my return I would pretend sometime that it was urgent that I should get up so I could taste the pleasure of a stolen nap without actually losing anything by it. I dozed off very sweetly over these thoughts to wake with a start, wondering anxiously if there was still time to catch the ship.

Of course I wanted to go, but I thought lazily that if some of these good people who spend so much time in trying to invent flying machines would only devote a little of the same energy towards promoting a system by which boats and trains would always make their start at noon or afterwards, they would be of greater assistance to suffering humanity.

I endeavored to take some breakfast, but the hour was too early to make food endurable. The last moment at home came. There was a hasty kiss for the dear ones and a blind rush downstairs trying to overcome the hard lump in my throat that threatened to make me regret the journey that lay before me.

"Don't worry," I said encouragingly, as I was unable to speak that dreadful word, goodbye; "only think of me as having a vacation and the most enjoyable time in my life."

Then to encourage myself I thought, as I was on my way to the ship: "It's only a matter of 28,000 miles, and seventy-five days and four hours until I shall be back again."

A few friends who were told of my hurried departure were there to say good-bye. The morning was bright and beautiful, and everything seemed very pleasant while the boat was still; but when they were warned to go ashore, I began to realize what it meant for me.

"Keep up your courage," they said to me while they gave my hand the farewell clasp. I saw the moisture in their eyes and I tried to smile so that their last recollection of me would be one that would cheer them.

But when the whistle blew and they were on the pier, and I was on the Augusta Victoria, which was slowly but surely moving away from all I knew, taking me to strange lands and strange people, I felt lost. My head felt dizzy and my heart felt as if it would burst. Only seventy-five days! Yes, but it seemed an age and the world lost its roundness and seemed a long distance with no end, and— well, I never turn back.

I looked as long as I could at the people on the pier. I did not feel as happy as I have at other times in life. I had a sentimental longing to take farewell of everything.

"I am off," I thought sadly, "and shall I ever get back?"

Intense heat, bitter cold, terrible storms, shipwrecks, fevers, all such agreeable topics had been drummed into me until I felt much as I imagine one would feel if shut in a cave of midnight darkness and told that all sorts of horrors were waiting to gobble one up.

The morning was beautiful and the bay never looked lovelier. The ship glided out smoothly and quietly, and the people on deck looked for their chairs and rugs and got into comfortable positions, as if determined to enjoy themselves while they could, for they did not know what moment someone would be enjoying themselves at their expense.

When the pilot went off, everybody rushed to the side of the ship to see him go down the little rope ladder. I watched him closely, but he climbed down and into the rowboat that was waiting to carry him to the pilot boat, without giving one glance back to us. It was an old story to him, but I could not help wondering if the ship should go down whether there would not be some word or glance he would wish he had given.

"You have now started on your trip," someone said to me. "As soon as the pilot goes off and the captain assumes command, then, and only then, our voyage begins, so now you are really started on your tour around the world."

Something in his words turned my thoughts to that demon of the sea— sea-sickness.

Never having taken a sea voyage before, I could expect nothing else than a lively tussle with the disease of the wave.

"Do you get sea-sick?" I was asked in an interested, friendly way. That was enough; I flew to the railing.

Sick? I looked blindly down, caring little what the wild waves were saying, and gave vent to my feelings.

People are always unfeeling about sea-sickness. When I wiped the tears from my eyes and turned around, I saw smiles on the face of every passenger. I have noticed that they are always on the same side of the ship when one is taken suddenly, overcome, as it were, with one's own emotions.

The smiles did not bother me, but one man said sneeringly:

"And she's going around the world!"

I too joined in the laugh that followed. Silently I marveled at my boldness to attempt such a feat wholly unused, as I was, to sea-voyages. Still I did not entertain one doubt as to the result.

Of course I went to luncheon. Everybody did, and almost everybody left very hurriedly. I joined them, or, I don't know, probably I made the start. Anyway I never saw as many in the dining room at any one time during the rest of the voyage.

When dinner was served I went in very bravely and took my place on the Captain's left. I had a very strong determination to resist my impulses, but yet, in the bottom of my heart was a little faint feeling that I had found something even stronger than my will power.

Dinner began very pleasantly. The waiters moved about noiselessly, the band played an overture. Captain Albers, handsome and genial, took his place at the head, and the passengers who were seated at his table began dinner with a relish equaled only by enthusiastic wheelmen when roads are fine. I was the only one at the Captain's table who might be called an amateur sailor. I was bitterly conscious of this fact. So were the others.

I might as well confess it, while soup was being served, I was lost in painful thoughts and filled with a sickening fear. I felt that everything was just as pleasant as an unexpected gift on Christmas, and I endeavored to listen to the enthusiastic remarks about the music made by my companions, but my thoughts were on a topic that would not bear discussion.

I felt cold, I felt warm; I felt that I should not get hungry if I did not see food for seven days; in fact, I had a great, longing desire not to see it, nor to smell it, nor to eat of it, until I could reach land or a better understanding with myself.

Fish was served, and Captain Albers was in the midst of a good story when I felt I had more than I could endure.

"Excuse me," I whispered faintly, and then rushed, madly, blindly out. I was assisted to a secluded spot where a little reflection and a little unbridling of pent up emotion restored me to such a courageous state that I determined to take the Captain's advice and return to my unfinished dinner.

"The only way to conquer sea-sickness is by forcing oneself to eat," the Captain said, and I thought the remedy harmless enough to test.

They congratulated me on my return. I had a shamed feeling that I was going to misbehave again, but I tried to hide the fact from them. It came soon, and I disappeared at the same rate of speed as before.

Once again I returned. This time my nerves felt a little unsteady and my belief in my determination was weakening, Hardly had I seated myself when I caught an amused gleam of a steward's eye, which made me bury my face in my handkerchief and choke before I reached the limits of the dining hall.

The bravos with which they kindly greeted my third return to the table almost threatened to make me lose my bearings again. I was glad to know that dinner was just finished and I had the boldness to say that it was very good!

I went to bed shortly afterwards. No one had made any friends yet, so I concluded sleep would be more enjoyable than sitting in the music hall looking at other passengers engaged in the same first-day-at-sea occupation.

I went to bed shortly after seven o'clock. I had a dim recollection afterwards of waking up enough to drink some tea, but beyond this and the remembrance of some dreadful dreams, I knew nothing until I heard an honest, jolly voice at the door calling to me.

Opening my eyes I found the stewardess and a lady passenger in my cabin and saw the Captain standing at the door.

"We were afraid that you were dead," the Captain said when he saw that I was awake.

"I always sleep late in the morning," I said apologetically.

"In the morning!" the Captain exclaimed, with a laugh, which was echoed by the others, "It is half-past four in the evening!"

"But never mind," he added consolingly, "as long as you slept well it will do you good. Now get up and see if you can't eat a big dinner."

I did. I went through every course at dinner without flinching, and stranger still, I slept that night as well as people are commonly supposed to sleep after long exercise in the open air.

The weather was very bad, and the sea was rough, but I enjoyed it. My sea-sickness had disappeared, but I had a morbid, haunting idea, that although it was gone, it would come again, still I managed to make myself comfortable.

Almost all of the passengers avoided the dining-room, took their meals on deck and maintained reclining positions with a persistency that grew monotonous. One bright, clever, American-born girl was traveling alone to Germany, to her parents. She entered heartily into anything that was conducive to pleasure. She was a girl who talked a great deal and she always said something. I have rarely, if ever, met her equal. In German as well as English, she could ably discuss anything from fashions to politics. Her father and her uncle are men well-known in public affairs, and by this girl's conversation, it was easy to see that she was a father's favorite child; she was so broad and brilliant and womanly. There was not one man on board who knew more about politics, art, literature or music, than this girl with Marguerite hair,[1] and yet there was not one of us more ready and willing to take a race on deck than was she.

---

1   Victorian headdress: braided coils wrapped around the top of the head while two braids (sometimes made of velvet instead of hair) were arranged and tied under the chin, resting on the woman's chest

I think it is only natural for travelers to take an innocent pleasure in studying the peculiarities of their fellow companions. We were not out many days until everybody that was able to be about had added a little to their knowledge of those that were not. I will not say that the knowledge acquired in that way is of any benefit, nor would I try to say that those passengers who mingled together did not find one another as interesting and as fit subjects for comment. Nevertheless it was harmless and it afforded us some amusement.

I remember when I was told that we had among the passengers one man who counted his pulse after every meal, and they were hearty meals, too, for he was free from the disease of the wave, that I waited quite eagerly to have him pointed out, so that I might watch him. If it had been my pulse, instead of his own, that he watched so carefully, I could not have been more interested thereafter. Every day I became more anxious and concerned until I could hardly refrain from asking him if his pulse decreased before meals and increased afterwards, or if it was the same in the evening as it was in the morning.

I almost forgot my interest in this one man, when my attention was called to another, who counted the number of steps he took every day. This one in turn became less interesting when I found that one of the women, who had been a great sufferer from sea-sickness, had not undressed since she left her home in New York.

"I am sure we are all going down," she said one day in a burst of confidence, "and I am determined to go down dressed!"

I was not surprised after this that she was so dreadfully sea-sick.

One family who were removing from New York to Paris, had with them a little silver skye terrier, which bore the rather odd name of "Home, Sweet Home." Fortunately for the dog, as well as for those who were compelled to speak to him, they had shortened the name into "Homie."

"Homie's" passage was paid, but according to the rules of the ship, "Homie" was confined to the care of the butcher, much to the disgust of his master and mistress. "Homie" had not been accustomed to such harsh measures before, and the only streaks of happiness that came into his life were when permission was obtained for him to come on deck. Permission was granted with a provision that if "Homie" barked, he was to be taken instantly below. I fear that many hours of "Homie's" imprisonment might be laid at our door, for he knew how to dig most frantically when anyone said, "Rats," and when he did dig, he usually punctuated his attempt with short, crisp barks. With dismay we daily noted "Homie's" decrease in flesh. We marveled at his losing weight while confined in the butcher's quarters, and at last put it down to sea-sickness, which he, like some of the passengers, confined to the secrecy of his cabin. Towards the end of the voyage, when we were all served with sausage and Hamburger steak, there would be many whispered inquiries as to whether "Homie" had been seen that day. So anxious became those whispers that sometimes I thought they were rather tinged with a personal concern that was not wholly friendship for the wee dog.

When everything else grew tiresome, Captain Albers would always invent something to amuse us. He made a practice every evening after dinner, of putting the same number of lines on a card as there were gentlemen at the table. One of these lines he would mark and then partly folding the card over so as to prevent the marked line from being seen. He would pass it around for the men to take their choice.

After all had marked, the card was passed to the Captain, and we would wait breathlessly for the verdict. The gentleman whose name had been marked paid for the cigars or cordials for the others.

Many were the discussions about the erroneous impression entertained by most foreigners about Americans and America. Someone remarked that the majority of people in foreign lands were not able to tell where the United States is.

"There are plenty of people who think the United States is one little island, with a few houses on it," Captain Albers said. "Once there was delivered at my house, near the wharf, in Hoboken, a letter from Germany, addressed to,

'CAPTAIN ALBERS,
FIRST HOUSE IN AMERICA.'"

"I got one from Germany once," said the most bashful man at the table, his face flushing at the sound of his own voice, "addressed to,

'HOBOKEN, OPPOSITE THE UNITED STATES.'"

While at luncheon on the 21st of November, someone called out that we were in sight of land. The way everyone left the table and rushed on deck was surely not surpassed by the companions of Columbus when they discovered America. I cannot give any good reason for it, but I know that I looked at the first point of bleak land with more interest than I would have bestowed on the most beautiful bit of scenery in the world.

We had not been long in sight of land until the decks began to fill with dazed-looking, wan-faced people. It was just as if we had taken on new passengers. We could not realize that they were from New York and had been enjoying a season of seclusion since leaving that port.

Dinner that evening was a very pleasant affair. Extra courses had been prepared in honor of those that were leaving at Southampton. I had not known one of the passengers when I left New York seven days before, but I realized, now that I was so soon to separate from them, that I regretted the parting very much.

Had I been traveling with a companion I should not have felt this so keenly, for naturally then I would have had less time to cultivate the acquaintance of my fellow passengers.

They were all so kind to me that I should have been the most ungrateful of women had I not felt that I was leaving friends behind. Captain Albers had served many years as commander of a ship in Eastern seas, and he cautioned me as to the manner in which I should take care of my health. As the time grew shorter for my stay on the Augusta Victoria, some teased me gently as to the outcome of my attempt to beat the record made by a hero of fiction, and I found myself forcing a false gaiety that helped to hide my real fears.

The passengers on the Augusta Victoria all stayed up to see us off. We sat on deck talking or nervously walking about until half—past two in the morning. Then some one said the tugboat had come alongside, and we all rushed over to see it. After it was made secure we went down to the lower deck to see who would come on and to get some news from land.

One man was very much concerned about my making the trip to London alone. He thought, as it was so late, or rather so early, that the London correspondent, who was to have met me, would not put in an appearance.

"I shall most certainly leave the ship here and see you safely to London, if no one comes to meet you," he protested, despite my assurances that I felt perfectly able to get along safely without an escort.

More for his sake than my own, I watched the men come on board, and tried to pick out the one that had been sent to meet me. Several of them were passing us in a line just as a gentleman made some remark about my trip around the world. A tall young man overheard the remark, and turning at the foot of the stairs, looked down at me with a hesitating smile.

"Nellie Bly?" he asked inquiringly.

"Yes," I replied, holding out my hand, which he gave a cordial grasp, meanwhile asking if I had enjoyed my trip, and if my baggage was ready to be transferred.

The man who had been so fearful of my traveling to London alone, took occasion to draw the correspondent into conversation. Afterwards he came to me and said with the most satisfied look upon his face:

"He is all right. If he had not been so, I should have gone to London with you anyway. I can rest satisfied now for he will take care of you."

I went away with a warm feeling in my heart for that kindly man who would have sacrificed his own comfort to insure the safety of an unprotected girl.

A few warm handclasps, and interchanging of good wishes, a little dry feeling in the throat, a little strained pulsation of the heart, a little hurried run down the perpendicular plank to the other passengers who were going to London, and then the tug cast off from the ship, and we drifted away in the dark.

CHAPTER III.
SOUTHAMPTON TO JULES VERNE'S.

"MR. & MRS. JULES VERNE have sent a special letter asking that, if possible, you will stop to see them," the London correspondent said to me, as we were on our way to the wharf.

"Oh, how I should like to see them!" I exclaimed, adding in the same breath, "Isn't it hard to be forced to decline such a treat?"

"If you are willing to go without sleep and rest for two nights, I think it can be done," he said quietly.

"Safely? Without making me miss any connections? If so, don't think about sleep or rest."

"It depends on our getting a train out of here to-night. All the regular trains until morning have left, and unless they decide to run a special mail train for the delayed mails, we will have to stay here all night and that will not give us time to see Verne. We shall see when we land what they will decide to do."

The boat that was landing us left much to be desired in the way of comfort. The only cabin seemed to be the hull, but it was filled with mail and baggage and lighted by a lamp with a smoked globe. I did not see any place to sit down, so we all stood on deck, shivering in the damp, chilly air, and looking in the gray fog like uneasy spirits.

The dreary, dilapidated wharf was a fit landing place for the antique boat. I silently followed the correspondent into a large empty shed, where a few men with sleep in their eyes and uniforms that bore ample testimony to the fact that they had slept in their clothes, were stationed behind some long, low tables.

"Where are your keys?" the correspondent asked me as he sat my solitary bag down before one of these weary looking inspectors.

"It is too full to lock," I answered simply.

"Will you swear that you have no tobacco or tea?" the inspector asked my escort lazily.

"Don't swear," I said to him; then turning to the inspector I added: "It's my bag."

He smiled and putting a chalk mark upon the bag freed us.

"Declare your tobacco and tea or tip the man," I said teasingly to a passenger who stood with poor, thin, shaking "Homie" under one arm, searching frantically through his pockets for his keys.

"I've fixed him!" he answered with an expressive wink.

Passing through the custom house we were made happy by the information that it had been decided to attach a passenger coach to the special mail train to oblige the passengers who wished to go to London without delay. The train was made up then, so we concluded to get into our car and try to warm up.

A porter took my bag and another man in uniform drew forth an enormous key with which he unlocked the door in the side of the car instead of the end, as in America. I managed to compass the uncomfortable long step to the door and striking my toe against some projection in the floor, went most ungracefully and unceremoniously on to the seat.

My escort, after giving some order to the porter, went out to see about my ticket, so I took a survey of an English railway compartment. The little square in which I sat looked like a hotel omnibus and was about as comfortable. The two red leather seats in it run across the car, one backing the engine, the other backing the rear of the train. There was a door on either side and one could hardly have told that there was a dingy lamp there to cast a light on the scene had not the odor from it been so loud. I carefully lifted the rug that covered the thing I had fallen over, curious to see what could be so necessary to an English railway carriage as to occupy such a prominent position. I found a harmless object that looked like a bar of iron and had just dropped the rug in place when the door opened and the porter, catching the iron at one end, pulled it out, replacing it with another like it in shape and size.

"Put your feet on the foot warmer and get warm, Miss," he said, and I mechanically did as he advised.

My escort returned soon after, followed by a porter who carried a large basket, which he put in our carriage. The guard came afterwards and took our tickets. Pasting a slip of paper on the window, which backwards looked like "etavirP," he went out and locked the door.

"How should we get out if the train ran the track?" I asked, not half liking the idea of being locked in a box like an animal in a freight train.

"Trains never run off the track in England," was the quiet, satisfied answer.

"Too slow for that," I said teasingly, which only provoked a gentle inquiry as to whether I wanted anything to eat.

With a newspaper spread over our laps for a table-cloth, we brought out what the basket contained and put in our time eating and chatting about my journey until the train reached London.

As no train was expected at that hour, Waterloo Station was almost deserted. It was some little time after we stopped before the guard unlocked the door of our compartment and released us. Our few fellow-passengers were just about starting off in shabby cabs when we alighted. Once again we called goodbye and good wishes to each other, and then I found myself in a four-wheeled cab, facing a young Englishman who had come to meet us and who was glibly telling us the latest news.

I don't know at what hour we arrived, but my companions told me that it was daylight. I should not have known it. A gray, misty fog hung like a ghostly pall over the city. I always liked fog, it lends such a soft, beautifying light to things that otherwise in the broad glare of day would be rude and commonplace.

"How are these streets compared with those of New York?" was the first question that broke the silence after our leaving the station.

"They are not bad," I said with a patronizing air, thinking shame-facedly of the dreadful streets of New York, although determined to hear no word against them.

Westminster Abbey and the Houses of Parliament were pointed out to me, and the Thames, across which we drove. I felt that I was taking what might be called a bird's-eye view of London. A great many foreigners have taken views in the same rapid way of America, and afterwards gone home and written books about America, Americans, and Americanisms.

We drove first to the London office of the New York World. After receiving the cables that were waiting for my arrival, I started for the American Legation to get a passport as I had been instructed by cable.

Mr. McCormick, Secretary of the Legation, came into the room immediately after our arrival, and after welcoming and congratulating me on the successful termination of the first portion of my trip, sat down and wrote out a passport.

My escort was asked to go into another part of the room until the representative could ask me an important question. I had never required a passport before, and I felt a nervous curiosity to know what secrets were connected with such proceedings.

"There is one question all women dread to answer, and as very few will give a truthful reply, I will ask you to swear to the rest first and fill in the other question afterwards, unless you have no hesitancy in telling me your age."

"Oh, certainly," I laughed. "I will tell you my age, swear to it, too, and I am not afraid; my companion may come out of the corner."

"What is the color of your eyes?" he asked.

"Green," I said indifferently.

He was inclined to doubt it at first, but after a little inspection, both the gentlemen accepted my verdict as correct.

It was only a few seconds until we were whirling through the streets of London again. This time we went to the office of the Peninsular and Oriental Steamship Company, where I bought tickets that would cover at least half of my journey. A few moments again and we were driving rapidly to the Charing Cross station.

I was faint for food, and while my companion dismissed the cab and secured tickets, I ordered the only thing on the Charing Cross bill of fare that was prepared, so when he returned, his breakfast was ready for him. It was only ham and eggs, and coffee, but what we got of it was delicious. I know we did not get much, and when we were interrupted by the announcement that our train was starting, I stopped long enough to take another drink of coffee and then had to run down the platform to catch the train.

There is nothing like plenty of food to preserve health. I know that cup of coffee saved me from a headache that day. I had been shaking with the cold as we made our hurried drive through London, and my head was so dizzy at times that I hardly knew whether the earth had a chill or my brains were attending a ball. When I got comfortable, seated in the train, I began to feel warmer and more stable.

The train moved off at an easy-going speed, and the very jog of it lulled me into a state of languor.

"I want you to see the scenery along here; it is beautiful," my companion said, but I lazily thought, "What is scenery compared with sleep when one has not seen bed for over twenty-four hours?" so I said to him, very crossly:

"Don't you think you would better take a nap? You have not had any sleep for so long and you will be up so late to-night, that, really, I think for the sake of your health you would better sleep now."

"And you?" he asked with a teasing smile. I had been up even longer.

"Well, I confess, I was saying one word for you and two for myself," I replied, with a laugh that put us at ease on the subject.

"Honestly, now, I care very little for scenery when I am so sleepy," I said apologetically. "Those English farm houses are charming and the daisy-dotted meadows (I had not the faintest conception as to whether there were daisies in them or not), are only equaled by those I have seen in Kansas, but if you will excuse me?—" and I was in the land that joins the land of death.

I slept an easy, happy sleep, filled with dreams of home until I was waked by the train stopping.

"We change for the boat here," my companion said, catching up our bags and rugs, which he hauled to a porter.

A little walk down to the pier brought us to the place where a boat was waiting. Some people were getting off the boat, but a larger number stood idly about waiting for it to move off.

The air was very cold and chilly, but still I preferred the deck to the close, musty-smelling cabin beneath. Two English women also remained on deck. I was much amused at the conversation they held with some friends who had accompanied them to the boat, and now stood on the wharf. One would have supposed, by hearing the conversation that they had only that instant met and having no time to spend together, were forced to make all further arrangements on the spot.

"You will come over to-morrow, now don't forget," the young woman on the boat called out.

"I won't forget. Are you certain that you have everything with you?" the one on the wharf called back.

"Look after Fido. Give him that compound in the morning if there is no appearance of improvement," the first one said.

"You will meet me to-morrow?" said number two on shore.

"Oh yes; don't forget to come," was the reply, and as the boat moved out they both talked at once until we were quite a distance off, then simultaneously the one turned to her chair and the other turned around and walked rapidly away from the wharf.

There has been so much written and told about the English Channel, that one is inclined to think of it as a stream of horrors. It is also affirmed that even hardy sailors bring up the past when crossing over it, so I naturally felt that my time would come.

All the passengers must have been familiar with the history of the channel, for I saw everyone trying all the known preventives of seasickness. The women assumed reclining positions and the men sought the bar.

I remained on deck and watched the sea-gulls, or what I thought were these useful birds— useful for millinery purposes— and froze my nose. It was bitterly cold, but I found the cold bracing until we anchored at Boulogne, France. Then I had a chill.

At the end of this desolate pier, where boats anchor and where trains start, is a small, dingy restaurant. While a little English sailor, who always dropped his h's and never forgot his "sir," took charge of our bags and went to secure accommodations for us in the outgoing train, we followed the other passengers into the restaurant to get something warm to eat.

I was in France now, and I began to wonder now what would have been my fate if I had been alone as I had expected. I knew my companion spoke French, the language that all the people about us were speaking, so I felt perfectly easy on that score as long as he was with me.

We took our places at the table and he began to order in French. The waiter looked blankly at him until, at last, more in a spirit of fun than anything else, I suggested that he give the order in English. The waiter glanced at me with a smile and answered in English.

We traveled from Boulogne to Amiens in a compartment with an English couple and a Frenchman. There was one foot-warmer and the day was cold. We all tried to put our feet on the one foot-warmer and the result was embarrassing. The Frenchman sat facing me and as I was conscious of having tramped on someone's toes, and as he looked at me angrily all the time above the edge of his newspaper, I had a guilty feeling of knowing whose toes had been tramped on.

During this trip I tried to solve the reason for the popularity of these ancient, incommodious railway carriages. I very shortly decided that while they may be suitable for countries where little traveling is done, they would be thoroughly useless in thinly populated countries where people think less of traveling 3,000 miles than they do about their dinner. I also decided that the reason why we think nothing of starting out on long trips, is because our comfort is so well looked after, that living on a first-class railway train is as comfortable as living at a first-class hotel. The English railway carriages are wretchedly heated. One's feet will be burning on the foot-warmer while one's back will be freezing in the cold air above. If one should be taken suddenly ill in an English railway compartment, it would be a very serious matter.

Still, I can picture conditions under which these ancient railway carriages might be agreeable, but they are not such as would induce a traveler to prefer them to those built on the American model.

Supposing one had the measles or a black eye, then a compartment in a railway carriage, made private by a tip to the porter, would be very consoling.

Supposing one was newly wed and was bubbling over in ecstasy of joy, then give one an English railway compartment, where two just made one can be secluded from the eyes of a cold, sneering public, who are just as great fools under the same conditions, although they would deny it if one told them so.

But talk about privacy! If it is privacy the English desire so much, they should adopt our American trains, for there is no privacy like that to be found in a large car filled with strangers. Everybody has, and keeps his own place. There is no sitting for hours, as is often the case in English trains, face to face and knees to knees with a stranger, offensive or otherwise, as he may chance to be.

Then too, did the English railway carriage make me understand why English girls need chaperones. It would make any American woman shudder with all her boasted self-reliance, to think of sending her daughter alone on a trip, even of a few hours' duration, where there was every possibility that during those hours she would be locked in a compartment with a stranger.

Small wonder the American girl is fearless. She has not been used to so-called private compartments in English railway carriages, but to large crowds, and every individual that helps to swell that crowd is to her a protector. When mothers teach their daughters that there is safety in numbers, and that numbers are the body—guard that shield all woman-kind, then chaperones will be a thing of the past, and women will be nobler and better.

As I was pondering over this subject, the train pulled into a station and stopped. My escort looking out, informed me that we were at Amiens. We were securely locked in, however, and began to think that we would be carried past, when my companion managed to get his head out of the window and shouted for the guard to come to our release. Freed at last, we stepped out on the platform at Amiens.

CHAPTER IV.
JULES VERNE AT HOME.

M. JULES VERNE and Mme. Verne, accompanied by Mr. R. H. Sherard, a Parisian journalist, stood on the platform waiting our arrival.

When I saw them I felt as any other woman would have done under the same circumstances. I wondered if my face was travel-stained, and if my hair was tossed. I thought regretfully, had I been traveling on an American train, I should have been able to make my toilet *en route*, so that when I stepped off at Amiens and faced the famous novelist and his charming wife, I would have been as trim and tidy as I would had I been receiving them in my own home.

There was little time for regret. They were advancing towards us, and in another second I had forgotten my untidiness in the cordial welcome they gave me. Jules Verne's bright eyes beamed on me with interest and kindliness, and Mme. Verne greeted me with the cordiality of a cherished friend. There were no stiff formalities to freeze the kindness in all our hearts, but a cordiality expressed with such charming grace that before I had been many minutes in their company, they had won my everlasting respect and devotion.

M. Verne led the way to the carriages, which waited our coming. Mme. Verne walked closely by my side, glancing occasionally at me with a smile, which said in the language of the eye, the common language of the whole animal world, alike plain to man and beast:

"I am glad to greet you, and I regret we cannot speak together." M. Verne gracefully helped Mme. Verne and myself into a coupé, while he entered a carriage with the two other gentlemen. I felt very awkward at being left alone with Mme. Verne, as I was altogether unable to speak to her.

Her knowledge of the English language consisted of "No" and my French vocabulary consisted of "Oui," so our conversation was limited to a few apologetic and friendly smiles interluded with an occasional pressure of the hand. Indeed, Mme. Verne is a most charming woman, and even in this awkward position she made everything go most gracefully.

It was early evening. As we drove through the streets of Amiens I got a flying glimpse of bright shops, a pretty park, and numerous nursemaids pushing baby carriages about.

When our carriage stopped I got out and gave my hand to Mme. Verne to help her alight. We stood on a wide, smooth pavement, before a high stone wall, over the top of which I could see the peaked outlines of the house.

M. Verne was not long behind us. He hurried up to where we were standing and opened a door in the wall. Stepping in, I found myself in a small, smoothly paved court-yard, the wall making two sides and the house forming the square.

A large, black shaggy dog came bounding forward to greet me. He jumped up against me, his soft eyes overflowing with affection, and though I love dogs and especially appreciated this one's loving welcome, still I feared that his lavish display of it would undermine my dignity by bringing me to my knees at the very threshold of the home of the famous Frenchman.

M. Verne evidently understood my plight, for he spoke shortly to the dog, who, with a pathetic droop of his tail, went off to think it out alone.

We went up a flight of marble steps across the tiled floor of a beautiful little conservatory that was not packed with flowers but was filled with a display just generous enough to allow one to see and appreciate the beauty of the different plants. Mme. Verne led the way into a large sitting-room that was dusky with the early shade of a wintry evening. With her own hands she touched a match to the pile of dry wood that lay in the wide-open fireplace.

Meanwhile M. Verne urged us to remove our outer wrappings. Before this was done a bright fire was crackling in the grate, throwing a soft, warm light over the dark room. Mme. Verne led me to a chair close by the mantel, and when I was seated she took the chair opposite. Cheered by the warmth I looked quietly on the scene before me.

The room was large and the hangings and paintings and soft velvet rug, which left visible but a border of polished hard wood, were richly dark. On the mantel, which towered above Mme. Verne's head, were some fine pieces of statuary in bronze and, as the fire gave frequent bright flashes as the flames greedily caught fresh wood, I could see another bronze piece on a pedestal in a corner. All the chairs artistically upholstered in brocaded silks, were luxuriously easy. Beginning at either side of the mantel they were placed in a semi-circle around the fire, which was only broken by a little table that held several tall silver candlesticks.

A fine white Angora cat came rubbing up against my knee, then seeing its charming mistress on the opposite side, went to her and boldly crawled up in her lap as if assured of a cordial welcome.

Next to me in this semi-circle sat Mr. Sherard. M. Jules Verne was next to Mr. Sherard. He sat forward on the edge of his chair, his snow-white hair rather long and heavy, was standing up in artistic disorder; his full beard, rivaling his hair in snowiness, hid the lower part of his face and the brilliancy of his bright eyes that were overshadowed with heavy white brows, and the rapidity of his speech and the quick movements of his firm white hands all bespoke energy—life— with enthusiasm.

The London correspondent sat next to Jules Verne. With a smile on her soft rosy lips, Mme. Verne sat nursing the cat, which she stroked methodically with a dainty, white hand, while her luminous black eyes moved alternately between her husband and myself.

She was the most charming figure in that group around the wood fire. Imagine a youthful face with a spotless complexion, crowned with the whitest hair, dressed in smooth, soft folds on the top of a dainty head that is most beautifully poised on a pair of plump shoulders. Add to this face pretty red lips, that opened disclose a row of lovely teeth, and large, bewitching black eyes, and you have but a faint picture of the beauty of Mme. Verne.

This day when she met me she wore a sealskin jacket and carried a muff, and on her white head was a small black velvet bonnet. On taking her wraps off in the house I saw she wore a watered-silk skirt, laid in side plaits in the front with a full straight black drapery, that was very becoming to her short, plump figure. The bodice was of black silk velvet.

Mme. Verne is, I should judge, not more than five feet two in height, M. Verne about five feet five. M. Verne spoke in a short, rapid way, and Mr. Sherard in an attractive, lazy voice translated what was said for my benefit.

"Has M. Verne ever been to America?" I asked.

"Yes, once;" the answer came translated to me. "For a few days only, during which time I saw Niagara. I have always longed to return, but the state of my health prevents my taking any long journeys. I try to keep a knowledge of everything that is going on in America and greatly appreciate the hundreds of letters I receive yearly from Americans who read my books. There is one man in California who has been writing to me for years. He writes all the news about his family and home and country as if I were a friend and yet we have never met. He has urged me to come to America as his guest. I know of nothing that I long to do more than to see your land from New York to San Francisco."

"How did you get the idea for your novel, 'Around the World in Eighty Days?'" I asked.

"I got it from a newspaper," was his reply. "I took up a copy of *Le Siécle*[1] one morning, and found in it a discussion and some calculations showing that the journey around the world might be done in eighty days. The idea pleased me, and while thinking it over it struck me that in their calculations they had not called into account the difference in the meridians and I thought what a denouement such a thing would make in a novel, so I went to work to write one. Had it not been for the denouement I don't think that I should ever have written the book."

"I used to keep a yacht, and then I traveled all over the world studying localities; then I wrote from actual observation. Now, since my health confines me to my home, I am forced to read up descriptions and geographies."

M. Verne asked me what my line of travel was to be, and I was very happy to speak one thing that he could understand, so I told him.

---

1   Daily newspaper published in France from 1836 to 1932

"My line of travel is from New York to London, then Calais, Brindisi, Port Said, Ismailia, Suez, Aden, Colombo, Penang, Singapore, Hong Kong, Yokohama, San Francisco, New York."

"Why do you not go to Bombay as my hero Phileas Fogg did?" M. Verne asked.

"Because I am more anxious to save time than a young widow," I answered.

"You may save a young widower before you return," M. Verne said with a smile.

I smiled with a superior knowledge as women, fancy free, always will at such insinuations.

I looked at the watch on my wrist and saw that my time was getting short. There was only one train that I could take from here to Calais, and if I missed it I might just as well return to New York by the way I came, for the loss of that train meant one week's delay.

"If M. Verne would not consider it impertinent I should like to see his study before I go," I said at last.

He said he was only too happy to show it me, and even as my request was translated Mme. Verne sprang to her feet and lighted one of the tall wax candles.

She started with the quick, springy step of a girl to lead the way. M. Verne, who walks with a slight limp, the result of a wound, followed, and we brought up the rear. We went through the conservatory to a small room up through which was a winding stair, or, more properly speaking, a spiral stair-case. Mme. Verne paused at every curve to light the gas.

Up at the top of the house and along a hall that corresponded in shape to the conservatory below, M. Verne went, Mme. Verne stopping to light the gas in the hall. He opened a door that led off the hall and I stepped inside after him.

I was astonished. I had expected, judging from the rest of the house, that M. Verne's study would be a room of ample proportions and richly furnished. I had read so many descriptions of the studies of famous authors, and have dwelt with something akin to envy (our space is so limited and expensive in New York) on the ample room, the beautiful hand-carved desks filled with costly trinkets, the rare etchings and paintings that covered the walls, the rich hangings, and, I will confess it, I have thought it small wonder that amid such surroundings authors were able to dream fancies that brought them fame.

But when I stood in M. Verne's study I was speechless with surprise. He opened a latticed window, the only window in the room, and Mme. Verne, hurrying in after us, lighted the gas jet that was fastened above a low mantel.

The room was very small; even my little den at home was almost as large. It was also very modest and bare. Before the window was a flat-topped desk. The usual litter that accompanies and fills the desks of most literary persons was conspicuously absent, and the waste-basket that is usually filled to overflowing with what one very often considers their most brilliant productions, in this case held but a few little scraps.

On the desk was a neat little pile of white paper, probably 8 by 10 inches in size. It was part of the manuscript of a novel that M. Verne is engaged on at present. I eagerly accepted the manuscript when he handed it to me, and when I looked at the neat penmanship, so neat in fact that had I not known it was prose I should have thought it was the work of a poet, I was more impressed than ever with the extreme tidiness of this French author. In several places he had most effectually blotted out something that he had written, but there was no interlining, which gave me the idea that M. Verne always improved his work by taking out superfluous things and never by adding.

One bottle of ink and one penholder was all that shared the desk with the manuscript. There was but one chair in the room, and it stood before the desk. The only other piece of furniture was a broad, low couch in the corner, and here in this room with these meagre surroundings, Jules Verne has written the books that have brought him everlasting fame.

I leaned over the desk and looked out of the little latticed window, which he had thrown open. I could see through the dusk the spire of a cathedral in the distance, while stretching down beneath me was a park, beyond which I saw the entrance to a railway tunnel that goes under M. Verne's house, and through which many Americans travel every year, on their way to Paris.

Leading off from the study, is an enormous library. The large room is completely lined with cases from ceiling to floor, and these glass-doored cases are packed with handsomely bound books, which must be worth a fortune.

While we were examining the wealth of literature that was there before us, M. Verne got an idea. Taking up a candle and asking us to follow, he went out into the hall; stopping before a large map that hung there, holding up with one hand the candle, he pointed out to us several blue marks. Before his words were translated to me, I understood that on this map he had, with a blue pencil, traced out the course of his hero, Phileas Fogg, before he started him in fiction to travel around the world in eighty days. With a pencil he marked on the map, as we grouped about him, the places where my line of travel differed from that of Phileas Fogg.

Our steps lagged as we descended the winding stair again. It had come time to take farewell, and I felt as if I was separating from friends. Down in the room where we had been before, we found wine and biscuit on the little table, and M. Jules Verne explained that, contrary to his regular rules, he intended to take a glass of wine, that we might have the pleasure of drinking together to the success of my strange undertaking.

They clinked their glasses with wine, and wished me "God speed."

"If you do it in seventy-nine days, I shall applaud with both hands," Jules Verne said, and then I knew he doubted the possibility of my doing it in seventy-five, as I had promised. In compliment to me, he endeavored to speak to me in English, and did succeed in saying, as his glass tipped mine:

"Good luck, Nellie Bly."

Mme. Verne was not going to be outdone by her gallant husband in showing kindness to me. She told Mr. Sherard that she would like to kiss me good-bye, and when he translated her kind request, he added that it was a great honor in France, for a woman to ask to kiss a stranger.

I was little used to such formalities, or familiarities, as one may deem them, but still I had not one thought of refusing such delicate attention, so I gave her my hand and inclined my head, for I am taller than she, and she kissed me gently and affectionately on either check. Then she put up her pretty face for me to kiss. I stifled a strong inclination to kiss her on the lips, they were so sweet and red, and show her how we do it in America. My mischievousness often plays havoc with my dignity, but for once I was able to restrain myself, and kissed her softly after her own fashion.

With uncovered heads, and despite our protestations, they followed us out into the cold court-yard, and as far as I could see I saw them standing at the gate waving farewell to me, the brisk winds tossing their white hair.

CHAPTER V.
ON TO BRINDISI.

WHEN M. and Mme. Verne were no longer visible, my thoughts turned to my trip. I feared that the enjoyment of my visit to their home had jeopardized the success of my tour.

The driver had been told to make the best speed back to the station, but the carriage seemed to be rolling along so quietly that I could not rest until it was urged again upon the coachman to reach the station in the shortest possible time.

Some few moments after we reached there the train came in. Bidding a hearty good-bye to Mr. Sherard, I started again on my tour of the world, and the visit to Jules Verne was a thing of the past. I had gone without sleep and rest; I had traveled many miles out of my way for the privilege of meeting M. and Mme. Verne, and I felt that if I had gone around the world for that pleasure, I should not have considered the price too high.

The train which carried us to Calais is, I infer from what I have heard, the pride of France. It is called the Club train, and is built on the plan of the vestibule trains in America. The carriages are so narrow, that after having been accustomed to wide ones, the Club train seems like a toy.

I have been curious to know why this train is called the Club train. I had a foolish idea at first that it was the private property of some club, run for the special benefit of its members, and I felt some hesitancy about traveling on a train devoted to the use of men. However, the presence of a number of women put me at ease, and though I made many inquiries about the train, all I could learn was that it was considered quite the finest equipped train in Europe.

The car in which we sat, as I said before, contained some women, and was besides liberally filled with men passengers. Shortly after we left Amiens, a porter announced that dinner was served in a front car. Everybody at once filed out and into the dining car. I have thought since that probably the train carried two dining cars, because the dinner, and an excellent one it proved to be, was served *table d'hôte,*[1] and there seemed to be accommodations for all.

After we had our cheese and salad, we returned to our drawing-room car, where we were served with coffee, the men having the privilege of smoking with it. I thought this manner of serving coffee a very pleasing one, quite an improvement on our own system, and quite worthy of adoption.

When I reached Calais, I found that I had two hours and more to spend in waiting. The train that I intended to take for Brindisi is a weekly mail train that runs to accommodate the mails and not passengers. It starts originally from London, at eight o'clock Friday evening of each week. The rule is that the persons desiring to travel on it must buy their tickets twenty-four hours in advance of the time of its departure. The mail and passengers are carried across the channel, and the train leaves Calais at 1.30 in the morning.

There are pleasanter places in the world to waste time in than Calais. I walked down along the pier and looked at the light-house, which I am told is one of the most perfect in the world, throwing its light farther away than any other. It is a revolving light, and it throws out long rays that seem so little above our heads that I found myself dodging to avoid being struck. Of course, that was purely imaginary on my part, for the rays are just the opposite to being near the ground, but they spread between the ground and the sky like the laths of an unfinished partition. I wonder if the people of Calais ever saw the moon and stars.

There is a very fine railway station built near the end of the pier. It is of generous size, but seemed, as far as I could judge, at this hour of the night, quite empty. There is a smoothly tiled enclosed promenade on the side of the station facing the pier that I should say would prove quite an attraction and comfort for passengers who were forced to wait in that place.

---

1   Literally, "table of the host" (French): A meal served with a fixed price and few (if any) options

My escort took me into the restaurant where we found something to eat, which was served by a French waiter who could speak some English and understand more. When it was announced that the boat from England was in we went out and saw the be-bundled and be-baggaged passengers come ashore and go to the train which was waiting alongside. One thousand bags of mail were quickly transferred to the train, and then I bade my escort good-bye, and was shortly speeding away from Calais.

There is but one passenger coach on this train. It is a Pullman Palace sleeping-car with accommodations for twenty-two passengers, but it is the rule never to carry more than twenty-one, one berth being occupied by the guard.

The next morning, having nothing else to occupy my time, I thought that I would see what my traveling companions looked like. I had shared the stateroom at the extreme end of the car with a pretty English girl who had the rosiest cheeks and the greatest wealth of golden brown hair I ever saw. She was going with her father, an invalid, to Egypt, to spend the winter and spring months. She was an early riser, and before I was awake had gotten up and joined her father in the other part of the car.

When I went out so as to give the porter an opportunity to make up my stateroom, I was surprised at the strange appearance of the interior of the car. All the head and foot boards were left in place, giving the impression that the coach was divided into a series of small boxes. Some of the passengers were drinking, some were playing cards, and all were smoking until the air was stifling. I never object to cigar smoke when there is some little ventilation, but when it gets so thick that one feels as if it is molasses instead of air that one is inhaling, then I mildly protest. It was soon this occasion, and I wonder what would be the result in our land of boasted freedom if a Pullman car should be put to such purposes. I concluded it is due to this freedom that we do not suffer from such things. Women travelers in America command as much consideration as men.

I walked down the car looking in the "boxes" only to find them all occupied by unsocial looking men. When I reached the middle of the car my little English room-mate, who was sitting with her father, saw me and kindly asked me to sit down with them.

Her father I remember as a cultured, broad-minded man, with a sense of humor that helped me to hear with less dread the racking cough that frequently stopped all speech and shook his thin frame as though he had the ague.

"Father," the little English girl said in a clear, musical voice, "the clergyman sent you his large prayer-book just before our departure, and I put it in your bag."

"My daughter is very thoughtful," he said to me, then turning to her he added, with a smile in his eye, "Please take the first opportunity to return the prayer-book to the clergyman, and tell him, with my compliments, that he might have saved himself that trouble; that I was grieved to deprive him of his book for so long."

The young girl's face settled into a look that spoke disapproval of her father's words, and a determination not to return the prayer-book. She held, clasped to her breast. a large prayer-book, and when her father jokingly told her she had bought the largest one she could find, which he looked on as wasting valuable packing space, when she could have carried a small one that would have been of as much service, I was actually startled by the hard, determined light on her face. In everything else she was the sweetest, most gentle girl I ever met, but her religion was of the hard, uncompromising kind, that condemns everything, forgives nothing, and swears the heathen is forever damned because he was not born to know the religion of her belief.

She spent all the afternoon trying to implant the seeds of her faith in my mind, and I listened, thinking from her words that if she was not the original Catherine Elsmere, she at least could not be more like that interesting character.

For the first day food was taken on the train at different stations, and the conductor, or guard, as they called him, served it to the passengers. A dining car was attached in the evening but I was informed by the women that it was not exactly the thing for us to eat in a public car with men, so we continued to be served in our state rooms.

I might have seen more while traveling through France if the car windows had been clean. From their appearance I judged that they had never been washed. We did not make many stops. The only purpose of stopping was for coal or water, as passengers are not taken on or off this train between Calais and Brindisi.

In the course of the afternoon we passed some high and picturesque mountains that were covered with a white frost. I found that
even wearing my ulster and wrapped in a rug I was none too warm.
About eight o'clock in the morning we reached Modena. The baggage
was examined there and all the passengers were notified in advance to
be prepared to get out and unlock the boxes that belonged to them.
The conductor asked me several times if I was quite certain that I had
no more than the handbag with me, telling me at the same time if any
boxes were found locked, with no owner to open them, they would be
detained by the custom inspectors. When partly assured that I had no
trunks he said that it was not necessary to get out with my hand-bag,
as no one would think it necessary to examine it.

Half an hour later we were in Italy. I was anxiously waiting to
see that balmy, sunny land, but though I pressed my face close to the
frosty window pane bleak night denied me even one glimpse of sunny
Italy and its dusky people. I went to bed early. It was so very cold that
I could not keep warm out of bed, and I cannot say that I got much
warmer in bed. The berths were provided with only one blanket each. I
piled all my clothing on the berth and spent half the night lying awake
thinking how fortunate the passengers were the week previous on this
train. Just in the very same place that we were traveling through Italian
bandits had attacked the train and I thought, with regretful envy, if
the passengers then felt the scarcity of blankets they at least had some
excitement to make their blood circulate.

When I got awake in the morning I hastily threw up the window
shade and eagerly looked out. I fell back in surprise, wondering, if for
once in my life I had made a mistake and waked up early. I could not
see any more than I had the night before on account of a heavy gray
fog that completely hid everything more than a yard away. Looking at
the watch on my wrist I found that it was ten o'clock, so I dressed with
some haste determined to find the guard and demand an explanation
of him.

"It is a most extraordinary thing," he said to me. "I never saw such
a fog in Italy before."

There was nothing for it except to sit quietly counting the days
I had been away from New York; subtracting them from the number that must elapse before my return. When this grew monotonous

I carefully thought over the advisability of trying to introduce brown uniforms for railroad employees in the United States. I thought with wearied frenzy of the universal employment of navy-blue uniforms in America, and I turned with rest to the neat brown uniforms brightened with a touching of gold braid on the collars and cuffs, that adorned the conductor and porter of the India mail.

But even this subject would not fill the day, so I began to notice the difference between the whistles employed on these engines and those at home. There was no deafening, ear-racking blast from these, but plaintive sounds, pitched in a high key that was very soprano indeed, compared with our bass whistles.

I noticed in Italy, as in all the other countries where I found railroads, that trains are started by a blast from a tin horn— horns such as those that take conspicuous places in political campaigns once every four years, succeeding, by the aid of enthusiastic campaigners, in making night hideous for several months preceding the election.

In most cases these horn-blowers seemed to be located at the station, but in France and Italy they occupied the front platform of a coach, and I noticed, with amusement, that the tin horns were chained to them.

All day I traveled through Italy—sunny Italy, along the Adriatic Sea. The fog still hung in a heavy cloud over the earth, and only once did I get a glimpse of the land I had heard so much about. It was evening, just at the hour of sunset, when we stopped at some station. I went out on the platform, and the fog seemed to lift for an instant, and I saw on one side a beautiful beach and a smooth bay dotted with boats bearing oddly-shaped and brightly-colored sails, which somehow looked to me like mammoth butterflies, dipping, dipping about in search of honey. Most of the sails were red, and as the sun kissed them with renewed warmth, just before leaving us in darkness, the sails looked as if they were composed of brilliant fire.

A high rugged mountain was on the other side of the train. It made me feel dizzy to look at the white buildings perched on the perpendicular side. I noticed the road that went in a winding line up the hill had been built with a wall on the ocean side; still I thought I would not care to travel up it.

I got out for a few minutes at the next station where we stopped to take our dinners. I walked into a restaurant to look about. It was very neat and attractive. Just as I stepped inside a little girl with wonderful large black eyes and enormous gold hoop-rings in her ears, ran forward to me with the fearless boldness of a child. I touched her pretty black hair, and then naturally felt in my pocket for something to give her. Just as I drew forth a large copper coin— the less the value of a coin generally, the larger its size— a small man with a delicately refined face, flashing black eyes, wide expanse of white shirt front, broken by a brilliant diamond, came up and spoke to the baby. In the way she drew back from me, although her little hand had been stretched out expectantly before, I knew he had told her not to accept anything from me.

I felt on first impulse like boxing his ears, he was so tiny and impudent. The guard coming in search of me, found us at this critical moment.

"You have insulted him," he said to me, as if I was not conscious of it! "The Italians are the poorest and proudest people on earth. They hate the English."

"I am an American," I said bluntly and abruptly. At this a waiter who had been standing close by apparently not listening, but catching every word just the same, came up and spoke to me in English. Then I determined to remedy the fault I had committed, but nevertheless I had a dogged determination that the child should yet take the coin.

"What a beautiful restaurant!" I exclaimed. "I am passing hurriedly through Italy and in my desire to see, judging from the samples of good cooking I have had *en route,* Italian eating houses are excellent. I hope I have not put you to any inconvenience. I almost forgot the restaurant when I saw that lovely baby. What exquisitely beautiful eyes! Exactly the same as her father's, at least I judge from the similarity of their eyes that he is her father, though he looks so young."

The waiter smiled and bowed and translated. I knew he would, and that is why I said it all. Then the little man's pride melted away, and a smile replaced the frown on his face. He spoke to the baby who came up and shook hands with me. I gave her the coin and our peace was sealed. Then the little father brought forth a bottle of wine, and with the most cordial smiles and friendliest words, begged me to accept it. I did not intend to be out—done, so I told the waiter that I must take some wine with me, insisted on paying for it, and with low bows and sweet smiles we took leave of one another, and I rushed after the guard to the train, boarding it just as the horn blew for it to continue on its way.

We arrived at Brindisi two hours late. When the train stopped, our car was surrounded with men wanting to carry us as well as our baggage to the boats. Their making no mention of hotels led me to wonder if people always passed through Brindisi without stopping. All these men spoke English very well, but the guard said he would get one omnibus and escort the English women, the invalid man and his daughter, and myself to our boats, and would see that we were not charged more than the right fare.

We drove first to the boat bound for Alexandria, where we took leave of my room-mate, and her father. Then we drove to the boat that we expected to sail on.

I alighted from the omnibus, and followed my companions up the gang plank. I dreaded meeting English people with their much-talked-of prejudices, as I knew I would shortly have to do. I was earnestly hoping that everybody would be in bed. As it was after one in the morning, I hardly expected the trial of facing them at once. The crowds of men on the deck dispelled my fond hope. I think every man on board that boat was up waiting to see the new passengers. They must have felt but illy paid for their loss of sleep, for besides the men who came on board, there were only the two large English women and my own plain, uninteresting self.

These women were more helpless than I. As they were among their own people, I waited for them to take the lead; but after we had stood at the foot of the stairs for some time, gazed at by the passengers, and no one came forward to attend to our wants, which were few and simple, I gently asked if that was the usual manner of receiving passengers on English boats.

"It is strange, very strange. A steward, or some one should come to our assistance," was all they could say.

At last a man came down below, and as he looked as if he was in some way connected with the boat, I ventured to stop him and inquire if it was expecting too much to ask if we might have a steward to show us to our cabins. He said there should be some about, and began lustily to call for one. Even this brought no one to us, and as he started to find one himself, I started in the opposite direction.

Among the crowd that stood about was but one man that dared to speak without waiting for an introduction before he could be commonly polite.

"You will find the purser in his office the first door to the left there," he said; and I went that way, followed by the guard from the train.

Sitting in the office was the purser and a man I supposed to be the doctor. I gave my ticket and a letter I had been given at the P. & O. office in London, to the purser. This letter requested that the commanders and pursers of all the P. & O. boats on which I traveled should give me all the care and attention it was in their power as such officers to bestow.

After leisurely reading the letter, the purser very carelessly turned around and told me the number of my cabin. I asked for a steward to show me the way, but he replied that there did not seen to be any about, that the cabin was on the port side, and with this meagre information, he impolitely turned his back and busied himself with some papers on the desk before him.

The train guard who still stood by my side, said he would help me find the cabin. After a little search, we did find it. I opened the door and stepped in, and the sight that met my eyes both amused me and dismayed me. At the opening of the door, two bushy heads were stuck out of the two lower berths, and two high pitched voices exclaimed simultaneously with a vexed intonation, "Oh!" I looked at the band-boxes, boots, hand bags, gowns and the upper berth that was also filled with clothes, and I echoed their "Oh!" in a little different tone and retired.

I returned to the purser and told him I could not sleep in an upper berth, and would not occupy a cabin with two other women. After looking again over the letter I had brought him, as if to see how much weight he should give it, he referred me to another cabin. This time a steward made his appearance and he took the part of an escort.

I found a pretty girl in that cabin, who lifted her head anxiously, and then gave me a friendly smile when I entered. I put my bag down and returned to the guard who was waiting to take me to the cable office. I stopped to ask the purser if I had time to make the trip, to which he replied in the affirmative, with the proviso, "If you hurry." The two women who had traveled with me from Calais, had by this time found their way to the purser's office, and I heard them telling that they had come away from home and left their purse and tickets lying on the table in the sitting-room, they had started in such a rush!

The guard took me down the gang plank, and along several dark streets. At last, coming to a building where a door stood open, he stopped and I followed him in. The room in which we stood was perfectly bare and lighted by a lamp whose chimney was badly smoked. The only things in the room were two stationary desks. On the one lay a piece of blank paper before an ancient ink well and a much used pen.

I thought that everybody had retired for the night, and the cable would have to wait until I reached the next port, until the guard explained to me that it was customary to ring for the operator, who would get up and attend to the message for me. Suiting the action to the words, the guard pulled at a knob near a small closed window, much like a postage stamp window. The bell made quite a clatter, still I had begun to think that hopeless, when the window opened with a clink, and a head appeared at the opening. The guard spoke in Italian, but hearing me speak English, the operator replied in the same language.

I told him I wanted to send a cable to New York. He asked me where New York was! I explained as best I could; then he brought out a lot of books, through which he searched first, to know by which line he could send the message; at least, so he explained; then what it would cost. The whole thing was so new and amusing to me that I forgot all about the departure of the boat until we had finished the business and stepped outside.

A whistle blew long and warningly. I looked at the guard, the guard looked at me. It was too dark to see each other, but I know our faces were the picture of dismay. My heart stopped beating and I thought with emotions akin to horror, "My boat was gone— and with it my limited wardrobe!"

"Can you run?" the guard asked in a husky voice. I said I could, and he taking a close grasp of my hand, we started down the dark street with a speed that would have startled a deer. Down the dark streets, past astonished watchmen and late pedestrians, until a sudden bend brought us in full view of my ship still in port. The boat for Alexandria had gone, but I was saved.

CHAPTER VI.
AN AMERICAN HEIRESS.

I HAD NOT been asleep long, it seemed to me, until I waked to find myself standing upright beside my berth. It required but a second, a glance at my drenched self, and the sounds of vigorous scrubbing on the deck above to explain the cause of my being out of bed before I knew it. I had gone to sleep with the port-hole open, and as my berth was just beneath it, I received the full force of the scrub-water as it came pouring over the sides. I managed to let the heavy window down and went back to bed, wet, but confident that I would not again be caught napping under such circumstances.

I had not been asleep many moments until I heard a voice call: "Miss, will you have your tea now?" I opened my eyes and saw a steward standing at the door awaiting a reply. I refused the tea, as did the English girl on the other side of my cabin, managing to answer her bright smile with a very tired one, and then I was off to sleep again.

"Miss, will you have your bath now?" a voice broke in on my slumbers shortly afterwards. I looked up in disgust at a little white-capped woman who was bending over me, tempted to say I had just had my bath, a shower-bath, but thought better of it before speaking. I know I said something about "in a few minutes," and then I was asleep again.

"Well, you are a lazy girl! You'll miss your bath and breakfast if you don't get up the instant," was my third greeting. My surprise at the familiarity of the remark got the better of my sleepiness, and I thought:

"Well, by all that is wonderful, where am I? Am I in school again that a woman dare assume such a tone to me?" I kept my thoughts to myself, and said stiffly:

"I generally get up when I feel so inclined."

I saw my room-mate was missing, but I felt like sleeping and I decided to sleep; whether it pleased the stewardess or not, it mattered little to me. The steward was the next one to put in an appearance.

"Miss, this ship is inspected every day and I must have this cabin made up before they come," he said complainingly. "The captain will be here presently."

There was nothing to do but to get up, which I did. I found my way to the bath-room, but soon saw that it was impossible for me to turn on the water, as I did not understand the mechanism of the faucet. I asked a steward I saw outside the door, the whereabouts of the stewardess, and was simply amazed to hear him reply:

"The stewardess is taking a rest and cannot be disturbed."

After dressing I wandered up on the next deck and was told that breakfast was over long ago. I went out on deck, and the very first glimpse of the lazy looking passengers in their summer garments, lounging about in comfortable positions, or slowly promenading the deck, which was sheltered from the heat of the sun by a long stretch of awnings, and the smooth, velvety looking water, the bluest I had ever seen, softly gurgling against the side of the ship as it almost imperceptibly steamed on its course, and the balmy air, soft as a rose leaf, and just as sweet, air such as one dreams about but seldom finds; standing there alone among strange people, on strange waters, I thought how sweet life is!

Before an hour had passed I was acquainted with several persons. I had thought and expected that the English passengers would hold themselves aloof from a girl who was traveling alone, but my cabin-companion saw me before I got away from the door, and came forward to ask me to join herself and friends. We first had an amusing search for the steamer-chair which I had told the guard to buy at Brindisi and send on before our departure. There were over three hundred passengers on the ship, and I suppose they averaged a chair apiece, so it can easily be pictured the trouble it would be to find a chair among that number. I asked where the deck-stewards were when at last I felt the search was useless, and was surprised to learn that a deck-steward was an unknown commodity on the P. & O. line.

"I presume the quarter-master has charge of the decks," my companion said in conclusion, "but we are expected to look after our own chairs and rugs, and if we don't it is useless to inquire for them if they disappear."

Shortly before noon I became acquainted with an Englishman who belongs to the Civil Service in Calcutta. He had been in India for the last twenty years, during which time he had repeatedly visited England, which made this trip an old story to him. He had made the same trip from Calais on the India express as I had, and said he noticed me on the train. Learning that I was traveling alone, he devoted most of his time looking out for my comfort and pleasure.

The bugle blew for luncheon, which is always called by the Indian title "*tiffin*" on ships traveling in Eastern seas. The Englishman asked if I would go with him to *tiffin*, and as I had gone without breakfast I was only too anxious to go at the first opportunity. The dining-hall is on the second deck. It is a small room nicely decorated with tropical foliage plants and looks quite cozy and pretty, but it was never intended to accommodate a ship carrying more than seven-five first-class passengers.

The head-waiter, who stood at the door, stared at us blankly as we went in. I hesitated, naturally thinking that he would show us to some table, but as he did not I suggested to the gentleman with me, that he ask before we take our places.

"Sit anywhere," was the polite reply we received, so we sat down at the table nearest.

We had just been served, when four women ranging from twenty-four to thirty-five came in, and with indignant snorts of surprise, seated themselves at the same table. They were followed by a short, fat woman with a sweeping walk and air of satisfied assurance, who eyed us in a supercilious way and then turned to the others with an air of injured dignity that was intensely amusing. They were followed by two men and as there were only places for seven at the table the elderly man went out. Two of the girls sat on a lounge at the end of the table, which made room for the young man. Then we were made to suffer. All kinds of rude remarks were made about us. "They did hate people coming to their table;" "Too bad Papa was robbed of his place;" "Shame people had to be crowded from their own table," and similar pleasant speeches were hurled at us. The young woman who sat at my left was not content to confine her rudeness to her tongue, but repeatedly reached across my plate, brushing my food with her sleeves without one word of apology. I confess I never had a more disagreeable meal. I thought at first that this rudeness was due to my being an American and that they had taken this means of showing their hatred for all Americans. Still I could not understand why they should subject an Englishman to the same treatment unless it was because he was with me. After-experiences showed me that my first conclusion was wrong; that I was not insulted because I was an American, but because the people were simply ill-bred. When dinner came we found that we were debarred from the dining-room. Passengers who got on at London were given the preference, and as there was not accommodations for all, the passengers who boarded the ship at Brindisi had to wait for second dinner.

One never realizes, until they face such contingencies, what an important part dinner plays in one's life. It was nine o'clock when the dining-room was cleared that night, and the Brindisi passengers were allowed to take their places at the table. I hardly believe they took much else. Everything was brought to us as it was left from the first dinner—cold soup, the remnants of fish, cut up bits of beef and fowl— all down the miserable course until at last came cold coffee! I had thought the food on the India Express might have been better until after my experience on the P. & O. steamer Victoria, and then I decided it might have been worse.

Such a roar of complaint as went up from those late dinner passengers. They wanted to get up a protest to serve on the captain, but I refused to take any part in it, and several of the more conservative ones followed my example.

The two women I have already referred to as having traveled on the India Express to Brindisi, were treated even worse than I was. When we made inquiries, we were told that at dinner only were the places reserved, but that at breakfast and tiffin, first there were first served. Acting on this information they went in to early tiffin the following day, and a young man who sat at the head of an empty table said to them as they went to sit down:

"You can't sit there. I've reserved those places for some of my friends." They went to another table and after sitting down, were requested by some late comers to get up and give the places to them. The one woman cried bitterly over it.

"I am a grandmother, and this is the sixth trip I have made to Australia, and I was never treated so insultingly in my life."

There are circumstances under which a trip on the Mediterranean would be like a dream of Paradise. If one were in love, for instance; for they do say that people in love do not eat, and aside from the food, the trip is perfect. Probably it is a hope of finding the cure that will help them to forget a stomach void, that makes love the principal subject on the P. & O. boats. Travelers who care to be treated with courtesy, and furnished with palatable food, will never by any chance travel on the Victoria.

It is all rule and no practice on that ship. The impudence and rudeness of the servants in America is a standing joke, but if the servants on the Victoria are a sample of English servants, I am thankful to keep those we have, such as they are. I asked the stewardess to assist a woman who looked as if she was dying of consumption, to the deck with her rugs, only to be told in reply, that she would not help any one unless they came and requested her to do so.

I heard her tell a passenger one day, that she did not believe it was sickness, but laziness that ailed the woman. If complaints were made about the conduct of the servants, they were always met by the assertion that the servants had been for a long time in the company's employ, and would take privileges.

The commander of the ship set an example for rudeness. A Spanish gentleman of high position who was traveling to China, where he represented his country in the diplomatic service, also got on at Brindisi. He thought that his first duty was to pay his respects to the Captain in charge of the ship, so he asked some one to point the Captain out to him. This was done on deck. He walked up to the Captain, and with a profound bow, hat in hand, begged the Captain's pardon, and said that he was *chargé d'affaires*[1] of China and Siam for the Spanish government, and he wished to pay his duty and respects to the Captain of the boat on which he was traveling. The Captain glared at him savagely for a moment after he had finished, and then asked rudely:

"Well, what of it?"

---

1   (French) A diplomatic offical acting temporarily in the place of an ambassador; a minor state's diplomatic representative

The Spaniard was speechless for a moment, but recovering, he said politely:

"I beg your pardon, I thought I was addressing a gentleman and the commander of this ship." Turning, he walked away, and they never spoke afterwards.

Although I had brought a letter to the Captain, he never noticed me in any way. A bright faced, jolly boy, who was going to Hong Kong to enter a banking house of his uncle's, brought a letter to the Captain. He presented himself one day on deck, stepping a foot or so away until the Captain should have time to read it and greet him. The Captain read the letter, folded it carefully, put it in his pocket, and walked away! He never spoke to the boy afterwards, and the boy was careful not to give him that trouble. The Captain had a tongue for gossip, too. Every time I heard a slighting story about any of the passengers, and would ask where it came from, the answer would always be the Captain had told it to somebody.

Notwithstanding all annoying trifles it was a very happy life we spent in those pleasant waters. The decks were filled all the day, and when the lights were put out at night the passengers reluctantly went to their cabins. The passengers formed two striking contrasts. There were some of the most refined and lovely people on board, and there were some of the most ill-bred and uncouth. Most of the women, whose acquaintance I formed, were very desirous of knowing all about American women, and frequently expressed their admiration for the free American woman, many going so far as to envy me, while admiring my unfettered happiness. Two clever Scotch women I met were traveling around the world, but are taking two years at it. One Irishwoman, with a laugh that rivaled her face in sweetness, was traveling alone to Australia. My cabin-mate was bound for New Zealand, but she was accompanied by her brother, a pleasant young Englishman, who insisted on relinquishing his place at first dinner in my favor, and who stayed away despite my protests and my determination not to deprive him of a warm dinner.

In the daytime the men played cricket and quoits. Sometimes, in the evenings, we had singing, and other times we went to the second-class deck and listened to better music given by second-class passengers. When there were no chairs we would all sit down on the deck, and I remember nothing that was more enjoyable than these little visits. There was one little girl with a pale, slender face, who was a great favorite with us all, though none of us ever spoke to her. She sang in a sweet, pathetic voice a little melody about "Who'll buy my silver herrings?"[1] until, I know, if she had tried to sell any, we should all have bought. The best we could do was to join her in the refrain, which we did most heartily.

Better than all to me, it was to sit in a dark corner on deck, above where the sailors had their food, and listen to the sounds of a tom-tom and a weird musical chanting that always accompanied their evening meal. The sailors were Lascars. They were not interesting to look at, and doubtless, if I could have seen as well as heard them at their evening meal, it would have lost its charm for me. They were the most untidy looking lot of sailors I ever saw. Over a pair of white muslin drawers they wore a long muslin slip very like in shape to the old-time night-shirt. This was tied about the waist with a colored handkerchief, and on their heads they wore gayly colored turbans, which are really nothing but a crown of straw with a scarf-shaped piece of bright cloth, often six feet in length, wound about the head. Their brown feet are always bare. They chant, as all sailors do, when hoisting sails, but otherwise are a grim, surly looking set, climbing about over the ship like a pack of monkeys.

When I boarded the boat at Brindisi the purser gave me some cables that had been sent to me, care of the Victoria. After we had been out several days, a young woman came to me with an unsealed cable and asked if I was Nellie Bly. Upon telling her I was, she said that the purser had given the cable to some of the passengers the day before, as he did not know who Nellie Bly was, and after two days traveling among them it reached me. Occasionally we would have a dance on deck to the worst music it has ever been my misfortune to hear. The members of the band also washed the dishes, and though I could not blame the passengers who always disappeared at the appearance of the musicians still I felt sorry for them; it was both ridiculous and pathetic that they should be required to cultivate two such inharmonious arts! One of the officers told me that the band they had before were com-

---

1   "Silver Herring" (Ca. 1800): Traditional peddler's song with variant verses about preparing herring

pelled to scrub the decks, and their hands became so rough from the work that it was impossible for them longer to fill the role of musicians, so they were discharged and the new band were turned into dish-washers instead of deck-scrubbers.

I had not been on the Victoria many days until some one who had become friendly with me, told me it was rumored on board that I was an eccentric American heiress, traveling about with a hair brush and a bank book. I judged that some of the attention I was receiving was due to the story of my wealth. I found it convenient, later on, to correct the report when a young man came to me to say that I was the kind of a girl he liked, and as he was the second son and his brother would get both the money and the title, his sole ambition was to find a wife who would settle £1,000 a year on him.

There was another young man on board who was quite as unique a character and much more interesting to me. He told me that he had been traveling constantly since he was nine years old, and that he had always killed the desire to love and marry because he never expected to find a woman who could travel without a number of trunks, and bundles innumerable. I noticed that he dressed very exquisitely and changed his apparel at least three times a day, so my curiosity made me bold enough to ask how many trunks he carried with him.

"Nineteen," was the amazing reply. I no longer wondered at his fears of getting a wife who could not travel without trunks.

CHAPTER VII.
"Two Beautiful Black Eyes."

It was in the afternoon when the Victoria anchored at Port Said. We were all on deck eagerly watching for the first sight of land, and though that sight showed us a wide, sandy beach, and some uninteresting two-storied white houses with arcade fronts, still it did not lessen our desire to go ashore. I suppose that would have been the result under the circumstances had Port Said been the most desolate place on earth. I know everybody was experiencing a slight weariness, though we should all have stoutly denied such a reflection on our constant companions, and gladly welcomed the change of a few hours on shore, where at least we might see new faces. A more urgent reason still, for our going to land, was the fact that this was a coaling port for the Victoria, and I never knew of anything that would make one more quickly feel that there are things in life much worse than death, if I may use the expression, than to have to stay on board a ship during the coaling operation.

Before the boat anchored the men armed themselves with canes, to keep off the beggars they said; and the women carried parasols for the same purpose. I had neither stick nor umbrella with me, and refused all offers to accept one for this occasion, having an idea, probably a wrong one, that a stick beats more ugliness into a person than it ever beats out.

Hardly had the anchor dropped than the ship was surrounded with a fleet of small boats, steered by half-clad Arabs, fighting, grabbing, pulling, yelling in their mad haste to be first. I never in my life saw such an exhibition of hungry greed for the few pence they expected to earn by taking the passengers ashore. Some boatmen actually pulled

150

others out of their boats into the water in their frantic endeavors to steal each other's places. When the ladder was lowered, numbers of them caught it and clung to it as if it meant life or death to them, and here they clung until the captain was compelled to order some sailors to beat the Arabs off, which they did with long poles, before the passengers dared venture forth. This dreadful exhibition made me feel that probably there was some justification in arming one's self with a club.

Our party were about the first to go down the ladder to the boats. It had been our desire and intention to go ashore together, but when we stepped into the first boat some were caught by rival boatmen and literally dragged across to other boats. The men in the party used their sticks quite vigorously; all to no avail, and although I thought the conduct of the Arabs justified this harsh course of treatment, still I felt sorry to see it administered so freely and lavishly to those black, half-clad wretches, and marveled at their stubborn persistence even while cringing under the blows. Having our party divided there was nothing to do under the circumstances but to land and reunite on shore, so we ordered the Arabs to pull away. Midway between the Victoria and the shore the boatmen stopped and demanded their money in very plain and forcible English. We were completely at their mercy, as they would not land us either way until we paid what they asked. One of the Arabs told me that they had many years' experience in dealing with the English and their sticks, and had learned by bitter lessons that if they landed an Englishman before he paid they would receive a stinging blow for their labor.

Walking up the beach, sinking ankle deep in the sand at every step, we came to the main street. Almost instantly we were surrounded by Arab boys who besought us to take a ride on the burros that stood patiently beside them. There were burros of all colors, sizes and shapes, and the boys would cry out, most beseechingly, "Here's Gladstone! Take a ride; see Gladstone with two beautiful black eyes."

This they would cry in such a soft plaintive way that one felt the "two beautiful black eyes" made the animals irresistible.

If one happened to be of a different political belief and objected to riding the Gladstone hobby, as it were, a choice could be made of almost any well-known, if not popular name. There were Mrs. Maybricks, Mary Andersons, Lillie Langtrys, and all the prominent men of the time.

I knew all about burros, having lived for some time in Mexico, but they proved to be quite a novelty to many of the passengers, almost all of whom were anxious to take a ride before returning to the boat. So, as many as could find animals to ride, mounted and went flying through that quaint, sleeping town, yelling with laughter, bouncing like rubber balls on their saddles, while half-naked Arab boys goaded the burros on by short, urgent hisses, and by prodding them from behind with a sharp stick.

After seeing about fifty of our passengers started off in this happy manner, a smaller number of us went to a gambling house, and in a short time were deep in the sport of placing our English gold on colors and numbers and waiting anxiously for the wheel to go 'round to see the money at last swept in by the man at the table. I do not think that any one of us knew anything about the game, but we recklessly put our money on the table and laughed to see it taken in by the man who gave the turn to the wheel.

There was another attraction in this place which helped to win a number of young men from that very expensive table. It was an orchestra composed of young women, some of whom were quite pleasing both in looks and manners.

The longer we remained at this gambling house the less money we had to spend in the shops. I went ashore with the determination not to buy anything as I was very anxious not to increase my baggage. I withstood the tempting laces which were offered at wonderfully low prices, the quaint Egyptian curios, and managed to content myself by buying a sun hat, as everybody else did; and a pugaree to wind about it, as is customary in the East.

Having bought a hat and seen all I cared to of the shops I went strolling about with some friends feasting my eyes on what were to me peculiarities of a peculiar people. I saw old houses with carved-wood fronts that would have been worth a fortune in America occupied by tenants that were unmistakably poor. The natives were apparently so accustomed to strangers that we attracted very little, if any attention, except from those who hoped to gain something from our visit. Unmolested we went about finding no occasion to use sticks on the natives.

We saw a great number of beggars who, true to their trade, whined forth, with outstretched hands, their plaintive appeals, but they were not so intrusive or bothersome that they necessitated our giving them the cane instead of alms. The majority of these beggars presented such repulsive forms of misery that in place of appealing to my sympathetic nature, as is generally the case, they had a hardening effect on me. They seemed to thrust their deformities in our faces in order to compel us to give money to buy their absence from our sight.

While standing looking after a train of camels that had just come in loaded with firewood I saw some Egyptian women. They were small in stature and shapelessly clad in black. Over their faces, beginning just below the eyes, they wore black veils that fell almost to their knees. As if fearing that the veil alone would not destroy all semblance of features they wear a thing that spans the face between the hair and the veil down the line of their noses. In some cases this appears to be of gold, and in others it is composed of some black material. One Egyptian woman carried a little naked baby with her. She held it on her hips, its little black legs clinging to her waist much after the fashion of a boy climbing a pole.

Down at the beach we came upon a group of naked men clustered about an alligator that they had caught. It was securely fastened in some knotted rope, the end of which was held by some half dozen black fellows. The public water-carriers, with well filled goat-skins flung across their backs, we met making their way to the town for the last trip that day.

Darkness came on us very suddenly and sent us rushing off for our ship. This time we found the boatman would not permit us even to enter their boats until we paid them to take us across to the Victoria. Their price now was just double what they had charged to bring us to land. We protested, but they said it was the law to double the price after sunset.

They were just finishing the coaling when we reached the ship, but the sight we caught of the coal barges, lighted by some sputtering, dripping stuff, held in iron cages on the end of long poles, that showed the hurrying naked people rushing with sacks of coal up a steep gangplank, between the barges and the ship, was one long to be remembered. Nor were they working quietly. Judging from the noise, every one of them was yelling something that pleased his own fancy and humor.

The next morning I got up earlier than usual so anxious was I to see the famous Suez Canal. Rushing up on deck, I saw we were passing through what looked like an enormous ditch, enclosed on either side with high sand banks. We seemed to be hardly moving, which made us feel the heat very intensely. They tell me, that according to law, a ship must not travel through the canal at a speed exceeding five knots an hour, because a rapid passage of the ship would make a strong current that would wash in the sand banks. One gentleman, who had traveled all his life, helped us to pass some of the tedious, stifling hours in the canal by telling us the history of it.

It was begun in 1859 and took ten years to build. The work is estimated to have cost nearly £18,250,000, although the poor blacks that were employed to do the labor commanded the lowest possible wages. It is claimed that the lives of 100,000 laborers were sacrificed in the building of this canal, which is only 100 English miles, 88 geographical miles, 5 in length.

When first completed the width of the surface of the canal was three hundred and twenty-five feet, but the constant washing in of the banks has reduced it to one hundred and ninety-five feet. The bottom is said to be seventy-two feet wide and the depth is but twenty-six feet. The trip through the canal can be made in from twenty to twenty-four hours.

About noon of our first day in the canal we anchored in the bay fronting Ismailia. Here passengers were taken on, which gave us time to see the Khedive's palace, which is built a little way back from the beach in the heart of a beautiful green forest. Continuing the journey through the canal we saw little of interest. The signal stations were the only green spots that met the eye, but they were proof of what could be done, even in this sandy desert by the expenditure of time and energy.

The one thing that enlivened this trip was the appearance of naked Arabs, who would occasionally run along the banks of the canal, crying in pitiful tones, "bahkshish."[1] This we understood meant money, which many of the kind hearted passengers would throw to them, but

---

1   Alternative spelling of "baksheesh" (Turkish)

the beggars never seemed to find it, and would keep on after us, still crying, "bahkshish" until they were exhausted.

We passed several ships in the canal. Generally the passengers would call to the passengers on the other ships, but the conversation was confined mainly to inquiries as to what kind of a voyage had been theirs. We saw at one place in the canal, a lot of Arabs, both men and women, at work. Among them were a number of camels that were employed in carrying stone with which the laborers were endeavoring to strengthen the banks.

In the night the boat hung an electric light from the front, and by the aid of this light, moving it from side to side, were able to continue on their way. Before the introduction of electric head lights for this purpose, the vessels were always compelled to tie up in the canal over night, because of the great danger of running into the sand banks. In addition to making the trip longer, this stoppage added greatly to the discomfort of the passengers, who found that even the slow motion of the boat, helped, in a measure, to lessen the stifling heat that seemed to come from out the sand banks during the night as well as when the blazing sun was in the cloudless sky.

We saw, when near the end of the canal, several Arab encampments. They were both picturesque and interesting. First we would notice a small dull red fire, and between that fire and us we could see the outlines of people and resting camels. At one encampment we heard music, but at the others we saw the people either working over the fire, as if preparing their evening meal, or in sitting positions crouching about it in company with their camels.

Shortly after this we dropped anchor in the Bay of Suez. Hardly had we done so when the ship was surrounded by a number of small sail boats that, in the semi-darkness, with their white sails before the breeze, reminded me of moths flocking to a light, both from their white, winged-like appearance, and the rapid way in which numbers of them floated down on us. These sail boats were filled with men with native fruits, photographs and odd shells to sell. They all came on board, and among them were a number of jugglers. The passengers took very little interest in the venders, but all had a desire to see what was to be offered by the jugglers. There was one among them, a black man, who wore little else than a sash, a turban and a baggy pocket, in the lining of which he carried two lizards and a small rabbit. He was very anxious to show us his tricks and to get the money for them. He refused, however, to do anything with the rabbit and lizards until after he had shown us what he could do with a handkerchief and some bangles that he brought along for this purpose. He selected me from among the crowd, to hold the handkerchief, which he had first shaken as if to show us that it contained nothing. He then showed us a small brass bangle, and pretended to put the bangle in the handkerchief; he then placed the handkerchief in my hand, telling me to hold it tightly. I did so, feeling the presence of the bangle very plainly. He blew on it and jerking the handkerchief loose from my grasp, shook it. Much to the amazement of the crowd the bangle was gone. Some of the passengers in the mean time stole the juggler's rabbit, and one of the lizards had quietly taken itself off to some secluded spot. He was very much concerned about the loss of them and refused to perform any more tricks until they were restored to his keeping. At last one young man took the rabbit from his pocket and returned it to the juggler, much to his gratification. The lizard was not to be found, and as it was time for the ship to sail, the juggler was forced to return to his boat. After he had gone, several people came to know if I had any idea how the trick with the handkerchief had been done. I explained to them that it was an old and very uninteresting trick; that the man had one bangle sewn in the handkerchief, and the other bangle, which he showed to the people, he slipped quietly out of sight. Of course, the one who held the handkerchief held the bangle, but when the juggler would jerk the handkerchief from the hand, and shake it, in full view of his audience, the bangle being sewn to the handkerchief, would naturally not fall to the floor, and as he carefully kept the side to which the bangle was attached turned towards himself, he successfully duped his audience into thinking, that by his magic, he had made the bangle disappear. One of the men who listened to this explanation became very indignant, and wanted to know if I knew positively how this trick had been done, and why I had not exposed the man. I merely explained that I wanted to see the juggler get his money, much to the disgust of the Englishman.

Where we anchored at Suez some claim is the historic place where the Israelites crossed the Red Sea. Some people who bother themselves greatly about facts, figures and ancient history, bought views, which showed that at certain stages of the tide, people, in even this day, can wade around there without any risk of life or comfort. The next morning when we arose we were out of sight of land and well out on the Red Sea. The weather now was very hot, but still some of the passengers did their best to make things lively on board. One evening a number of young men gave a minstrel show. They displayed both energy and perseverance in preparing for it as well as in the execution of it. One end of the deck was set aside for the show. A stage was put up and the whole corner was enclosed by awnings, and the customary green curtain hung in place during service, as drop curtain between acts, as well appearing before and after the performance.

The young men filled their different roles in a very commendable manner, but as the night was so dreadfully warm, the passengers feeling the heat more than usual, owing to the deck being enclosed by awnings, it was difficult to awake any enthusiasm on the part of the audience. We had an intermission, when all retired to the dining room for punch and biscuits, and I know that no one appreciated the refreshments more than the actors, who joined us, their blackened faces streaked with perspiration.

Towards the last the passengers could find very little to do that proved interesting or in any way aided them to forget the heat. A few of those who could sing, or imagined they could, were persuaded to exercise their vocal organs for the benefit of those who could sing and would not, and those who realized they had no voice and knew enough to remain quiet. At other times many of us went to the deck reserved for the second-class passengers and enjoyed the concerts given by them. When there were no chairs for us on this deck we would sit on the floor, and we all acknowledged that the first-class passengers could not furnish music that was any better.

The days were spent mainly on deck lounging about in easy chairs. I found that no one enjoyed as much comfort as I did. I had changed my heavy waist for my silk bodice, and I felt cool and comfortable and lazily happy. When dinner hour approached we would see a few rush off to dress for dinner and later they would appear in full dress, low bodice and long train, much to the amusement of that class of passengers who maintained that it was decidedly not the thing to appear in full dress on an ocean steamer.

The evening dress, made of white linen, in which the young men in the East generally made their appearance at dinner, impressed me as being not only comfortable and appropriate, but decidedly becoming and elegant.

It is very seldom that men do not get more enjoyment out of life than women under like circumstances. Between cricket, to which they were passionately attached, and quoits and the smoking-room, which was the scene of many exciting games for large stakes and, later on, an hour or so spent in a dark corner of the deck pleasing and being pleased by some congenial companion of the opposite sex, the enforced rest was quite an agreeable one to the men.

We were all very much interested and concerned about a small bird that had traveled with us from Suez, sometimes flying along a little way and then resting on the rigging of the ship. It was a pretty bird with a slender gray tail and a silver breast and a black ring about its throat, its back being a modest drabish brown. At first it was easily frightened but after awhile it became very tame and would light on the deck among the passengers, picking up the crumbs they threw to it. Beside the bird as a topic of interest we had the lizard which was left behind by the juggler.

It was found in a quiet corner of the deck by the quarter-master the morning following our stop at Suez. A sympathizing young man took charge of it and endeavored to feed it, but after living in sullen quietness for a few days, it ceased to breathe and its death was solemnly announced to the passengers.

The Victoria is said to be the finest boat on the P. & O. Line, still it could not be more unsuited for the trip. It is very badly planned, being built so that a great number of cabins inside are absolutely cut off from light and air. It is a compliment to call them cabins as they are really nothing more than small, dark, disagreeable, and unventilated boxes. The passengers are charged all the same rate of fare, and if they are consigned to one of these undesirable boxes there is no redress; they must simply bow before the dictates of this company, who trade on the fact of their being an old established line, and a very desirable one in many respects, and passengers are treated—I judge only by what I saw and heard— as if they should consider that a favor had been conferred upon them when they were permitted to pay for tickets to travel on that line. The prices to ports that are touched at by rival steamship lines are rather reasonable, while to ports where they have the monopoly they charge exorbitant rates. I have stated that the conduct of the officers and servants, and the quality of the food left much to be desired by travelers.

The nights were so warm while on the Red Sea that the men left their cabins and spent their nights on deck. It is usually customary for the women to sleep on deck, one side of which, at such times, is reserved exclusively for them. During this trip none of the women had the courage to set the example, so the men had the decks to themselves.

Sleeping down below was all the more reason why women arising early would go on the decks before the sun began to boil in search of a refreshing spot where they could get a breath of cool air. At this hour the men were usually to be seen promenading about in their pajamas, but I heard no objections raised until much to the dismay of the women the Captain announced that the decks belonged to the men until after eight o'clock in the morning, and that the women were expected to remain below until after that hour.

Just before we came to Aden we passed in the sea a number of high brown mountains. They are known as the Twelve Apostles. Shortly after this we came in sight of Aden. It looked to us like a large, bare mountain of wonderful height, but even by the aid of glasses we were unable to tell that it was inhabited. Shortly after eleven o'clock in the morning we anchored in the bay. Our boat was soon surrounded by a number of small boats, which brought to us men who had things to sell, and the wonderful divers of the East.

The passengers had been warned by the officers on board not to go ashore at Aden because of the intense heat. So the women spent their time bargaining with the Jews who came to the ship to sell ostrich feathers and feather boas. The men helped them to close with the sellers always to the sellers' advantage, much as they might congratulate themselves to the contrary.

I, in company with a few of the more reckless ones, decided to brave the heat and go ashore and see what Aden[1] had to offer.

---

1   City in modern Yemen, at the time a British Indian province, located on the southern Arabian Peninsula

CHAPTER VIII.
ADEN TO COLOMBO.

HIRING a large boat, I went ashore with a half dozen acquaintances who felt they could risk the sun. The four oarsmen were black fellows, thin of limb, but possessed of much strength and tireless good humor. They have, as have all the inhabitants of Aden, the finest white teeth of any mortals. This may be due to the care they take of them and the manner of that care. From some place, I am unable to state where, as I failed to see one living thing growing at Aden, they get tree branches of a soft, fibrous wood which they cut into pieces three and four inches in length. With one end of this stick, scraped free of the bark, they rub and polish their teeth until they are perfect in their whiteness. The wood wears into a soft pulp, but as one can buy a dozen sticks for a penny one can well afford to throw the stick away after once using; although, if necessary, a stick can be used many times. I bought several sticks and found them the most efficient as well as pleasant tooth brush I had ever tried. I felt a regret that some enterprising firm had not thought of importing this useful bit of timber to replace the tooth-destroying brush used in America.

The man in charge of the boat that carried us to land was a small black fellow with the thinnest legs I ever saw. Somehow they reminded me of smoked herrings, they were so black, flat and dried looking. He was very gay notwithstanding his lack of weight. Around his neck and over his bare breast were twined strings of beads, black and gold and silver. Around his waist was a highly colored sash, and on his arms and ankles were heavy bracelets, while his fingers and toes seemed to be trying to outdo one another in the way of rings. He spoke English quite well, and to my rather impertinent question as to what number

160

constituted his family told me that he had three wives and eleven children, which number, he added piously, by the grace of the power of his
faith, he hoped to increase.

His hair was yellow which, added to his very light dress of jewelry and sash, gave him rather a strange look. The bright yellow hair
and the black skin forming a contrast which was more startling than
the black eyes and yellow hair that flashed upon the astonished vision
of the American public some years ago, but has become since an old
and tiresome sight. Some of the boatmen had their black wool pasted
down and hidden under a coating of lime. I was very curious about it
until the first man explained that they were merely bleaching their hair;
that it was always done by covering the head with lime, which, being
allowed to remain on for several days, exposed to the hot sun and the
water, bleached the hair yellow or red at the expiration of that time.
This bleaching craze, he also informed me, was confined to the men
of Aden. So far, none of the women had tried to enhance their black
beauty in that way, but it was considered very smart among the men.

While we were talking our men were vigorously pulling to the time
of a rousing song, one line of which was sung by one man, the others
joining in the refrain at the end. Their voices were not unpleasant, and
the air had a monotonous rhythm that was very fascinating.

We landed at a well-built pier and walked up the finely-cut, white-
stone steps from the boat to the land. Instantly we were surrounded by
half-clad black people, all of whom, after the manner of hack-drivers at
railway stations, were clamoring for our favor. They were not all drivers, however. Mingling with the drivers were merchants with jewelry,
ostrich plumes and boas to sell, runners for hotels, beggars, cripples
and guides. This conglomeration besought us to listen to every individual one of them until a native policeman, in the Queen's uniform,
came forward and pushed the black fellows back with his hands, sometimes hastening their retreat with his boot.

A large board occupied a prominent position on the pier. On it
was marked the prices that should be paid drivers, boatmen, and like
people. It was, indeed, a praiseworthy thoughtfulness that caused the
erection of that board, for it prevented tourists being robbed. I looked
at it, and thought that even in that land there was more precaution
taken to protect helpless and ignorant strangers than in New York City,

where the usual custom of night hack-men is to demand exorbitant prices, and if they are not forthcoming, to pull off their coats and fight for it.

Perched on the side of this bleak, bare mountain is a majestic white building, reached by a fine road cut in the stone that forms the mountain. It is a club house, erected for the benefit of the English soldiers who are stationed on this barren spot. In the harbor lay an English man-of-war,[1] and near a point where the land was most level, numbers of white tents were pitched for soldiers.

From the highest peak of the black, rocky mountain, probably 1700 feet above sea level, floated the English flag. As I traveled on and realized more than ever before how the English have stolen almost all, if not all, desirable sea-ports, I felt an increased respect for the level-headedness of the English government, and I cease to marvel at the pride with which Englishmen view their flag floating in so many different climes and over so many different nationalities.

Near the pier were shops run by Parsees[2]. A hotel, post-office and telegraph office are located in the same place. The town of Aden is five miles distant. We hired a carriage and started at a good pace, on a wide, smooth road that took us along the beach for a way, passing low rows of houses, where we saw many miserable, dirty-looking natives; passed a large graveyard, liberally filled, which looked like the rest of that stony point, bleak, black and bare, the graves often being shaped by cobblestones.

The roads at Aden are a marvel of beauty. They are wide and as smooth as hardwood, and as they twist and wind in pleasing curves up the mountain, they are made secure by a high, smooth wall against mishap. Otherwise their steepness might result in giving tourists a serious roll down a rough mountain-side.

Just before we began to ascend we saw a black man at his devotions. He was kneeling in the centre of a little square formed by rocks. His face was turned heavenward, and he was oblivious to all else except the power before which he was laying bare his inmost soul, with a fervor

1   British Royal Navy ship armed with cannons and propelled by sails, used from the 16th century through the 19th century

2   Descendents of Zoroastrians who fled from Persia to India in the 7th and 8th centuries to avoid Muslim persecution

and devotion that commanded respect, even from those who thought of him as a heathen. I inferred that he was a sun worshipper from the way in which he constantly had his face turned upward, except when he bent forward to kiss the ground on which he knelt.

On the road we saw black people of many different tribes. A number of women I noticed, who walked proudly along, their brown, bare feet stepping lightly on the smooth road. They had long purple-black hair, which was always adorned with a long, stiff feather, dyed of brilliant red, green, purple, and like striking shades. They wore no other ornament than the colored feather, which lent them an air of pride, when seen beside the much-bejeweled people of that quaint town. Many of the women, who seemed very poor indeed, were lavishly dressed in jewelry. They did not wear much else, it is true, but in a place as hot as Aden, jewelry must be as much as anyone would care to wear.

To me the sight of these perfect, bronze-like women, with a graceful drapery of thin silk wound about the waist, falling to the knees, and a corner taken up the back and brought across the bust, was most bewitching. On their bare, perfectly modeled arms were heavy bracelets, around the wrist and muscle, most times joined by chains. Bracelets were also worn about the ankles, and their fingers and toes were laden with rings. Sometimes large rings were suspended from the nose, and the ears were almost always outlined with hoop rings, that reached from the inmost edge of the lobe to the top of the ear joining the head. So closely were these rings placed that, at a distance, the ear had the appearance of being rimmed in gold. A more pleasing style of nose ornament was a large gold ornament set in the nostril and fastened there as screw rings fasten in the ear. Still, if that nose ornamentation was more pleasing than the other, the ear adornment that accompanied it was disgusting. The lobe of the ear was split from the ear, and pulled down to such length that it usually rested on the shoulder. The enormous loop of flesh was partially filled with large gold knobs.

At the top of the hill we came to a beautiful, majestic, stone double gate, the entrance to the English fort and also spanning the road that leads to the town. Sentinels were pacing to and fro but we drove past them without stopping or being stopped, through a strange, narrow cut in the mountain, that towered at the sides a hundred feet above the road bed. Both these narrow, perpendicular sides are strongly fortified.

It needs but one glance at Aden, which is in itself a natural fort, to strengthen the assertion that Aden is the strongest gate to India.

The moment we emerged from the cut, which, besides being so narrow that two carriages pass with great difficulty, is made on a dangerous steep grade, we got a view of the white town of Aden, nestling in the very heart of what seems to be an extinct volcano. We were driven rapidly down the road, catching glimpses of gaudily attired mounted policemen, water-carriers from the bay, with their well-filled goat-skins flung across their backs, camels loaded with cut stone, and black people of every description.

When we drove into the town, which is composed of low adobe houses, our carriage was surrounded with beggars. We got out and walked through an unpaved street, looking at the dirty, uninviting shops and the dirty, uninviting people in and about them. Very often we were urged to buy, but more frequently the natives stared at us with quiet curiosity. In the heart of the town we found the camel market, but beyond a number of camels standing, lying, and kneeling about, the sight was nothing extraordinary. Near by was a goat market, but business seemed dull in both places.

Without buying anything we started to return to the ship. Little naked children ran after us for miles, touching their foreheads humbly and crying for money. They all knew enough English to be able to ask us for charity.

When we reached the pier, we found our driver had forgotten all the English he knew when we started out. He wanted one price for the carriage and we wanted to pay another. It resulted in our appealing to a native policeman, who took the right change from us, handed it to the driver, and gave him, in addition, a lusty kick for his dishonesty.

Our limited time prevented our going to see the water tanks, which are some miles distant from Aden. When we returned to the ship we found Jews there, selling ostrich eggs and plumes, shells, fruit, spears of sword-fish, and such things. In the water, on one side of the boat, were numbers of men, Somali boys, they called them, who were giving an exhibition of wonderful diving and swimming.

They would actually sit in the water looking like bronze statues, as the sun rested on their wet, black skins. They sat in a row, and turning their faces up towards the deck, would yell methodically, one after the other, down the entire line:

"Oh! Yo! Ho!"

It sounded very like a chorus of bull-frogs and was very amusing. After finishing this strange music they would give us a duet, half crying, persuasively, in a sing-song style:

"Have a dive! Have a dive! Have a dive!"

The other half, meanwhile, would put their hands before their widely opened mouths, yelling through their rapidly moving fingers with such energy that we gladly threw over silver to see them dive and stop the din.

The moment the silver flashed over the water all the bronze figures would disappear like flying fish, and looking down we would see a few ripples on the surface of the blue water— nothing more. After a time that seemed dangerously long to us, they would bob up through the water again. We could see them coming before they finally appeared on the surface, and one among the number would have the silver between his teeth, which would be most liberally displayed in a broad smile of satisfaction. Some of these divers were children not more than eight years old, and they ranged from that up to any age. Many of them had their hair bleached. As they were completely naked, excepting a small cloth twisted about the loins, they found it necessary to make a purse out of their cheeks, which they did with as much ease as a cow stows away grass to chew at her leisure.

I have often envied a cow this splendid gift. One wastes so much time eating, especially when traveling, and I could not help picturing the comfort it would be sometimes to dispose of our food wholesale and consume it at our leisure afterwards. I am certain there would be fewer dyspeptics[1] then.

No animal, waterborn and bred, could frisk, more gracefully in the water than do these Somali boys. They swim about, using the legs alone, or the arms alone, on their backs, or sides, and, in most cases, with their faces under water. They never get out of the way of a boat. They merely sink and come up in the same spot when the boat passes. The bay at Aden is filled with sharks, but they never touch these black men, so they tell me, and the safety with which they spend their lives in

1   One who suffers from indigestion

the water proves the truth of the assertion. They claim that a shark will not attack a black man, and after I had caught the odor of the grease with which these men annoint their bodies, I did not blame the sharks.

After a seven hours stay at Aden we left for Colombo,[1] being followed a long ways out from land by the divers. One little boy went out with us on the ship, and when he left us he merely took a plunge from the upper deck into the sea and went happily back towards Aden, on his side, waving a farewell to us with his free hand.

The passengers endeavored to make the time pass pleasantly between Aden and Colombo. The young women had some *tableaux vivants*[2] one evening, and they were really very fine. In one they wished to represent the different countries. They asked me to represent America, but I refused, and then they asked me to tell them what the American flag looked like! They wanted to represent one as nearly as possible and to rise it to drape the young woman who was to represent America. Another evening we had a lantern slide exhibition that was very enjoyable.

The loyalty of the English to their Queen on all occasions, and at all times, had won my admiration. Though born and bred a staunch American, with the belief that a man is what he makes of himself, not what he was born, still I could not help admiring the undying respect the English have for their royal family. During the lantern slide exhibition, the Queen's picture was thrown on the white sheet, and evoked warmer applause than anything else that evening. We never had an evening's amusement that did not end by everybody rising to their feet and singing "God Save the Queen." I could not help but think how devoted that woman, for she is only a woman after all, should be to the interests of such faithful subjects.

With that thought came to me a shamed feeling that there I was, a free born American girl, the native of the grandest country on earth, forced to be silent because I could not in honesty speak proudly of the rulers of my land, unless I went back to those two kings of manhood, George Washington and Abraham Lincoln.

---

1   Modern day Sri Lanka
2   Literally "living pictures" (French): A silent, motionless group of people arranged in a scene or incident

CHAPTER IX.
DELAYED FIVE DAYS.

ABOUT nine o'clock in the morning we anchored in the bay at Co-lombo, Ceylon. The island, with its abundance of green trees, was very restful and pleasing to our eyes after the spell of heat we had passed through on the ocean coming from Aden.

Preparations had been made by the passengers before we anchored, to go ashore, and as we came slowly into the small harbor, where a number of vessels were lying, we all stood impatiently on deck waiting for the first opportunity to desert the ship.

With all our impatience we could not fail to be impressed with the beauties of Colombo and the view from the deck of our incoming steamer. As we moved in among the beautiful ships laying at anchor, we could see the green island dotted with low arcaded buildings which looked, in the glare of the sun, like marble palaces. In the rear of us was the blue, blue sea, jumping up into little hills that formed into snow drifts which softly sank into the blue again. Forming the background to the town was a high mountain, which they told us was known as Adam's Peak. The beach, with a forest of tropical trees, looked as if it started in a point away out in the sea, curving around until near the harbor it formed into a blunt point, the line of which was carried out to sea by a magnificent breakwater surmounted by a light-house. Then the land curved back again to a point where stood a signal station, and on beyond a wide road ran along the water's edge until it was lost at the base of a high green eminence that stood well out over the sea, crowned with a castle—like building glistening in the sunlight.

Little boats filled with black-men, we could see coming out to-wards us from the shore, but my eyes were fastened on a strangely

167

shaped object, resting on the surface of the water in the bay. It seemed a living, feathered thing of so strange a shape that I watched it with feelings akin to horror. What horrible feathered monster could that lovely island produce, I wondered, noticing with dismay that the ship was heading for it. Just as we were upon it, there was a flutter of wings and a cloud of birds flew across and settled down upon the breakwater, where some fishermen, their feet overhanging the stony sides, were watching their lines. I looked back at what had raised so much consternation in my mind, and saw now that it was relieved of a feathered mass of birds—a harmless red buoy!

Accompanied by a friend, I was the first to step ashore. Some passengers who started in advance of us, took a steam launch. My escort said that he would give me a novel experience, and also show me a small boat that traveled faster than a steam launch. The gentleman who had offered to be my escort during our jaunt on land was a traveler of vast experience. He has averaged a yearly tour of the world for several years, and knows the eastern countries as he knows his home. Still, when I saw the boat in which he intended to take me ashore, I rather doubted his judgment, but I said nothing.

The boat was a rudely constructed thing. The boat proper was probably five feet in length and two feet in width across the top, narrowing down to the keel, so that it was not wide enough to allow one's feet to rest side by side in the bottom. There were two seats in the middle of the boat facing one another. They are shaded by a bit of coffee sack that must be removed to give room for passengers to get in. The two men sit at either end of this peculiar boat, and with one paddle each. The paddle is a straight pole, with a board the shape and size of a cheese-box head tied to the end of it, and with both those paddles on the same side they row us ashore. The boat is balanced by a log the length of the boat and fastened out by two curved poles, probably three feet from the boat. These boats are called by tourists, outriggers, but are called by the people of Ceylon, *catamarans*.

With but slight exertion the men sent the boat cutting through the water, and in a few moments we had distanced the steam launch and had accommodations engaged at the hotel before the launch had landed its passengers. It is said at Colombo that *catamarans* are used by the native fisherman, who go out to sea in them, and that they are so seaworthy and so secure against capsizing that no case of an accident to a catamaran has ever been reported.

A nearer view of the hotel, the Grand Oriental, did not tend to lessen its attractiveness—in fact it increased it. It was a fine, large hotel, with tiled arcades, corridors airy and comfortable, furnished with easy chairs and small marble topped tables which stood close enough to the broad arm-rests, for one to sip the cooling lime squashes or the exquisite native tea, or eat of the delicious fruit while resting in an attitude of ease and laziness. I found no place away from America where smoking was prohibited, and in this lovely promenade the men smoked, consumed gallons of whiskey and soda and perused the newspapers, while the women read their novels or bargained with the pretty little copper-colored women who came to sell dainty hand-made lace, or with the clever, high-turbaned merchants who would snap open little velvet boxes and expose, to the admiring gaze of the charmed tourists, the most bewildering gems. There were deeply-dark emeralds, fire-lit diamonds, exquisite pearls, rubies like pure drops of blood, the lucky cat's-eye with its moving line, and all set in such beautiful shapes that even the men, who would begin by saying, "I have been sold before by some of your kind," would end by laying down their cigars and papers and examining the glittering ornaments that tempt all alike. No woman who lands at Colombo ever leaves until she adds several rings to her jewel box, and these rings are so well known that the moment a traveler sees one, no difference in what part of the globe, he says to the wearer, inquiringly:

"Been to Colombo, eh?"

For the first time since leaving America I saw American money. It is very popular in Colombo and commands a high price—as jewelry! It goes for nothing as money. When I offered it in payment for my bills I was told it would be taken at sixty per cent discount. The Colombo diamond merchants are very glad to get American twenty dollar gold pieces and pay a high premium on them. The only use they make of the money is to put a ring through it and hang it on their watch chains for ornaments. The wealth of the merchant can be estimated by his watch chain, they tell me; the richer the merchant the more American gold dangles from his chain. I saw some men with as many as twenty pieces on one chain. Most of the jewelry bought and sold in Colombo is sold in the corridor of the Grand Oriental Hotel. Merchants bring their wares with them and tourists find it pleasanter than visiting the shops.

Leading off from this corridor, pleasant in its coolness, interesting in its peculiarities, is the dining-hall, matching the other parts of the hotel with its picturesque stateliness. The small tables are daintily set and are richly decorated daily with the native flowers of Colombo, rich in color, exquisite in form, but void of perfume. From the ceiling were suspended embroidered *punkas*, that invention of the East which brings comfort during the hottest part of the day. The *punkas* are long strips of cloth, fastened to bamboo poles that are suspended within a short distance of the tables. They are kept in motion by a rope pulley, worked by a man or boy. They send a lazy, cooling air through the building, contributing much to the ease and comfort of the guest. *Punkas* are also used on all the ships that travel in the East.

Very good food was served at the hotel—which was all the more palatable to the passengers from the Victoria after the trials they had had for the past fortnight in eating the same kind of food under daily different names. Singalese waiters were employed, and they were not only an improvement on the English stewards, to whose carelessness and impudence we had been forced to submit, but they were interesting to the Westerner.

They managed to speak English very well and understood everything that was said to them. They are not unpleasing people, being small of stature and fine of feature, some of them having very attractive, clean-cut faces, light bronze in color. They wore white linen apron-like skirts and white jackets. Noiselessly they move over the smooth tile floor, in their bare, brown feet. Their straight black hair is worn long, twisted in a Psyche knot[1] at the back of the head. On the crown of the head, instead of circling it from ear to ear, is always set a tortoise shell comb, like those worn by American school children. It was some time before I could tell a Singalese man from a Singalese woman. It is not difficult to distinguish the different sexes after one knows that the Singalese men wear the comb, which is as distinct a feature of their dress as men's trousers in America. Singalese women would not think

---

1   Hairstyle in which a coil or knot of hair projects from the back of the wearer's head

of donning this little comb any more than a sensitive American woman would think of wearing men's apparel.

I did not hear the term waiter, or *garçon*, after leaving America. After leaving the English ships I did not hear the word steward, but instead, in the hotels and ships in the East, all the servants were called "boy." We can call "steward! .... waiter! .... *garçon!*" until we are weary, without any result, but the moment we whisper "boy!" a pleasant black fellow says, "yes, sir," at our side, and is ready to do our bidding.

At tiffin I had some real curry, the famous native dish of India. I had been unable to eat it on the Victoria, but those who knew said it was a most delicious dish when prepared rightly and so I tested it on shore. First a divided dish containing shrimps and boiled rice was placed before me. I put two spoonfuls of rice on my plate, and on it put one spoonful of shrimps; there was also chicken and beef for the meat part of the curry, but I took shrimps only. Then was handed me a much divided plate containing different preserved fruits, chuddah[1] and other things hot with pepper. As instructed, I partook of three of this variety and put it on top of what had been placed first on my plate. Last came little dried pieces of stuff that we heard before we saw, its odor was so loud and unmistakable. They called it Bombay duck. It is nothing more or less than a small fish, which is split open, and after being thoroughly dried, is used with the curry. One can learn to eat it.

After all this is on the plate it is thoroughly mixed, making a mess very unsightly, but very palatable, as I found. I became so given to curry that I only stopped eating it when I found, after a hearty meal, curry threatened to give me palpitation of the heart. A story is told concerning the Bombay duck that is very amusing.

The Shah of Persia was notified that some high official in India intended to send him a lot of very fine Bombay duck. The Shah was very much pleased and, in anticipation of their arrival, had some expensive ponds built to put the Bombay ducks in! Imagine his consternation when he received those ill-smelling, dried fish!

After tiffin we drove to mount Lavania. We went along the smoothest, most perfectly made roads I ever saw. They seemed to be made of red asphalt, and I was afterwards told that they are constructed by convicts. Many of these roads were picturesque bowers, the over-reaching

1   Alternative spelling of "chuda:" easily digestible flattened rice

branches of the trees that lined the waysides forming an arch of foliage above our heads, giving us charming telescopic views of people and conveyances along the road. Thatched huts of the natives and glimpses of the dwellers divided our attention with the people we passed on the road.

Mount Lavania we found to be the place we had noticed on entering the harbor. It is a fine hotel situated on an eminence overlooking the sea, and is a favorite resort during the hot seasons. It is surrounded by a smooth green lawn and faces the blue sea, whence it gets a refreshing breeze all the year through.

After dinner, everybody at the Grand Oriental Hotel went out for a drive, the women, and many of the men, going bare-headed. Driving through the town, down the wide streets, past beautiful homes set well back in tropical gardens, to the Galle Face drive that runs along the beach just out of reach of the waves that break on the sandy banks with a more musical roar than I ever heard water produce before. The road lies very close to the water's edge, and by the soft rays of the moon its red surface was turned to silver, the deep blue of the sea was black, and the foamy breakers were snow drifts. In the soft, pure light we would see silent couples strolling along arm and arm, apparently so near the breakers that I felt apprehensive lest one, stronger than the others, should catch them unawares and wash them out to that unknown land where we all travel to rest. Lounging on the benches that face the sea were occasional soldiers in the Queen's uniform, whom I looked at anxiously, unable to tell whether their attitude of weariness bespoke a rest from labor or hungry home-sickness. One night I saw a native standing waist deep fishing in the roaring breakers. They tell me that many of the fish bite more freely after night, but I thought how easily the fisherman might be washed away, and no one would be the wiser until his absence was noticed by his friends.

Where the Galle Face drive merges into another road, stands the Galle Face Hotel surrounded by a forest of palm trees. Lounging on long-bottomed, easy chairs, on the stone-floored and stone-pillared verandah, one can see through the forest of tall palms where the ocean kisses the sandy beach, and while listening to the music of the wave, the deep, mellow roar, can drift— drift out on dreams that bring what life has failed to give; soothing pictures of the imagination that blot out for a moment the stern disappointment of reality. Or, when the dreams fade away, one can drown the sigh with the cooling lime squash which the noiseless, bare-footed, living bronze has placed on the white arm-rest, at the same time lazily watching the jinrickshas come silently in through the gas-lit gate, the naked black runners coming to a sudden stop, letting the shafts drop so the passenger can step out.

Lazily I sat there one sweet, dusky night, only half hearing my escort's words that came to me mingled with the sound of the ocean. A couple stood close together, face bending over a face up-turned, hand clasped in hand and held closely against a manly heart, standing, two dark figures, beneath an arch of the verandah, outlined against the gate lamp. I felt a little sympathy for them as wrapped in that delusion that makes life heaven or hell, that forms the foundation for every novel, play or story, they stood, until a noisy new arrival wakened her from blissful oblivion, and she rushed, scarcely waiting for him to kiss the hand he held, away into the darkness. I sighed again, and taking another sip of my lime squash, turned to answer my companion.

Early next morning I was awakened by a Singalese waiter placing coffee and toast on a small table which he drew up close to my cur-tained bed, after which he went out. I knew from the dim light that crept in through the open glass door which led to the balcony, that it was still early, and I soon went off to sleep. I was awakened shortly by a rattling of the dishes on the table, and opening my eyes I saw, standing on the table, quietly enjoying my toast, a crow!

I was not then used to having toast and tea before arising, as is the custom in Ceylon, so I let the crow satisfy his appetite and leisurely take his departure without a protest. I arose earlier than was my habit, because I had a desire to see what there might be to see while I had the opportunity.

After a cool, refreshing bath, I dressed hastily and went down be-low. I found almost all of my friends up, some having already started out to enjoy the early morning. I regretted my generosity to the crow when I learned that breakfast was never served until nine o'clock, and as everybody endeavored to have the benefit of the cool, sweet morn-ing, toast and tea was very sustaining.

In a light wagon we again drove down Galle Face road, and out past a lake in which men, women, children, oxen, horses, buffalo and dogs were sporting. It was a strange sight. Off on a little green island we saw the laundry folk at work, beating, sousing and wringing the clothes, which they afterwards spread upon the grass to dry. Almost all of the roads through which we drove were perfect with their picturesque curves, and often bordered and arched with magnificent trees, many of which were burdened with beautiful brilliant blossoms.

Everybody seemed to be out. The white people were driving, riding, riding bicycles, or walking. The breakwater, which is a good half mile in length, is a favorite promenade for the citizens of Colombo. Morning and evening gaily dressed people can be seen walking back and forth between the light-house and the shore. When the stormy season comes the sea dashes full forty feet above this promenade, which must be cleansed of a green slime, after the storms are over, before it can be traveled with safety. The Prince of Wales laid the first stone of this beautiful breakwater in 1875, and ten years later it was finished.

It is considered one of the finest in existence.

Colombo reminded me of Newport, R. I. Possibly— in my eyes, at least— Colombo is more beautiful. The homes may not be as expensive, but they are more artistic and picturesque. The roads are wide and perfect; the view of the sea is grand, and while unlike in its tropical aspect, still there is something about Colombo that recalls Newport.

After breakfast, which usually leaves nothing to be desired, guests rest in the corridor of the hotel; the men who have business matters to attend to look after them and return to the hotel not later than eleven. About the hour of noon everybody takes a rest, and after luncheon they take a nap. While they sleep the hottest part of the day passes, and at four they are again ready for a drive or a walk, from which they return after sunset in time to dress for dinner. After dinner there are pleasant little rides in jinrickshas or visits to the native theaters.

I went one night to a Parsee theatre. At the entrance were groups of people, some of whom were selling fruits, and some were jinricksha men waiting to haul the people home after the performance. There was no floor in the building. The chairs were placed in rows on the ground. the house was quite well filled with native men, women and children who were deeply interested in the performance which had begun before we reached there.

The actors were all men; my escort had told me women never think of going on the stage in that country. The stage was not unlike any other stage, and the scenery, painted by native artists, was quite as good as is usually seen. On the left of the stage, close to the wing, was a man, sitting cross-legged on a raised platform, beating a tom-tom. A tom-tom was undoubtedly the mother to the drum. It is made on the same principle, but instead of being round is inclined to be long in shape, The player uses his hands instead of drum-sticks, and when one becomes accustomed to it I do not think the sound of a tom-tom can be called unmusical. The musician who presided over the tom-tom this night was dressed in a thin white material, and he wore a very large turban of the same stuff on his head. His copper-colored face was long and earnest, and he beat the tom-tom with a will that was simply amazing when one was informed that he had been constantly engaged at it since nine in the morning. If his hands did not tire his legs did. Several times I saw him move, as if to find ease by shifting his squatting position, and every time I saw his bare feet turn up, in full view of the audience, I felt an irresistible desire to laugh.

On the right, directly opposite to the tom-tom player, was a man, whose duty it was to play a strange looking organ. He only used one hand, the left, for playing, and with the right he held a book, which he steadily perused throughout the entire performance, reading and playing mechanically without once looking at the actors.

The actors were amusing, at least. The story of the opera was not unlike those in other countries. The basis or plot of the play was a tale of love and tragedy. A tall young man, with his face painted a deathlike white, sang shrilly through his very high-arched nose to another young man, dressed in the costume of a native woman. The latter was the lady, and the heroine of the play, and he sang sharply through his nose like his, or her, lover. All the actors sang through their noses, and the thinner their voices and the more nasal sound they employed the more the audience applauded.

The heroine of the play was a maid-servant employed by a very wealthy tea planter, who was the father of the lover who sang through his nose. The lover, like all lovers urged the girl to be his in songs that were issued through his nose for fifteen minutes at a time. He, the heroine, would endeavor to look shy all through this unsufferably long song of nasal sound, and then she would take up the same refrain, and to the same tune sing back at him for the same length, and after his own style, while he would hang his head and listen. Their gestures were very few, and they usually stood in one spot on the stage. Sometimes they would embrace, but only to fall apart and sing at each other again.

The play goes on. A bold, bad robber, whose chalk-whitened face has a most Jewish cast, sees the maid-servant and falls in love with her. She repels his advances and goes into her master's house. Then the robber puts a cross on the house and vows that he will return with his men to kill the inhabitants, for the heroine, in her simplicity, confesses to the truth of his supposition that she loves another, and that other is her master's son, so the villain swears that he will return, kill the people of the house, and not only carry off the wealth but the maidservant as well.

After the robber departs, the heroine comes out, and spies the cross upon her house. With a crafty look upon her face, she picks up the chalk which the robber had dropped, and marks all the other houses in the street in just the same way, so that when the robber returns he is foiled in his bold, bad game, for he cannot tell which house holds his charmer, and her wealthy lover and master. He is a patient robber, and lies in wait until the lovers come forth to coo on the street. While they are busy, making love through their noses, the man plays the organ with energy, the turbaned musician beats the tom-tom as if his life depended upon it, and the bold, bad robber clutches at his stomach, twists his face into the most agonized expressions, and otherwise shows his agony to the audience. When they go into the house he is about to follow, when the master appears, and, as he is going in, the robber approaches and, saying that he is a wealthy tea-merchant, begs to be permitted to rest at his house that night. The master most cordially consents, just as the heroine appears, and she, having heard the conversation tells her master not to allow the man to stay. The master becomes very angry at her boldness and promises her a liberal punishment, to take effect later in the day.

The merchant begs to be permitted to have his cases of tea placed within the garden-walls of his host, that the tea may be safe through the night. Of course the host consents, and the next scene shows the chests of tea in the garden, and the bold robber puts out the light at the door and goes into the house to bide his time. Even that heroine dreams, and, like other heroines, selects the cool, sweet night and the garden to dream in. She is surprised to find the garden in darkness, and lays her finger to the side of her nose when she sees the lamp is not burning. As she skips about, smelling the artificial flowers, the lid of a tea-chest is raised slightly, and a man sings something through his nose. She starts back in surprise, but instead of screaming, she answers the inquiry in nasal tones, and she learns that the chests are not filled with tea, but with men who belong to the robber, for whom they mistook her. When the man closes the lid again to wait the bidding to come forth, she deftly locks all the cases, and then calls upon a man servant who helps her, the heroine, to carry these cases containing men into a house in which they are securely locked.

The next scene shows a room in which the people are gathered and making merry. They are all sitting on the floor, and among them is the chief robber. The heroine, and other maidservants are brought in to give a dagger dance. They have bracelets of bells around their wrists and ankles, and the dance is very pleasing. The heroine and another servant dance while battling with each other with their knives. Occasionally they break apart and encircle the room, and the heroine makes motions as if she intended to give the guests a playful thrust. She sees the robber slyly poison her master's wine, and so she dances around the robber's way, and sticks her dagger in his heart and goes on with her dance. The guests laugh until they see the robber rise to his feet and fall dead. They see then the thrust was not playful but real, and the girl is caught and the master says she shall die. Then she screeches out the story of the men in the tea-cases and tells about the poisoned wine, and the guests applaud her brave act, and she is told to ask for any favor she wishes. She asks for her master's son! She gets him, to the music of the tom-tom and the organ, and I suppose they live happy ever afterwards.

I rode home from the theatre in a bullock hackery. It was a very small springless cart on two wheels with a front seat for the driver, and on the back seat, with our backs to the driver and out feet hanging over, we drove to the hotel. The bullock is a strange, modest-looking little animal with a hump on its back and crooked horns on its head. I feared that it could not carry us all, but it traveled at a very good pace. There was a sound of grunt, grunt, grunting that concerned me very much until l found it was the driver and not the bullock that was responsible for the noise. With grunts he urged the bullock to greater speed.

The drive, along tree-roofed roads, was very quiet and lovely. The moonlight fell beautiful and soft over the land, and nothing disturbed the stillness except the sound of the sea and an occasional soldier we met staggering along towards the barracks. At one place we saw a mosque with low, dim lamps hanging about. We went in and found the priests lying about on the stone floor, some at the very foot of the altar. We talked with them in whispers and then returned to the cart, which soon carried us back to the hotel. Just as we turned a corner to go to the hotel, an officer rushed up and, catching hold of a wheel, tried to stop the hackery, telling the driver that we were all under arrest.

The candles in one of the lamps had burned out and we were arrested for driving with a dark side. My companion made it right with the policeman, and we went to the hotel instead of the jail.

Among the natives that haunt the hotel are the snake charmers. They are almost naked fellows, sometimes with ragged jackets on and sometimes turbans on their heads, but more often the head is bare. They execute a number of tricks in a very skillful manner. The most wonderful of these tricks, to me, was that of growing a tree. They would show a seed, then they would place the seed on the ground, cover it with a handful of earth, and cover this little mound with a handkerchief, which they first passed around to be examined, that we might be positive there was nothing wrong with it. Over this they would chant, and after a time the handkerchief is taken off and then up through the ground is a green sprout. We look at it incredulously, while the man says:

"Tree no good; tree too small," and covering it up again he renews his chanting. Once more he lifts the handkerchief and we see the sprout is larger, but still it does not please the trickster, for he repeats: "Tree no good; tree too small," and covers it up again. This is repeated until he has a tree from three to five feet in height. Then he pulls it up, shows us the seed and roots.

Although these men always asked us to "See the snake dance?" we always saw every other trick but the one that had caught us. One morning, when a man urged me to "See the snake dance?" I said that I would, but that I would pay to see the snake dance and for nothing else. Quite unwillingly the men lifted the lid of the basket, and the cobra crawled slowly out, curling itself up on the ground. The "charmer" began to play on a little fife, meanwhile waving a red cloth which attracted the cobra's attention. It rose up steadily, darting angrily at the red cloth, and rose higher at every motion until it seemed to stand on the tip end of its tail. Then it saw the charmer and it darted for him, but he cunningly caught it by the head and with such a grip that I saw the blood gush from the snake's month. He worked for some time, still firmly holding the snake by the head before he could get it into the basket, the reptile meanwhile lashing the ground furiously with its tail. When at last it was covered from sight, I drew a long breath, and the charmer said to me sadly:

"Cobra no dance, cobra too young, cobra too fresh!"

I thought quite right; the cobra was too fresh!

At Colombo I saw the jinricksha for the first time. The jinricksha is a small two-wheel wagon, much in shape like a sulky, except that it has a top which can be raised in rainy weather. It has long shafts joined at the end with a crossbar. The jinricksha men are black and wear little else than a sash. When the sun is hot they wear large hats that look like enormous mushrooms, but most of the time these hats are hanging to the back of the 'ricksha. There are stands at different places for these men as well as carriage stands. While waiting for patrons they let their 'rickshas rest on the shafts and they sit in the bottom, their feet on the ground. Besides dressing in a sash these men dress in an oil or grease, and when the day is hot and they run, one wishes they wore more clothing and less oil! The grease has an original odor that is entirely its own.

One day I was going out in a 'ricksha and an acquaintance was going with me. The man put his foot on the shaft when I got in, and as he raised it, ready to start, I saw my friend step into her 'ricksha. She sat down and instantly went out— the other way! The man did not have his foot on the shaft and she overbalanced.

I had a shamed feeling about going around the town drawn by a man, but after I had gone a short way, I decided it was a great improvement on modern means of travel; it was so comforting to have a horse that was able to take care of itself! When we went into the shops it was so agreeable not to have the worry of fearing the horses were not blankcted, and when we made them run we did not have to fear we might urge them into a damaging speed. It is a great relief to have a horse whose tongue can protest.

I have spoken about the perfect roads in Ceylon. I found the roads in the same state of perfection in almost all the Eastern ports at which I stopped. I could not decide, to my own satisfaction, whether the smoothness of the road was due to the entire and blessed absence of beer wagons, or to the absence of the New York street commissioners.

I visited at the temples in Colombo, finding little of interest, and always having to pay liberally for the privilege of looking about. One day I went to the Buddhist college, and while there I met the famous high priest of Ceylon. He was sitting on a verandah, that surrounded his low bungalow, writing on a table placed before him. His gown consisted of a straight piece of old gold silk wrapped deftly around the body and over the waist. The silk had fallen to his waist, but after he greeted us he pulled it up around his shoulders. He was a copper-colored old fellow, with gray hair that was shaved very close to the head. He spoke English quite well, and among other things told me he received hundreds of letters from the United States every year, and that they found more converts to the Buddhist religion in America than in any other land.

The two newspapers in Colombo are in charge of two young Englishmen who are very clever. They are very kind to strangers, and I am indebted to them for a great deal of pleasure during my stay in Ceylon. The hotel manager is a German of high birth. He is untiring in his efforts to make his guests comfortable. His wife is a very pretty little woman, with a beautiful voice. Through her kindness I learned of a tailor in Ceylon who makes gowns, that for style and fit are not excelled. I have seen gowns from Worth that could not equal them, and this man charges for making a gown, five rupees! Five rupees are about two dollars and a half. He will make a gown in two days.

The praises of Kandy had been sung to me, so one morning at seven o'clock I started for Kandy with the Spanish representative, who was going to Pekin, and a jolly Irish lad who was bound for Hong Kong, both of whom had traveled with me from Brindisi. We drove to the station and were passed with the people, through the gate to the train. English cars, and ones that leave everything to be desired, are used on this line. We got into a compartment where there was but one seat, which, luckily for us, happened to be facing the way we traveled. Our tickets were taken at the station, and then the doors were locked and the train started. Before the start, we had entered our names in a book which a guard brought to us with the information that we could have breakfast on the train if so desired. As it was too early for breakfast at the hotel, we were only too glad to get an opportunity to eat. At eight o'clock the train stopped and the guard unlocked our door, telling us to go front to the dining-car. It seemed strange to be compelled to get out of a train, instead of walking through it, in order to get to the other end of it.

The dining-car was fitted up with stationary tables which almost spanned the car, leaving a small space for people to walk along. There were more people than could be accommodated, but as the train had started, they were obliged to stand. Several persons had told me that the breakfast served on this train was considered remarkably good. I thought, on seeing the bill of fare, they had prepared a feast for a chicken hawk. First, there was fish dressed in vinegar and onions, followed by chicken soup, chicken aspic, grilled chicken, boned chicken, fried chicken, boiled chicken, cold chicken and chicken pie!

After we had finished our breakfast we were compelled to remain where we were until the train arrived at some station. Then the dining-car was unlocked and we returned to the other car, being again locked in until the end of our journey. The road to Kandy is spoken of as being very beautiful. It winds up the mountain side and is rather pretty, but nothing wonderful in that respect. It is a tropical land, but the foliage and flowers are very ordinary. About the prettiest things to be seen are the rice beds. They are built in terraces, and when one looks down into the deep valley, seeing terrace after terrace of the softest, lightest green, one is forced to cry: "How beautiful!"

Arriving at Kandy at last, we hired a carriage and went to see the lake, the public library and the temples. In one old temple, surrounded by a moat, we saw several altars, of little consequence, and a bit of ivory which they told us was the tooth of Buddha. Kandy is pretty, but far from what it is claimed to be. They said it was cool, but we found it so hot that we thought with regret of Colombo. Disgusted with all we found worth seeing we drove to Parathenia to see the great botanical garden. It well repaid us for the visit. That evening we returned to Colombo. I was tired and hungry and the extreme heat had given me a sick headache. On the way down, the Spanish gentlemen endeavored to keep our falling spirits up, but every word he said only helped to increase my bad temper, much to the amusement of the Irish boy. He was very polite and kind, the Spaniard, I mean, but he had an unhappy way of flatly contradicting one, that, to say the least, was very exasperating. It was to me, but it only made the Irish boy laugh. When we were going down the mountain side the Spaniard got up, and standing, put his head through the open window in the door to get a view of the country.

"We are going over," he said, with positive conviction, turning around to us. I was leaning up in a corner trying to sleep and the Irish boy, with his feet braced against the end of the compartment, was trying to do the same.

"We won't go over," I managed to say, while the Irish boy smiled.

"Yes, we will," the Spaniard shouted back, "Make your prayers!"

The Irish boy screamed with laughter, and I forgot my sickness as I held my sides and laughed. It was a little thing, but it is often little things that raise the loudest laughs. After that all I needed to say to upset the dignity of the Irish boy was: "Make your prayers!"

I went to bed that night too ill to eat my dinner. The next morning I had intended to go to the pearl market, but felt unequal to it, and when my acquaintances returned and told me that at the very end of the sale a man bought some left over oysters for one rupee and found in them five hundred dollars worth of pearls, I felt sorry that I had not gone, although there was great danger of getting cholera.

One day I heard a man ask another if he knew the meaning of the word "jinricksha." the first replied the word meant "Draw man power," and the second said, with innocent surprise, "I thought it was 'Pull man car!'" I heard a passenger who came ashore from an Australian boat ask Andrew, a clever native who stands at the hotel door, to get him one of those carts to take a ride. Andrew did not know just what the man wanted as there were many different kinds of carts about.

"I don't recall the name of them," the passenger said, in a hesitating manner, "but I believe you call them Jim-Jams!"

He got a jinricksha.

CHAPTER X.
IN THE PIRATE SEAS.

ONE night, after I had been five days in Colombo, the blackboard in the hotel corridor bore the information that the Oriental would sail for China the following morning, at eight o'clock. I was called at five o'clock and some time afterwards left for the ship. The "Spanish minister," as we called the Spaniard, wanted me to go to some of the shops with him until he should buy some jewelry, but I was so nervous and anxious to be on my way that I could not wait a moment longer than was necessary to reach the boat that was to carry me to China.

When farewells had been said, and I was on the Oriental, I found my patience had given way under the long delay. The ship seemed to be deserted when I went on deck, with the exception of a handsome, elderly man, accompanied by a young blonde man in a natty white linen suit, who slowly promenaded the deck, watching out to sea while they talked. I was trying to untie my steamer chair so as to have some place to sit, when the elderly man came up and politely offered to assist me.

"When will we sail," I asked shortly.

"As soon as the Nepaul comes in," the man replied. "She was to have been here at daybreak, but she hasn't been sighted yet. Waiting for the Nepaul has given us this five days' delay. She's a slow old boat."

"May she go to the bottom of the bay when she does get in!" I said savagely. "The old tub! I think it an outrage to be kept waiting five days for a tub like that."

"Colombo is a pleasant place to stay," the elderly man said with a twinkle in his eye.

"It may be, if staying there does not mean more than life to one. Really, it would afford me the most intense delight to see the Nepaul go the bottom of the sea."

Evidently my ill humor surprised them, and their surprise amused me, for I thought how little anyone could realize what this delay meant to me, and the mental picture of a forlorn little self creeping back to New York ten days behind time, with a shamed look on her face and afraid to hear her name spoken, made me laugh outright. They gazed at me in astonishment, while I laughed immoderately at my own unenviable position. My better nature surged up with the laugh, and I was able to say, once again: "Everything happens for the best."

"There is the Nepaul," I said, pointing out a line of smoke just visible above the horizon. They doubted it, but a few moments proved that I was correct. "I am very ill-natured," I said, glancing from the kindly blue eyes of the elderly man to the laughing blue eyes of the younger man; "but I could not help it. After being delayed for five days I was called at five o'clock because they said the ship was to sail at eight, and here it is nine o'clock and there's no sign of the ship sailing and I am simply famished."

As they laughed at my woes the gong sounded for breakfast and they took me down. The Irish lad, with his sparkling eyes and jolly laugh, was there, as was a young Englishman who had also traveled on the ship Victoria to Colombo. I knew him by sight, but as he was a sworn woman-hater I did not dare to speak to him. There were no women on board. I was the only woman that morning, and a right jolly breakfast we had.

The captain, a most handsome man, and as polite and courteous as he was good looking, sat at the head of the table. Officers, that any ship might boast of, were gathered about him. Handsome, good natured, intelligent, polite, they were, every single one of them. I found the elderly man I had been talking to was the chief engineer, and the young man was the ship's doctor.

The dining-hall was very artistic and pleasant, and the food was good. The ship, although much smaller than the Victoria, was very much better in every way. The cabins were more comfortable, the ship was better ventilated, the food was vastly superior, the officers were polite and good natured, the captain was a gentleman in looks and manners, and everything was just as agreeable as it could be. For several days I let things go on and said nothing about myself, nor did I give them the letter which the London agent had kindly sent. It had brought me no attention or courtesy on the Victoria, and I decided to take my chances on the Oriental. When I saw that uniform kindness and politeness was the rule on this ship, I then gave them the letter, and though the captain was pleased to receive it, still, it could not have made his treatment of me any kinder than it was at first.

It was well on to one o'clock before the passengers were transferred from the Nepaul to the Oriental. In the meantime the ship was amply peopled with merchants from the shore, who were selling jewels and lace. How they did cheat the passengers! They would ask, and sometimes get, fabulous prices for things, and when the ship was ready to sail, they offered to sell at any price. They were quite saucy chaps, too. I heard a vender reply to a man who offered him a small price for some so-called precious stones:

"I am not charging you for looking at these."

In fact they grew so impudent and bold, that I am surprised that the steamship lines do not issue orders prohibiting their presence on board.

At one o'clock we sailed. The first day and the two days following were passed lazily on deck. I found it a great relief to be again on the sweet, blue sea, out of sight of land, and free from the tussle and worry and bustle for life which we are daily, hourly even, forced to gaze upon on land. Although the East is, in a very great measure, free from the dreadful crowding for life, still one is bound to see signs of it even among the most indolent of people. Only on the bounding blue, the grand, great sea, is one rocked into a peaceful rest at noon of day, at dusk of night, feeling that one is drifting, drifting, not seeing, or knowing, or caring, about fool mortals striving for life. True, the sailors do this and that, but it has an air far from that of elbowing each other for a living. To the lazy passengers it seems that they merely hoist a sail or pull it down, that they may drift— dream— sleep—talk— live for happiness and not for gain.

The fourth day out was Sunday. The afternoon was spent on deck looking at the most beautiful green islands which we slowly passed.

Sometimes we would lazily conjecture as to whether they were inhabited or not.

The next day we anchored at Penang, or Prince of Wales Island, one of the Straits Settlements. As the ship had such a long delay at Colombo, it was said that we would have but six hours to spend on shore. With an acquaintance as escort, I made my preparations and was ready to go to land the moment we anchored. We went ashore in a Sampan, an oddly shaped flat boat with the oars, or rather paddles, fastened near the stern. The Malay oarsman rowed hand over hand, standing upright in the stern, his back turned towards us as well as the way we were going. Frequently he turned his head to see if the way was clear, plying his oars industriously all the while. Once landed he chased us to the end of the pier demanding more money, although we had paid him thirty cents, just twenty cents over and above the legal fare.

Hiring a carriage we drove to where a waterfall comes bounding down the side of a naturally verdant mountain which has been transformed, half way up, into a pleasing tropical garden. The picturesque waterfall is nothing marvelous. It only made me wonder from whence it procured its water supply, but after walking until I was much heated, and finding myself apparently just as far from the fount, I concluded the waterfall's secret was not worth the fatigue it would cost.

On the way to the town we visited a Hindoo temple. Scarcely had we entered when a number of half-clad, bare-footed priests rushed frantically upon us, demanding that we remove our shoes. The temple being built open, its curved roof and rafters had long been utilized by birds and pigeons as a bed-room. Doubtless ages had passed over the stone floor, but I could swear nothing else had, so I refused emphatically and unconditionally to un-boot myself. I saw enough of their idols to satisfy me. One was a black god in a gay dress, the other was a shapeless black stone hung with garlands of flowers, the filthy stone at its base being buried 'neath a profusion of rich blossoms.

English is spoken less in Penang than in any port I visited. A native photographer, when I questioned him about it, said:

"The Malays are proud, Miss. They have a language of their own and they are too proud to speak any other."

That photographer knew how to use his English to advantage. He showed me cabinet-sized proofs for which he asked one dollar each.

"One dollar!" I exclaimed in astonishment, "That is very high for a proof."

"If Miss thinks it is too much she does not need to buy. She is the best judge of how much she can afford to spend," he replied with cool impudence.

"Why are they so expensive?" I asked, nothing daunted by his impertinence.

"I presume because Penang is so far from England," he rejoined, carelessly.

I was told afterwards that a passenger from the Oriental pulled the photographer's long, thin, black nose for his impudence, and I was pleased to hear it.

A Chinese joss-house, the first I had seen, was very interesting. The pink and white roof, curved like a canoe, was ornamented with animals of the dragon tribe, with their mouths open and their tails in the air. The straggling worshippers could be plainly seen from the streets through the arcade sides of the temple. Chinese lanterns and gilt ornaments made gay the dark interior. Little josses, with usual rations of rice, roast pig and smouldering joss-sticks disbursing a strangely sweet perfume, were no more interesting than a dark corner in which the superstitious were trying their luck, a larger crowd of dusky people than were about the altars. In fact, the only devoutee was a waxed-haired Chinese woman, with a slit-eyed brown babe tied on her back, bowing meekly and lowly before a painted, be-bangled joss.

Some priests with shaven heads and old-gold silk garments, who were in a summer-house in the garden, saw us when we were looking at the gold-fish ponds. One came forth, and, taking me by the hand, gracefully led me to where they were gathered. They indicated their wish that we should sit with them and drink tea with them, milkless and sugarless, from child-like China cups, which they re-filled so often that I had reasons for feeling thankful the cups were so like unto play-dishes. We were unable to exchange words, but we smiled liberal smiles, at one another.

Mexican silver is used almost exclusively in Penang. American silver will be accepted at the same value, but American gold is refused and paper money is looked on with contempt. The Chinese jinricksha men in Penang, compared with those in Colombo, are like over-fed pet horses besides racers in trim. They were the plumpest Chinamen I ever saw; such round fat legs and arms!

When we started back to the ship the bay was very rough. Huge waves angrily tossed our small boat about in a way that blotted the red from my escort's checks and caused him to hang his head in a care-for-nothing way over the boat's side. I could not help liking the sea to a coquette, so indifferent and heedless is it to the strange emotions it raises in the breast of man. It was a reckless spring that landed us on the ship's ladder, the rolling of the coal barge helping to increase the swell which had threatened to engulf us. Hardly had we reached deck when the barge was ordered to cut loose; even as this was being done the ship hoisted anchor and started on its way. Almost immediately there was a great commotion on board. About fifty ragged black men rushed frantically on deck to find that while depositing their last sacks of coal in the regions below, their barge and companions had cast off and were rapidly nearing the shore. Then followed dire chattering, wringing of hands, pulling of locks and crying after the receding barge, all to no avail. The tide was coming in, a very strong tide it was, too, and despite the efforts of those on it the barge was steadily swept inland.

The captain appeased the coolies' fears by stating that they should go off in the pilot's boat. We all gathered to see the sight and a funny one it was! The tug being lashed to the ship they first tried to take the men off without slowing down but after one man got a dangerous plunge bath and the sea threatened to bury the tug then the ship was forced to slow down. Some coolies slid down a cable, their comrades grabbing and pulling them wet and frightened white on to the tug. Others went down the ladder which lacked five feet of touching the pilot boat. Those already on board would clutch the hanging man's bare legs, he meanwhile clinging despairingly to the ladder, fearing to loosen his grasp and only doing so when the ship officers would threaten to knock him off.

The pilot, a native, was the last to go down. Then the cable was cast off and we sailed away seeing the tug, so overloaded that the men were afraid to move even to bail it out, swept back by the tide towards the place where we had last seen the land.

I had a cabin down below at first and I found little rest owing to the close proximity of a nurse and two children whose wise parents selected a cabin on the other side of the ship. They could rest in peace. After I had been awakened several mornings at daybreak by the squabbling of the children I cherished a grudge against the parents. The mother made some show of being a beauty. She had a fine nose, everybody confessed that, and she had reduced her husband to such a state of servitude and subjection that she needed no maids.

I have always confessed that I like to sleep in the morning as well as I like to stay up at night, and to have my sleep disturbed makes me as ill-natured as a bad dinner makes a man. The fond father of these children had a habit of coming over early in the morning to see his cherubs, before he went to his bath. I know this from hearing him tell them so. He would open their cabin door and in the loudest, coldest, most unsympathetic voice in the world, would thoroughly arouse me from my slumbers by screaming:

"Good morning. How is Papa's family this morning?"

A confused conglomeration of voices sounded in reply; then he would shout:

"What does baby say to Mamma? Say; what does baby say to Mamma?"

"Mamma!" baby would at length shout back in a coarse, unnatural baby voice.

"What does baby say to Papa? Tell me, baby, what does baby say to Papa?"

"Papa!" would answer back the shrill treble.

"What does the moo-moo cow say, my treasure; tell Papa what the moo-moo cow says?"

To this the baby would make no reply and again he would shout:

"What does the moo-moo cow say, darling; tell Papa what the moo-moo cow says?"

If it had been once, or twice even, I might have endured it with civilized forbearance but after it had been repeated, the very same identical word every morning for six long weary mornings, my temper gave way and when he said: "Tell papa what the moo-moo cow says?" I shouted frantically:

"For heaven's sake, baby, tell Papa what the moo-moo cow says and let me go to sleep."

A heavy silence, a silence that was heavy with indignation and surprise, followed and I went off to sleep to dream of being chased down a muddy hill by babies sitting astride cows with crumpled horns, and straight horns and no horns at all, all singing in a melodious cow-like voice, moo! moo! moo!

The fond parents did not speak to me after that. They gazed on me in disdain and when the woman got sea-sick I persuaded an acquaintance of hers to go in and see her one day by telling her it was her Christian duty. The fond mother would not allow the ship doctor to see her although her husband had to relate her ills to the doctor and in that way get him to prescribe for them. I knew there was something she wished to keep secret. The woman, true to my counsel, knocked on the door; hearing no voice and thinking it lost in the roar of the ocean opened the door. The fond mother looked up, saw, and screaming buried her face in the pillows. She was toothless and hairless! The frightened Samaritan did not wait to see if she had a cork limb! I felt repentant afterwards and went to a deck cabin where I soon forgot the moo-moo cow and the fond parents. But the woman's fame as a beauty was irrevocably ruined on the ship.

It was so damply warm in the Straits of Malacca that for time first time during my trip I confessed myself uncomfortably hot. It was sultry and foggy and so damp that everything rusted, even the keys in one's pockets, and the mirrors were so sweaty that they ceased to reflect. The second day out from Penang we passed beautiful green islands. There were many stories told about the straits being once infested with pirates, and I regretted to hear that they had ceased to exist, I so longed for some new experience.

We expected to reach Singapore that night. I was anxious that we should, for the sooner we got in the sooner we should leave, and every hour lost meant so much to me. The pilot came on at six o'clock. I waited tremblingly for his verdict. A wave of despair swept over me when I heard that we should anchor outside until morning, because it was too dangerous to try to make the port after dark. And this was the result of slowing down to leave off the coolies at Penang. The mail contract made it compulsory for the ship to stay in port twenty-four hours, and while we might have been consuming our stay and so helping me on in my race against time I was wasting precious hours lying outside the gates of hope, as it were, merely because some black men had been too slow. Those few hours might mean time loss of my ship at Hong Kong; they might mean days to my record. What agony of suspense and impatience I suffered that night!

When I came on deck time next morning the ship lay along side the wharf, and naked Chinese coolies carrying, two by two, baskets of coal suspended between them on a pole, were constantly traversing the gang-plank between the ship and shore, while in little boats about were peddlers with silks, photographs, fruits, laces and monkeys to sell.

The doctor, a young Welshman, and I hired a gharry, a light wagon with latticed windows and comfortable seating room for four with the driver's seat on the same level outside. They are drawn by a pretty spotted Malay pony whose speed is marvelous compared with its diminutive size, and whose endurance is of such quality that the law confines their working hours to a certain limit.

Driving along a road as smooth as a ball-room floor, shaded by large trees, made picturesque by native houses built on pins in marshy land on either side, which tended to dampen our surprise at the great number of graveyards and the generous way in which they were filled, we drove to the town. The graves were odd, being round mounds with walls shaped like horse-shoes. A flat stone where the mound ends and the wall begins bears the inscriptions done in colored letters.

There are no sidewalks in Singapore, and blue and white in the painting of the houses largely predominate over other colors. Families seem to occupy the second story, the lower being generally devoted to business purposes. Through latticed windows we got occasional glimpses of peeping Chinese women in gay gowns, Chinese babies bundled in shapeless, wadded garments, while down below through widely opened fronts we could see people pursuing their trades. Barbering is the principal trade. A chair, a comb, a basin and a knife are all the tools a man needs to open shop, and he finds as many patrons if he sets up shop in the open street as he would under shelter. Sitting doubled over, Chinamen have their heads shaven back almost to the crown, when a spot about the size of a tiny saucer is left to bear the crop of hair which forms the pig-tail. When braided and finished with a silk tassel the Chinaman's hair is "done" for the next fortnight.

The people here, as at other ports where I stopped, constantly chew betel nut, and when they laugh one would suppose they had been drinking blood. The betel nut stains their teeth and mouthfuls blood-red. Many of the natives also fancy tinting their finger-nails with it.

Nothing is patronized more than the 'rickshas in Singapore, and while they are to be had for ten cents an hour it is no unusual sight to see four persons piled in one jinricksha and drawn by one man. We visited a most interesting museum, and saw along the suburban roads the beautiful bungalows of the European citizens. People in dog-carts and wheelmen on bicycles crowded the splendid drives.

We found the monkey-cage, of course. There was besides a number of small monkeys one enormous orang-outang. It was as large as a man and was covered with long red hair. While seeming to be very clever he had a way of gazing off in the distance with wide, unseeing eyes, meanwhile pulling his long red hair up over his head in an aimless, insane way that was very fetching. The doctor wanted to give him a nut, but feared to put his hand through the bars. The grating was too small for the old fellow to get his hand through, but he did not intend to be cheated of his rights, so he merely stuck his lips through the gratings until they extended fully four inches. I burst into laughter at the comical sight. I had heard of mouths, but that beat anything I ever saw, and I laughed until the old fellow actually smiled in sympathy. He got the nut!

The doctor offered him a cigar. He did not take it, but touched it with the back of his hand, afterwards smelling his hand, and then subsided into that dreamy state, aimlessly pulling his hair up over the back of his head.

At the cable office, in the second story of a building, I found the agents conversant with the English language. They would accept American silver at par, but they did not care to handle our other money. The bank and post-office are open places on the ground floor with about as much comfort and style as is found in ordinary wharf warehouses. Chinese and English are employed in both places.

We had dinner at the *Hotel de l'Europe*, a long, low, white building set back in a wide, green lawn, with a beautiful esplanade, faced by the sea, fronting it. Upon the verandah were long white tables where a fine dinner was served by Chinamen.

On our return from the Governor's House, I heard a strange, weird din as of many instruments in dire confusion and discord, very like in sound to a political procession the night after the presidential election.

"That's a funeral," my Malay driver announced.

"Indeed! If that is the way you have funerals here, I'll see one," I said. So he pulled the gharry to one side where we waited eagerly for a funeral that was heralded by a blast of trumpets. First came a number of Chinamen with black and white satin flags which, being flourished energetically, resulted in clearing the road of vehicles and pedestrians. They were followed by musicians on Malay ponies, blowing fifes, striking cymbals, beating tom-toms, hammering gongs, and pounding long pieces of iron, with all their might and main. Men followed carrying on long poles roast pigs and Chinese lanterns, great and small, while in their rear came banner-bearers. The men on foot wore white trousers and sandals, with blue top dress, while the pall-bearers wore black garments bound with blue braid. There were probably forty pall-bearers. The casket, which rested on long poles suspended on the shoulders of the men, was hidden beneath a white-spotted scarlet cloth with decorations of Chinese lanterns or inflated bladders on arches above it. The mourners followed in a long string of gharries, They were dressed in white satin from head to toe and were the happiest looking people at the funeral. We watched until the din died away in the distance when we returned to town as delighted as if we had seen a circus parade.

"I would not have missed that for anything," Doctor Brown said to me.

"You could not," I replied laughingly, "I know they got it up for our special benefit."

And so laughing and jesting about what had to us no suggestion of death, we drove back to see the temples. None of us were permitted to pass beneath the gate of the Mahommedan temple, so we went on to a Hindoo temple. It was a low stone building, enclosed by a high wall. At the gateway leading to it were a superfluity of beggars, large and small, lame and blind, who asked for alms, touching their foreheads respectfully. The temple was closed but some priests rushed forth to warn us not step on the sacred old dirty stone-passage leading to it with our shoes on. Its filth would have made it sacred to me with my shoes off! My comrades were told that removing their shoes would give them admission but I should be denied that privilege because I was a woman.

"Why?" I demanded, curious to know why my sex in heathen lands should exclude me from a temple, as in America it confines me to the side entrances of hotels and other strange and incommodious things.

"No, *Señora*, no mudder," the priest said with a positive shake of the head.

"I'm not a mother!" I cried so indignantly that my companions burst into laughter, which I joined after a while, but my denials had no effect on the priest. He would not allow me to enter.

In some sheds which lined the inner part of the high wall we saw a number of fantastically shaped carts of heavy build. Probably they were juggernauts. Near by we saw through the bars a wooden image of a woman. Her shape was neither fairy-like nor girlish; her features were fiendish in expression and from her mouth fell a long string of beads. As the mother of a poor man's family she would have been a great success. Instead of one pair of arms she had four. One pair was employed in holding a stiff wooden baby before her and the other three pairs were taking care of themselves much like the legs of a crab. They showed us a white wooden horse mounted on wheels, images of most horrible devils, in short, we saw so many images of such horrible shapes that it would be impossible to recall them all. I remember one head that I was very much interested in and the limited English of the priest failed to satisfy my curiosity as to who, what, and for what purpose the thing was invented.

It was only a head but must have been fully twelve feet high and wide in proportion. The face was a fiery scarlet and the eyes were tightly closed. On the lawn, fastened to a slight pin, was a white cow, the only presentable cow I saw during my trip.

I noticed the doctor gave her wide range keeping his eye on her as she playfully tossed her head.

"Be careful," he said nervously to me. "I believe that's the sacred white cow."

"She looks old enough— and tough enough— to make her sacred in the eye of a butcher!" I replied.

"If she is the sacred cow," he continued, despite my levity, "and went for us they would consider it their duty to let the old beast kill an infidel. That pin does not look very strong."

So to quiet the fears of the doctor we left the old cow and the gods behind.

The people in Singapore have ranks as have people in other lands. There they do not wait for one neighbor to tell another or for the newspapers to inform the public as to their standing but every man, woman, and child carries his mark in gray powder on the forehead so that all the world may look and read and know his caste.

We stopped at the driver's humble home on our way to the ship and I saw there on the ground floor, his pretty little Malay wife dressed in one wrapping of linen, and several little brown naked babies. The wife had a large gold ring in her nose, rings on her toes and several around the rim of her ears, and gold ornaments on her ankles. At the door of their home was a monkey. I did resist the temptation to buy a boy at Port Said and also smothered the desire to buy a Singalese girl at Colombo, but when I saw the monkey my will-power melted and I began straightway to bargain for it. I got it.

"Will the monkey bite?" I asked the driver, and he took it by the throat, holding it up for me to admire as he replied:

"Monkey no bite." But he could not under the circumstances.

CHAPTER XI.
AGAINST THE MONSOON.

THAT evening we sailed for Hong Kong. The next day the sea was rough and head winds made the run slower than we had hoped for. Towards noon almost all the passengers disappeared. The roughness increased and the cook enjoyed a holiday. There was some chaffing among the passengers who remained on deck. During dinner the chief officer began to relate the woes of people he had seen suffering from the dire disease that threatened now to even overpower the captain. I listened for quite a while, merely because I could not help hearing; and if there was anything the chief could do well it was relating anecdotes. At last one made me get up and run, it was so vivid, and the moment the doctor, who sat opposite, saw me go he got up and followed. I managed to overcome my faintness without really being sick, but the doctor gave way entirely. I went back to dinner to find the cause of our misery had disappeared. When I saw him later, his face was pale and he confessed contritely that his realistic joke had made even him seasick.

During the roughness that followed the doctor would always say to me pleadingly:

"Don't make a start, for if you do I will have to follow."

The terrible swell of the sea during the Monsoon was the most beautiful thing I ever saw. I would sit breathless on deck watching the bow of the ship standing upright on a wave then dash headlong down as if intending to carry us to the bottom. Some of the men made no secret of being seasick and were stretched out in their chairs on deck where they might hope to catch the first breath of air. Although there was a dreadful swell, still the atmosphere was heavy and close. Sometimes I felt as if I would smother. One man who had been quite attentive to me became seasick. I was relieved when I heard it, still I felt very cruel when I would see his pale face and hear him plead for sympathy. As heartless as I thought it was I could not sympathize with a seasick man. There was an effort on the part of others to tease the poor fellow. When I sat down on deck they would carefully take away all the chairs excepting those occupied by themselves, but it mattered little to the seasick man. He would quietly curl up on his rugs at my feet and there lie, in all his misery, gazing at me.

"You would not think that I am enjoying a vacation, but I am," he said plaintively to me one day.

"You don't know how nice I can look," he said pathetically at another time. "If you would only stay over at Hong Kong for a week you would see how pretty I can look."

"Indeed, such a phenomenon might induce me to remain there six weeks," I said coldly.

At last some one told him I was engaged to the chief officer, who did not approve of my talking to other men, thinking this would make him cease following me about, but it only served to increase his devotion. Finding me alone on deck one stormy evening he sat down at my feet and holding to the arms of my chair began to talk in a wild way.

"Do you think life is worth living?" he asked.

"Yes, life is very sweet. The thought of death is the only thing that causes me unhappiness," I answered truthfully.

"You cannot understand it or you would feel different. I could take you in my arms and jump overboard, and before they would know it we would be at rest," he said passionately.

"You can't tell. It might not be rest—" I began and he broke in hotly.

"I know, I know. I can show you. I will prove it to you. Death by drowning is a peaceful slumber, a quiet drifting away."

"Is it?" I said, with a pretense of eagerness. I feared to get up for I felt the first move might result in my burial beneath the angry sea.

"You know, tell me about it. Explain it to me," I gasped, a feeling of coldness creeping over me as I realized that I was alone with what for the time was a mad man. Just as he began to speak I saw the chief officer come on deck and slowly advance towards me. I dared not call. I dared not smile, lest he should notice. I feared the chief would go away, but no, he saw me, and with a desire to tease the man who had been so devoted he came up on tip-toe, then, clapping the poor fellow on the back, he said: "What a very pretty love scene!"

"Come," I shouted, breaking away before the startled man could understand. The chief, still in a spirit of fun, took my hand and we rushed down below. I told him and the captain what had occurred and the captain wanted to put the man in irons but I begged that he be left free. I was careful afterwards not to spend one moment alone and unprotected on deck.

The Parsees, traveling first class, were compelled to go below when a heavy swell was on. We welcomed the storm on that account if on no other, because they had a peculiar habit of dropping off their slippers when they sat down. As they wore no hose, this habit was annoying.

The doctor seriously affirmed that every time he sat down anywhere a Parsee was sure to squat alongside, drop his shoes and turn his bare, brown feet up to be gazed upon.

The monkey proved a good seaman. One day when I visited it I found the young men had been toasting its health. It was holding its aching head when I went in, and evidently thinking I was the cause of the swelling, it sprang at me, making me seek safety in flight.

The hurricane deck was a great resort for lovers, so Chief Officer Sleeman told me; and evidently he knew, for he talked a great deal about two American girls who had traveled to Egypt, I believe, on the Thames when he was first officer of it. He had lost their address but his heart was true, for he had lost a philopoena to one and though he did not know her habitation he bought the philopoena and put it in a bank in London where it awaits some farther knowledge of the fair young American's whereabouts.

Lovers were not plentiful on the Oriental, there were so few passengers. The "Spanish minister" had an eye for beauty and a heart for romance, though he led a most quiet life on shipboard, and was the very essence of gallantry.

"I was very much in love with a woman once. Traveling on the same ship with me was a woman, a beautiful woman, most beautiful, indeed. I watched her, she watched me, and my eyes told her I admired her and her eyes said back to me they were pleased that it should be so. Two men were traveling with her. One day I awkwardly knocked against her in a corridor and I said, 'I beg your pardon, Miss!' To which she answered lowly and sadly: 'I beg YOUR pardon,— Mrs!' When she came to dinner that night her eyes were red from weeping. I caught her glance; it spoke so sadly to me, her lips trembling like a grieved child's. She started in to drink a great deal of wine but one look from me made her push her glass away. Her husband, for she was married, was a very brutal fellow and my love for the beautiful woman almost made me forget my family and hers in my longing to claim her as my heart's companion. They left us at the first port. I stood on deck as they came up to go ashore. Her husband and his comrade went down the steps. Starting to follow she saw me, and stopped. Her eyes said to me as plain as speech, 'Say but the word and I am yours,' and although my feelings made me spring towards her, I paused before touching her and my aching eyes said: 'Go! be a good woman.' She went slowly down into the boat. Rising to her feet as it moved off, she held out her arms to me and with a great despairing cry fell back in the boat insensible! I never saw her since, I never knew her name, but I know as well as I know you are there that beautiful woman loved me!"

"And you?" I said inquiringly.

"I!" with a slight shrug of the shoulders, accompanied by a little cold laugh, which was not unpleasant to hear; it somehow reminded me of the sound of dripping water on a hot day. "Ah, she was a beautiful lady, very, ver—ry beautiful, most beautiful, indeed, but Señorita, I have a son older than you and I am devoted to my family."

Impatiently I turned to an Englishman who was sitting on the other side.

"Why do Englishmen always say 'Deah me!' " I lazily asked.

"Deah me! Do they? I can't say, don't you know."

"Well, I can. It's because they think so wonderfully much of themselves," I said with a laugh.

"Deah me! Really?" was all he said in reply.

"You are so jolly clever, now; can you tell me why Eve did not take the measles?" he asked after a time.

"'Cause she'd 'ad 'em," I said in a Bowery tone.

"I sai, now, you are jolly clever, but can you tell me why Cain did not take them? Hasten, now, I cannot dwell."

"Because he wasn't Abel. Now don't dwell, but move on and tell me what chestnuts are?" I said, teasingly.

"Oh come, now—"

"I'm here."

"I sai, really, you Americans have such a jolly queer language. Deah me, I can't tell."

"I thought you could, you have such a jolly supply of them, 'don't you know.' "

"Deah me!" he exclaimed, as he rushed down below to brace on a whiskey and soda.

It is wonderful the amount of whiskey and soda Englishmen consume. They drink it at all times and places. There was an Englishman on the Oriental who drank whiskey and soda all the day, half a dozen different wines at dinner, and then complained, as he invariably staggered away from the table, that the wine list had no variety!

Talk about cranks! One woman told the chief officer one day that she wanted a cabin just over the ship's screw so she could tell that the ship was going! She got it, and she was the worst sea-sick woman I ever saw. Another passenger complained because the berths had spring mattresses!

One night during the monsoon the sea washed over the ship in a frightful manner. I found my cabin filled with water, which, however, did not touch my berth. Escape to the lower deck was impossible, as I could not tell the deck from the angry, pitching sea. As I crawled back into my bunk a feeling of awe crept over me and with it a conscious feeling of satisfaction. I thought it very possible that I had spoken my last word to any mortal, that the ship would doubtless sink, and with it all I thought, if the ship did go down, no one would be able to tell whether I could have gone around the world in seventy-five days or not. The thought was very comforting at that time, for I felt then I might not get around in one hundred days.

I could have worried myself over my impending fate had I not been a great believer in letting unchangeable affairs go their way. "If the ship does go down," I thought, "there is time enough to worry when it's going. All the worry in the world cannot change it one way or the other, and if the ship does not go down, I only waste so much time." So I went to sleep and slumbered soundly until the breakfast hour.

The ship was making its way laboriously through a very frisky sea when I looked out, but the deck was drained, even if it was not dry.

When I went out, the jolly Irish lad, for whom I had a great fondness, was stretched out languidly in a willow chair with a bottle of champagne on one arm-rest and a glass on the other. Every little motion of the ship made him vow that when he reached Hong Kong he would stay there until he could return to England overland!

"You should have seen my cabin-mate last night," he said with a laugh when I sat down beside him. The man he spoke of, a very clever Englishman, was the man who posed as a woman-hater, and naturally we enjoyed any joke at his expense.

"Finding our cabin filling with water, he got out of bed, put on a life preserver and bailed out the cabin with a cigarette box!"

I laughed until my sides ached at the mental picture presented to me of the little chunky Englishman in an enormous life preserver, bailing out his cabin with a tiny cigarette box! Even the box of the deadly cigarette seems to have its christian mission to perform. While I was wiping away the tears brought there by the strength of my laughter, the Englishman came up, and hearing what had amused us, said: "While I was bailing out the cabin, 'the boy,' "as we fondly called him, "clung to the upper berth all the time groaning and praying! He was certain the ship would sink, and I could not persuade him to get out of the top berth to help bail. He would do nothing but groan and pray."

The boy answered with a laugh, "I did not want to sleep the rest of the night in wet pajamas," which caused the woman-hater to flee!

Later in the day the rolling was frightful. I was sitting on deck when all at once the ship went down at one side like a wagon in a deep rut. I was thrown in my chair clear across the deck. A young man endeavored to come to my assistance just as the ship went the other way in a still deeper sea-rut. It flung me back again, and only by catching hold of an iron bar did I save my neck at least, for in another moment I would have been dashed through the skylight into the dining hall on the deck below.

As I caught the bar, I saw the man who had rushed to my assistance turned upside down and land on his face. I began to laugh, his position was so ludicrous. When I saw he made no move to get up, I ran to his side, still convulsed with laughter. I found his nose was bleeding profusely, but I was such an idiot that the sight of the blood only served to make the scene to me the more ridiculous. Helping him to a chair, I ran for the doctor and from laughing could hardly tell him what I wanted. The man's nose was broken, and the doctor said he would be scarred for life. Even the others laughed when I described the accident, and, although I felt a great pity for the poor fellow, hurt as he was in my behalf, still an irresistible impulse to laugh would sweep over me every time I endeavored to express my appreciation of his attempt to assist me.

Our passengers were rather queer. I always enjoy the queerness of people. One day, when speaking about the boat, I said:

"Everything is such an improvement on the Victoria. The food is good, the passengers are refined, the officers are polite and the ship is comfortable and pleasant."

When I finished my complimentary remarks about the ship, a little bride who had been a source of interest to us looked up and said:

"Yes, everything is very nice; but the life preservers are not quite comfortable to sleep in."

Shocked amazement spread over the countenances of all the passengers, and then in one grand shout that dining-room resounded with laughter. The bride said that ever since they left home on their bridal tour they had been sleeping in the life preservers. They thought it was the thing to do on board a ship.

But I never knew how queer our passengers were until we reached Hong Kong, which we did two days ahead of time, although we had the monsoon against us. When we landed, a man sued the company for getting him in ahead of time. He said he bought his tickets to cover a certain length of time, and if the company got him in before it expired they were responsible for his expenses, and they had to pay his hotel bill.

The captain asked a minister who was on board to read the service one Sunday. He did so, and when he reached Hong Kong he put in a bill for two pounds! He said he was enjoying a vacation and did not propose to work during that time unless he was paid for it! The company paid, but warned the officers not to let ministers read the service thereafter until they knew their price.

The evening of December 22 we all sat on deck in a dark corner. The men were singing and telling stories. The only other woman who was able to be up and I were the interested and appreciative audience. We all felt an eagerness for morning and yet the eagerness was mingled with much that was sad. Knowing that early in the day we would reach Hong Kong, and while it would bring us new scenes and new acquaintances, it would take us from old friends.

CHAPTER XII.
BRITISH CHINA.

WE first saw the city of Hong Kong in the early morning. Gleaming white were the castle-like homes on the tall mountain side. We fired a cannon as we entered the bay, the captain saying that this was the custom of mail ships. A beautiful bay was this magnificent basin, walled on every side by high mountains. Once within this natural fortified harbor we could discern, in different directions, only small outlets between the mountains, but so small, indeed, they appeared that one could hardly believe a ship would find space large enough for passage. In fact, these outlets are said to be dangerously narrow, the most vigilant care being necessary until the ship is safely beyond on the ocean blue. Mirror-like was the bay in the bright sun, dotted with strange craft from many countries. Heavy iron-clads, torpedo boats, mall steamers, Portuguese lorchas, Chinese junks and sampans. Even as we looked, a Chinese ship wended its way slowly out to sea. Its queer, broad stern hoisted high out of the water and the enormous eye gracing its bow, were to us most interesting. A graceful thing I thought it, but I heard an officer call it most ungraceful and unshapely.

Hong Kong is strangely picturesque. It is a terraced city, the terraces being formed by the castle-like, arcaded buildings perched tier after tier up the mountain's verdant side. The regularity with which the houses are built in rows made me wildly fancy them a gigantic staircase, each stair made in imitation of castles.

The doctor, another gentleman, and I left the boat, and walking to the pier's end selected sedan chairs, in which we were carried to the town. The carriers were as urgent as our hackmen around railway stations in America. There is a knack of getting into a chair properly.

It is placed upon the ground, the carrier tilts the shafts down, and the patron steps inside, back towards the chair, and goes into it backward. Once seated, the carriers hoist the chair to their shoulders and start off with a monotonous trot, which gives the chair a motion not unlike that of a pacing saddle-horse.

We followed the road along the shore, passing warehouses of many kinds and tall balconied buildings filled with hundreds of Chinese families, on the flat-house plan. The balconies would have lent a pleasing appearance to the houses had the inhabitants not seemed to be enjoying a washing jubilee, using the balconies for clotheslines. Garments were stretched on poles, after the manner of hanging coats so they will not wrinkle, and those poles were fastened to the balconies until it looked as if every family in the street had placed their old clothing on exhibition.

The town seemed in a state of untidiness, the road was dirty, the mobs of natives we met were filthy, the houses were dirty, the numberless boats lying along the wharf, which invariably were crowded with dirty people, were dirty, our carriers were dirty fellows, their untidy pig-tails twisted around their half-shaven heads. They trotted steadily ahead, snorting at the crowds of natives we met to clear the way. A series of snorts or grunts would cause a scattering of natives more frightened than a tie-walker would be at the tooting of an engine's whistle.

Turning off the shore road our carriers started up one of the roads which wind about from tier to tier up the mountain.

My only wish and desire was to get as speedily as possible to the office of the Oriental and Occidental Steamship Company to learn the earliest possible time I could leave for Japan, to continue my race against time around the world. I had just marked off my thirty-ninth day. Only thirty-nine days since leaving New York and I was in China. I was leaving particularly elated, because the good ship Oriental not only made up the five days I had lost in Colombo, but reached Hong Kong two days before I was due, according to my schedule. And that with the northeast monsoon against her. It was the Oriental's maiden trip to China, and from Colombo to Hong Kong she had broken all previous records.

I went to the O. & O. office feeling very much elated over my good fortune, with never a doubt but that it would continue.

"Will you tell me the date of the first sailing for Japan?" I asked a man in the office.

"In one moment," he said, and going into an inner office he brought out a man who looked at me inquiringly, and when I repeated my question, said:

"What is your name?"

"Nellie Bly," I replied in some surprise.

"Come in, come in," he said nervously. We followed him in, and after we were seated he said:

"You are going to be beaten."

"What? I think not. I have made up my delay," I said, still surprised, wondering if the Pacific had sunk since my departure from New York, or if all the ships on that line had been destroyed.

"You are going to lose it," he said with an air of conviction.

"Lose it? I don't understand. What do you mean?" I demanded, beginning to think he was mad.

"Aren't you having a race around the world?" he asked, as if he thought I was not Nellie Bly.

"Yes; quite right. I am running a race with Time," I replied.

"Time? I don't think that's her name."

"Her! Her!!" I repeated, thinking, "Poor fellow, he is quite unbalanced," and wondering if I dared wink at the doctor to suggest to him the advisability of our making good our escape.

"Yes, the other woman; she is going to win. She left here three days ago."

I stared at him; I turned to the doctor; I wondered if I was awake; I concluded the man was quite mad, so I forced myself to laugh in an unconcerned manner, but I was only able to say stupidly:

"The other woman?"

"Yes," he continued briskly; "Did you not know? The day you left New York another woman started out to beat your time, and she's going to do it. She left here three days ago. You probably met somewhere near the Straits of Malacca. She says she has authority to pay any amount to get ships to leave in advance of their time. Her editor offered one or two thousand dollars to the O. & O. if they would have the Oceanic leave San Francisco two days ahead of time. They would not do it, but they did do their best to get her here in time to catch the

English mail for Ceylon. If they had not arrived long before they were due, she would have missed that boat, and so have been delayed ten days. But she caught the boat and left three days ago, and you will be delayed here five days."

"That is rather hard, isn't it?" I said quietly, forcing a smile that was on the lips, but came from nowhere near the heart.

"I'm astonished you did not know anything about it," he said. "She led us to suppose that it was an arranged race."

"I do not believe my editor would arrange a race without advising me," I said stoutly. "Have you no cables or messages for me from New York?"

"Nothing," was his reply.

"Probably they do not know about her," I said more cheerfully.

"Yes they do. She worked for the same newspaper you do until the day she started."

"I do not understand it," I said quietly, too proud to show my ignorance on a subject of vital importance to my well-doing. "You say I cannot leave here for five days?"

"No, and I don't think you can get to New York in eighty days. She intends to do it in seventy. She has letters to steamship officials at every point requesting them to do all they can to get her on. Have you any letters?"

"Only one, from the agent of the P. & O., requesting the captains of their boats to be good to me because I am traveling alone. That is all," I said with a little smile.

"Well, it's too bad; but I think you have lost it. There is no chance for you. You will lose five days here and five in Yokohoma, and you are sure to have a slow trip across at this season.

Just then a young man, with the softest black eyes and a clear pale complexion, came into the office. The agent, Mr. Harmon, introduced him to me as Mr. Fuhrmann, the purser of the Oceanic, the ship on which I would eventually travel to Japan and America. The young man took my hand in a firm, strong clasp, and his soft black eyes gave me such a look of sympathy that it only needed his kind tone to cheer me into a happier state.

"I went down to the Oriental to meet you; Mr. Harmon thought it was better. We want to take good care of you now that you are in our charge, but, unfortunately, I missed you. I returned to the hotel, and as they knew nothing about you there I came here, fearing that you were lost."

"I have found kind friends everywhere," I said, with a slight motion towards the doctor, who was speechless over the ill-luck that had befallen me. "I am sorry to have been so much trouble to you."

"Trouble! You are with your own people now, and we are only too happy if we can be of service," he said kindly. "You must not mind about the possibility of some one getting around the world in less time than you may do it. You have had the worst connections it is possible to make, and everybody knows the idea originated with you, and that others are merely trying to steal the work of your brain, so, whether you get in before or later, people will give you the credit of having originated the idea."

"I promised my editor that I would go around the world in seventy-five days, and if I accomplish that I shall be satisfied," I stiffly explained. "I am not racing with anyone. I would not race. If someone else wants to do the trip in less time, that is their concern. If they take it upon themselves to race against me, it is their lookout that they succeed. I am not racing. I promised to do the trip in seventy-five days, and I will do it; although had I been permitted to make the trip when I first proposed it over a year ago, I should then have done it in sixty days."

We returned to the hotel, where a room had been secured for me, after arranging the transfer of my luggage and the monkey from the Oriental to the Oceanic. I met a number of people after tiffin, who were interested in my trip, and were ready and anxious to do anything they could to contribute to my pleasure during my enforced stay.

Having but the one dress I refused to attend any dinners or receptions that were proposed in my honor. During the afternoon the wife of a prominent Hong Kong gentleman waited upon me to place herself and her home at my disposal. She was anxious that I should make her home mine during my stay, but I told her I could not think of accepting her kindness, because I would wish to be out most of the time, and could not make my hours conform to the hours of the house, and still feel free to go, come and stay, as I pleased. Despite her pleadings I assured her I was not on pleasure bent, but business, and I considered it my duty to refrain from social pleasures, devoting myself to things that lay more in the line of work.

I had dinner on the Oriental. As I bade the captain and his officers farewell, remembering their kindness to me, I had a wild desire to cling to them, knowing that with the morning light the Oriental would sail, and I would be once again alone in strange lands with strange people.

That evening the purser of the Oceanic, another acquaintance and I were carried in chairs up a winding road, arched with green trees, on which the leaves hung motionless and still in the silent night.

Our lazy voices, as occasionally we spoke softly to each other, and the steady, monotonous slap-slap-slap of the bare-feet of our carriers made the only break in the slumbering stillness. All earth seemed to have gone to rest. Silently we went along, now getting, by dim gas lamps at garden gates, glimpses of comfortable homes in all their Eastern splendor, and then, for a moment emerging from beneath the over-lapping arch of verdant trees, we would get a faint glimmer of the quivering stars and cloudless heavens. The ascent was made at last. We were above the city, lying dark and quiet, but no nearer the glorious starlit sky. A little rush through a wide gate in a high wall, a sudden blindness in a road banked and roofed by foliage, a quick lowering to the ground at the foot of wide steps that led to an open door through which a welcoming light shed its soft, warm rays upon us and we had reached our journey's end.

Inside, where a cordial welcome awaited us, was a bright wood fire before which I longed to curl up on a rug and be left alone to dream—dream. But there were friends instead of dreams, and realities in the shape of a splendid dinner. A table, graced with a profusion of tropical blossoms—a man, handsomer than an ideal hero, at its head—a fine menu, guests, handsome, witty and just enough in number to suit my ideas, were the items of what made up an ideal evening.

It is said people do not grow old in Hong Kong. Their youthful looks bear ample testimony to the statement. I asked the reason why, and they said it is because they are compelled to invent amusements for themselves, and by inventing they find, not time to grow blasé, but youth and happiness.

The theatre in Hong Kong knows few professional troupes, but the amateur actors in the English colony leave little to be desired in the way of splendid entertainments. The very best people in the town take part, and I believe they all furnish their own stage costumes. The regiments stationed there turn out very creditable actors in the persons of the young officers. I went one night to see "Ali Baba and the Forty Thieves" as given by the Amateur Dramatic Club of Hong Kong. It was a new version of the old story filled with local hits arranged for the club by a military captain; the music was by the band— master of the Argyll and Sutherland Highlanders. The beautiful and artistic scenery was designed and executed by two army men, as were the lime-light effects. Spectators came to the theatre in their chairs instead of carriages.

Inside, the scene was bewitching. A rustling of soft gowns, the odor of flowers, the fluttering of fans, the sounds of soft, happy whispering, a maze of lovely women in evening gowns mingling with handsome men in the regulation evening dress— what could be prettier? If American women would only ape the English in going bonnetless to the theatres, we would forgive their little aping in other respects, and call it even. Upon the arrival of the Governor the band played "God Save the Queen," during which the audience stood. Happily, they made it short. The play was pleasantly presented, the actors filling their roles most creditably, especially the one taking the part of Ally Sloper.[1]

Afterwards, the sight of handsomely dressed women stepping into their chairs, the daintily-colored Chinese lanterns, hanging fore and aft, marking the course the carriers took in the darkness, was very oriental and affective. It is a luxury to have a carriage, of course, but there is something even more luxurious in the thought of owning a chair and carriers. A fine chair with silver mounted poles and silk hangings can be bought, I should judge, for a little more than twenty dollars. Some women keep four and eight carriers; they are so cheap that one can afford to retain a number. Every member of a well established household in Hong Kong has his or her own private chair. Many men prefer a coverless willow chair with swinging step, while many women have chairs that close entirely, so they can be carried along the streets secure against the gaze of the public. Convenient pockets, umbrella stands and places for parcels are found in all well-appointed chairs.

---

1   A popular comic strip character with a large red nose, a parody of the lazy schemer archetype

At every port I touched I found so many bachelors, men of position, means and good appearance, that I naturally began to wonder why women do not flock that way. It was all very well some years ago to say, "Go West, young man;" but I would say, "Girls, go East!" There are bachelors enough and to spare! And a most happy time do these bachelors have in the East. They are handsome, jolly and good natured. They have their own fine homes with no one but the servants to look after them. Think of it, and let me whisper, "Girls, go East!"

The second day after my arrival, Captain Smith, of the Oceanic, called upon me. I expected to see a hard-faced old man; so, when I went into the drawing-room and a youthful, good-looking man, with the softest blue eyes that seemed to have caught a tinge of the ocean's blue on a bright day, smiled down at me, I imagine I must have looked very stupid indeed. I looked at the smooth, youthful face, with its light-brown moustache, and I felt inclined to laugh at the long iron-gray beard my imagination had put upon the Captain of the Oceanic. I caught a laughing gleam of the bluest of blue eyes, and I thought of imaginary stern ones, and had to smother another insane desire to laugh. I looked at the tall, slender, shapely body, and recalled the imaginary short legs, holding upright a wide circumference under an ample waistcoat, and I laughed audibly.

"You were so different to what I imagined you would be," I said afterwards, when we talked over our first meeting.

"And I could not believe you were the right girl, you were so unlike what I had been led to believe," he said, with a laugh, in a burst of confidence. "I was told that you were an old maid with a dreadful temper. Such horrible things were said about you that I was hoping you would miss our ship. I said if you did come I supposed you would expect to sit at my table, but I would arrange so you should be placed elsewhere."

The Captain took me out to see "Happy Valley" that day before we separated. In jinrickshas we rode by the parade and cricket grounds where some lively games are played, the city hall, and the solid, unornamented barracks; along smooth, tree-lined roads, out to where the mountains make a nest of one level, green space. This level has been converted into a race-course. The judges' stand was an ordinary, commonplace race-course stand, but the stands erected by and for private families, were built of palms and were more pleasing because they were out of the usual.

During the month of February races are held here annually. They last three days, and during that period everybody stops work, rich and poor alike flocking to the race-course. They race with native-bred Mongolian ponies, having no horses, and the racing is pronounced most exciting and interesting.

"Happy Valley" lines the hillside. There are congregated the grave-yards of all the different sects and nationalities in Hong Kong. The Fire Worshipers lie in ground joining the Presbyterians, the Episcopalians, the Methodists and the Catholics, and Mahommedans are just as close by. That those of different faiths should consent to place their dead together in this lovely tropical valley is enough to give it the name of Happy Valley, if its beauty did not do as much. In my estimation it rivals in beauty the public gardens, and visitors use it as a park. One wanders along the walks looking at the beautiful shrubs and flowers, never heeding that they are in the valley of death, so thoroughly is it robbed of all that is horrible about graveyards. We rode back to town through the crowded districts, where the natives huddle together in all their filth. It is said that over 100,000 people live within a certain district in Hong Kong not exceeding one-half square mile, and they furthermore positively affirm, that sixteen hundred people live in the space of an acre. This is a sample of the manner in which the Chinese huddle together. They remind me of a crowd of ants on a lump of sugar. An effort is being made in Hong Kong to compel owners to build differently, so as to make the huddling and packing impossible, for the filth that goes with it invariably breeds disease.

Queen's road is interesting to all visitors. In it is the Hong Kong Club, where the bachelors are to be found, the post office, and greater than all, the Chinese shops. The shops are not large, but the walls are lined with black-wood cabinets, and one feels a little thrill of pleasure at the sight of the gold, the silver, ivory carvings, exquisite fans, painted scrolls and the odor of the lovely sandal-wood boxes, coming faintly to the visitor, creates a feeling of greed. One wants them all— everything.

The Chinese merchants cordially show their goods, or follow as one strolls around, never urging one to buy, but cunningly bringing to the front the most beautiful and expensive part of their stock.

"Chin chin," which means "good day," "good bye," "good night," "How are you?" or anything one may take from it, is the greeting of Chinamen. They all speak mongrel English, called "pidgin" or "pigeon" English. It is impossible to make them understand pure English, consequently Europeans, even housekeepers, use pidgin English when addressing the servants. The servants are men, with the exception of the nurses, and possibly the cooks. To the uninitiated it sounds absurd to hear men and women addressing servants and merchants in the same idiotic language with which fond parents usually cuddle their offspring; but even more laughable is it to hear men swear in "pigeon English," at an unkind or unruly servant. Picture a man with an expression of frenzied rage upon his countenance, saying:

"Go to hellee, savey?"

Pidgin or pigeon, is applied to everything. One will hear people say: " Hab got pigeon," which means they have business to look after; or if a Chinaman is requested to do some work which he thinks is the duty of another, he will say: "No belongee boy pigeon."

While strolling about the Chinese localities, seeing shops more worthy a visit, being more truly Chinese, I came upon an eating house, from which a conglomeration of strange odors strolled out and down the road. Built around a table in the middle of the room, was a circular bench. The diners perched on this bench like chickens on a fence, not letting their feet touch the floor, or hang over, nor "hunkering" down, nor squatting crossed-legged like a Turk or tailor, but sitting down with their knees drawn up until knees and chin met; they held large bowls against their chins, pushing the rice energetically with their chop-sticks into their mouths. Cup after cup of tea is consumed, not only at meals, but at all hours during the day. The cup is quite small and saucerless, and the tea is always drank minus sugar and cream.

Professional writers, found in nooks and recesses of prominent thoroughfares, are interesting personalities. Besides writing letters for people they tell fortunes, and their patrons never go away without having their fates foretold. I noticed when paying for articles, merchants invariably weigh the money. It is also customary for merchants to put their private stamp upon silver dollars as an assurance of its legality and worth. Much silver is beaten into such strange shapes by this queer practice that at first I was afraid to accept it in change.

I saw a marriage procession in Hong Kong. A large band of musicians, who succeeded in making themselves heard, were followed by coolies carrying curious looking objects in blue and gilt, which, I was told, represent mythical and historical scenes. A number of very elegant Chinese lanterns and gorgeous looking banners were also carried along. I was told that in such processions they carry roast pig to the temples of the josses, but it is afterwards very sensibly carried off by the participants.

It would be a hopeless thing for a man to go to Hong Kong in search of employment. The banking and shipping houses, controlled by Europeans, certainly employ numbers of men, but they are brought from England under three and five years' contracts. When a vacancy occurs from a death, or a transfer, the business house immediately consults its representatives in London, where another man signs an agreement, and comes out to Hong Kong to work.

One day I went up to Victoria Peak, named in honor of the Queen. It is said to be 1,800 feet high, the highest point on the island. An elevated tramway is built from the town to Victoria Gap, 1,100 feet above the sea. It was opened in 1887. Before that time people were carried up in sedans.

The first year after its completion 148,344 passengers were carried up the mountain side. The fare is thirty cents up and fifteen cents down. During the summer months Hong Kong is so hot that those who are in a position to do so seek the mountain top, where a breeze lives all the year round. Level places for buildings are obtained by blasting, and every brick, stone, and bit of household furniture is carried by coolies from the town up to the height of 1,600 feet.

At the Gap we secured sedan chairs, and were carried to the Hotel Craigiburn, which is managed by a colored man. The hotel— Oriental in style— is very liberally patronized by the citizens of Hong Kong, as well as visitors. After the proprietor had shown us over the hotel and given us a dinner that could not be surpassed we were carried to Victoria Peak. It required three men to a chair ascending the peak. At the Umbrella Seat, merely a bench with a peaked roof, everybody stops long enough to allow the coolies to rest, then we continue on our way, passing sight-seers and nurses with children. After a while they stop again, and we travel on foot to the signal station.

The view is superb. The bay, in a breastwork of mountains, lies calm and serene, dotted with hundreds of ships that seem like tiny toys. The palatial white houses come half way up the mountain side, beginning at the edge of the glassy bay. Every house we notice has a tennis-court blasted out of the mountain side. They say that after night the view from the peak is unsurpassed. One seems to be suspended between two heavens. Every one of the several thousand boats and sampans carries a light after dark. This, with the lights on the roads and in the houses, seems to be a sky more filled with stars than the one above.

Early one morning a gentleman, who was the proud possessor of a team of ponies, the finest in Hong Kong, called at the hotel to take me for a drive. In a low, easy phaeton behind the spirited ponies that seem like playthings in their smallness but giants in their strength, we whirled along through the town and were soon on the road edging the bay. We had a good view of the beautiful dry dock on the other side, which is constructed entirely of granite and is said to be of such size that it can take in the largest vessels afloat. I thought there were other things more interesting, so I refused to go over to it.

During our drive we visited two quaint and dirty temples. One was a plain little affair with a gaudy altar. The stone steps leading to it were filled with beggars of all sizes, shapes, diseases and conditions of filth. They were so repulsive that instead of appealing to one's sympathy they only succeed in arousing one's disgust.

At another temple, near by a public laundry where the washers stood in a shallow stream slapping the clothes on flat stones, was a quaint temple hewed, cave-like, in the side of an enormous rock. A selvage of rock formed the altar, and to that humble but picturesque temple Chinese women flock to pray for sons to be born unto them that they may have some one to support them in their old age.

After seeing everything of interest in Hong Kong I decided to go to a real Simon-pure Chinese city. I knew we were trying to keep the Chinamen out of America, so I decided to see all of them I could while in their land. Pay them a farewell visit, as it were! So, on Christmas eve, I started for the city of Canton.

CHAPTER XIII.
CHRISTMAS IN CANTON.

THE O. & O. agent escorted me to the ship Powan, on which I was to travel to Canton. He gave me in charge of Captain Grogan, the Powan's commander, an American, who has lived for years in China. A very bashful man he was, but a most kindly, pleasant one. I never saw a fatter man, or a man so comically fattened. A wild inclination to laugh crept over me every time I caught a glimpse of his roly-poly body, his round red face embedded, as it were, in the fat of his shoulders and breast. The thoughts of how sensitive I am concerning remarks about my personal appearance, in a measure subdued my impulse to laugh. I have always said to critics, who mercilessly write about the shape of my chin, or the cut of my nose, or the size of my mouth, and such personal attributes that can no more be changed than death can be escaped:

"Criticise the style of my hat or my gown, I can change them, but spare my nose, it was born on me."

Remembering this, and how nonsensical it is to blame or criticise people for what they are powerless to change, I pocketed my merriment, letting a kindly feeling of sympathy take its place.

Soon after we left, night descended. I went on deck where everything was buried in darkness. Softly and steadily the boat swam on, the only sound— and the most refreshing and restful sound in the world— was the lapping of the water.

To sit on a quiet deck, to have a star-lit sky the only light above or about, to hear the water kissing the prow of the ship, is, to me, paradise. They can talk of the companionship of men, the splendor of the sun, the softness of moonlight, the beauty of music, but give me a willow chair on a quiet deck, the world with its worries and noise and

216

prejudices lost in distance, the glare of the sun, the cold light of the moon blotted out by the dense blackness of night. Let me rest rocked gently by the rolling sea, in a nest of velvety darkness, my only light the soft twinkling of the myriads of stars in the quiet sky above; my music, the round of the kissing waters, cooling the brain and easing the pulse; my companionship, dreaming my own dreams. Give me that and I have happiness in its perfection.

But away with dreams. This is a work-a-day world and I am racing Time around it. After dinner, when the boat anchored, waiting for the tide which was to carry us safely over the bar, I went below to see the Chinese passengers. They were gambling, smoking opium, sleeping, cooking, eating, reading and talking, all huddled together on one deck, which was in one large room, not divided into cabins. They carry their own beds, a bit of matting, and their own food, little else than rice and tea.

Before daybreak we anchored at Canton. The Chinamen went ashore the moment we landed, but the other passengers remained for breakfast.

While we were having breakfast, the guide whom the captain had secured for us, came on board and quietly supervised the luncheon we were to take with us. A very clever fellow was that guide, Ah Cum. The first thing he said to us was "A Merry Christmas!" and as it had even slipped our minds, I know we all appreciated the polite thoughtfulness of our Chinese guide. Ah Cum told me later that he had been educated in an American mission located in Canton, but he assured me, with great earnestness, that English was all he learned. He would have none of the Christian religion. Ah Cum's son was also educated in an American mission, and, like his father, has put his learning to good account. Besides being paid as guide, Ah Cum collects a percentage from merchants for all the goods bought by tourists. Of course the tourists pay higher prices than they would otherwise, and Ah Cum sees they visit no shops where he is not paid his little fee.

Ah Cum is more comely in features than most Mongolians, his nose being more shapely and his eyes less slit-like than those of most of his race. He had on his feet beaded black shoes with white soles. His navy-blue trousers, or tights, more properly speaking, were tied around the ankle and fitted very tight over most of the leg. Over this he wore a blue, stiffly starched shirt-shaped garment, which reached his heels, while over this he wore a short padded and quilted silk jacket, somewhat similar to a smoking jacket. His long, coal-black queue, finished with a tassel of black silk, touched his heels, and on the spot where the queue began rested a round black turban.

Ah Cum had chairs ready for us. His chair was a neat arrangement in black, black silk hangings, tassels, fringe and black wood-poles finished with brass knobs. Once in it, he closed it, and was hidden from the gaze of the public. Our plain willow chairs had ordinary covers, which, to my mind, rather interfered with sightseeing. We had three coolies to each chair. Those with us were bare-footed, with tousled pigtail and navy-blue shirts and trousers, much the worse for wear both in cleanliness and quality. Ah Cum's coolies wore white linen garments, gayly trimmed with broad bands of red cloth, looking very much like a circus clown's costume.

Ah Cum led the way, our coolies following. For a time I was only conscious of a confused mass of black faces and long pig tails, though shortly I became accustomed to it, and was able to distinguish different objects along the crowded thoroughfare; could note the different stands and the curious looks of the people. We were carried along dark and dirty narrow ways, in and about fish stands, whence odors drifted, filling me with disgust, until we crossed a bridge which spanned a dark and sluggish stream.

This little island, guarded at every entrance, is Shameen, or Sandy Face, the land set aside for the habitation of Europeans. An unchangeable law prohibits Celestials from crossing into this sacred precinct, because of the hatred they cherish for Europeans. Shameen is green and picturesque, with handsome houses of Oriental design, and grand shade trees, and wide, velvety green roads, broken only by a single path, made by the bare feet of the chair-carriers.

Here, for the first time since leaving New York, I saw the stars and stripes. It was floating over the gateway to the American Consulate. It is a strange fact that the further one goes from home the more loyal one becomes. I felt I was a long ways off from my own dear land; it was Christmas day, and I had seen many different flags since last I gazed upon our own. The moment I saw it floating there in the soft, lazy breeze I took off my cap and said: "That is the most beautiful flag in the world, and I am ready to whip anyone who says it isn't."

No one said a word. Everybody was afraid! I saw an Englishman in the party glance furtively towards the Union Jack, which was floating over the English Consulate, but in a hesitating manner, as if he feared to let me see.

Consul Seymour received our little party with a cheery welcome. He was anxious that we should partake of his hospitality, but we assured him our limited time only gave us a moment to pay our respects, and then we must be off again.

Mr. Seymour was an editor before he went to China with his wife and only daughter, to be consul. Since then he has conceived a hobby for embroideries and carved ivories, which he is able to ride to the top of his bent in Canton. When tourists go there he always knows some place where he can guide them to bargains. Mr. Seymour is a most pleasant, agreeable man, and a general favorite. It is to be hoped that he will long have a residence in Shameen, where he reflects credit upon the American Consulate.

What a different picture Canton presents to Shameen. They say there are millions of people in Canton. The streets, many of which are roughly paved with stone, seem little over a yard in width. The shops, with their gayly colored and handsomely carved signs, are all open, as if the whole end facing the street had been blown out. In the rear of every shop is an altar, gay in color and often expensive in adornment. As we were carried along the roads we could see not only the usually rich and enticing wares, but the sellers and buyers. Every shop has a book-keeper's desk near the entrance. The book-keepers all wear tortoise-shell rimmed glasses of an enormous size, which lend them a look of tremendous wisdom. I was inclined to think the glasses were a mark of office, for I never saw a man employed in clerical work without them.

I was warned not to be surprised if the Chinamen should stone me while I was in Canton. I was told that Chinese women usually spat in the faces of female tourists when the opportunity offered. However, I had no trouble. The Chinese are not pleasant appearing people; they usually look as if life had given them nothing but trouble; but as we were carried along the men in the stores would rush out to look at me. They did not take any interest in the men with me, but gazed at me as if I was something new. They showed no sign of animosity, but the few women I met looked as curiously at me, and less kindly.

The thing that seemed to interest the people most about me were my gloves. Sometimes they would make bold enough to touch them, and they would always gaze upon them with looks of wonder.

The streets are so narrow that I thought at first I was being carried through the aisles of some great market. It is impossible to see the sky, owing to the signs and other decorations, and the compactness of the buildings; and with the open shops, just like stands in a market, except that they are not even cut off from the passing crowd by a counter, the delusion is a very natural one. When Ah Cum told me that I was not in a market-house, but in the streets of the city of Canton, my astonishment knew no limit. Sometimes our little train would meet another train of chairs, and then we would stop for a moment and there would be great yelling and fussing until we had safely passed, the way being too narrow for both trains to move at once in safety.

Coolie number two of my chair was a source of great discomfort to me all the day. He had a strap spanning the poles by which he upheld his share of the chair. This band, or strap, crossed his shoulders, touching the neck just where the prominent bone is. The skin was worn white and hard-looking from the rubbing of the band; but still it worried me, and I watched all the day expecting to see it blister. His long pig-tail was twisted around his head, so I had an unobstructed view of the spot. He was not an easy traveler, this coolie, there being as much difference in the gait of carriers as there is in the gait of horses. Many times he shifted the strap, much to my misery, and then he would turn and, by motions, convey to me that I was sitting more to one side than to the other.

As a result, I made such an effort to sit straight and not to move that when we alighted at the shops I would be cramped almost into a paralytic state. Before the day was over I had a sick headache, all from thinking too much about the comfort of the Chinamen.

A disagreeable thing about the coolies is that they grunt like pigs when carrying one. I can't say whether the grunt has any special significance to them or not, but they will grunt one after the other along the train, and it is anything but pleasant.

I was very anxious to see the execution ground, so we were carried there. We went in through a gate where a stand erected for gambling was surrounded by a crowd of filthy people. Some few idle ones left it to saunter lazily after us. The place is very unlike what one would naturally suppose it to be. At first sight it looked like a crooked back alley in a country town. There were several rows of half dried pottery. A woman, who was moulding in a shed at one side, stopped her work to gossip about us with another female who had been arranging the pottery in rows. The place is probably seventy-five feet long by twenty-five wide at the front, and narrowing down at the other end. I noticed the ground in one place was very red, and when I asked Ah Cum about it he said indifferently, as he kicked the red-colored earth with his white-soled shoe:

"It's blood. Eleven men were beheaded here yesterday."

He added that it was an ordinary thing for ten to twenty criminals to be executed at one time. The average number per annum is something like 400. The guide also told us that in one year, 1855, over 50,000 rebels were beheaded in this narrow alley.

While he was talking I noticed some roughly fashioned wooden crosses leaned up against the high stone wall, and supposing they were used in some manner for religious purposes before and during the executions, I asked Ah Cum about them. A shiver waggled down my spinal cord when he answered:

"When women are condemned to death in China they are bound to wooden crosses and cut to pieces."

"Men are beheaded with one stroke unless they are the worst kind of criminals," the guide added, "then they are given the death of a woman to make it the more discreditable. They tie them to the crosses and strangle or cut them to pieces. When they are cut to bits, it is done so deftly that they are entirely dismembered and disemboweled before they are dead. Would you like to see some heads?"

I thought that Chinese guide could tell as large stories as any other guides; and who can equal a guide for highly-colored and exaggerated tales? So I said coldly:

"Certainly; bring on your heads!"

I tipped a man, as he told me, who, with the clay of the pottery on his hands, went to some barrels which stood near to the wooden crosses, put in his hand and pulled out a head!

Those barrels are filled with lime, and as the criminals are beheaded their heads are thrown into the barrels, and when the barrels become full they empty them out and get a fresh supply. If a man of wealth is condemned to death in China he can, with little effort, buy a substitute. Chinamen are very indifferent about death; it seems to have no terror for them.

I went to the jail and was surprised to see all the doors open. The doors were rather narrow, and when I got inside and saw all the prisoners with thick, heavy boards fastened about their necks, I no longer felt surprised at the doors being unbarred. There was no need of locking them.

I went to the court, a large, square, stone-paved building. In a small room off one side I was presented to some judges who were lounging about smoking opium! In still another room I met others playing fan tan! At the entrance I found a large gambling establishment! They took me into a room to see the instruments of punishment. Split bamboo to whip with, thumb screws, pulleys on which people are hanged by their thumbs, and such pleasant things. While I was there they brought in two men who had been caught stealing. The thieves were chained with their knees meeting their chins, and in that distressing position were carried in baskets suspended on a pole between two coolies. The judges explained to me that as these offenders had been caught in the very act of taking what belonged not to them, their hands would be spread upon flat stones and with smaller stones every bone in their hands would be broken. Afterwards they would be sent to the hospital to be cured. Prisoners dying in jail are always beheaded before burial.

An American who has lived many years near Canton told me there is a small bridge spanning a stream in the city where it is customary to hang criminals in a fine wire hammock, first removing all their clothing. A number of sharp knives are laid at the end of the bridge, and every one crossing while the man is there is compelled to take a knife and give a slash to the wire-imprisoned wretch. As I saw none of this myself, I only give these stories as they were given to me.

They tell me bamboo punishment (I cannot now recall the name they gave it) is not as uncommon in China as one would naturally suppose from its extreme brutality. For some crimes offenders are pinioned in standing position with their legs astride, fastened to stakes in the earth. This is done directly above a bamboo sprout. To realize this punishment in all its dreadfulness it is necessary to give a little explanation of the bamboo. A bamboo sprout looks not unlike the delicious asparagus, but is of a hardness and strength not equaled by iron. When it starts to come up, nothing can stop its progress. It is so hard that it will go through anything on its way up; let that anything be asphalt or what it will, the bamboo goes through it as readily as though the obstruction didn't exist. The bamboo grows with marvelous rapidity straight up into the air for thirty days, and then it stops. When its growth is finished it throws off a shell-like bark, its branches slowly unfolding and falling into place. They are covered with a soft airy foliage finer than the leafage of a willow. From a distance a bamboo forest is a most beautiful thing, exquisitely soft and fine in appearance, but adamant is not harder in reality. As I have said, nothing can stop a bamboo sprout when it intends to come up. Nothing ever equaled the rapidity of its growth, it being affirmed that it can really be seen growing! In the thirty days that it grows it may reach a height of seventy-five feet.

Picture then a convict pinioned above a bamboo sprout and in such a position that he cannot get away from it. It starts on its upward course never caring for what is in its way; on it goes through the man who stands there dying, dying, worse than by inches, conscious for a while, then fever mercifully kills knowledge, and at last, after days of suffering, his head drops forward, and he is dead. But that is not any worse than tying a man in the boiling sun to a stake, covering him with quick-lime and giving him nothing but water to quench hunger and thirst. He holds out and out, for it means life, but at last he takes the water that is always within his reach. He drinks, he perspires, and the lime begins to eat. They also have a habit of suspending a criminal by his arms, twisting them back of him. As long as a man keeps his muscles tense he can live, but the moment he relaxes and falls, it ruptures blood vessels and his life floats out on a crimson stream. The unfortunate is always suspended in a public place, where magistrates watch so that no one may release him. Friends of the condemned flock around the man of authority, bargaining for the man's life; if they can pay the price extorted by him the man is taken down and set free; if not, he merely hangs until the muscles give out and he drops to death. They also have a way of burying the whole of criminals except their heads. The eyelids are fastened back so that they cannot close them, and so facing the sun they are left to die. Sticking bamboo splints under the finger nails and then setting fire to them is another happy way of punishing wrongdoers.

I had no idea what I was to see when we mounted the filthy stone steps leading to the Temple of Horrors. I concluded it most be an exhibition of human monstrosities. The steps were filled with dirty Mongolians of all sizes, ages, shapes and afflictions. When they heard our steps, those who could see and walk, rushed up to us, crying for alms, and those who were blind and powerless raised their voices the louder because they could not move. Inside, a filthy stone court was crowded with a mass of humanity. There were lepers, peddlers, monstrosities, fortune tellers, gamblers, quacks, dentists with strings of horrid teeth, and even pastry cooks! It is said the Chinese worship here occasionally and consult idols. In little, dirty cells were dirty figures, representing the punishment of the Buddhists' hell. They were being whipped, ground to death, boiled in oil, beheaded, put under red hot bells, being sawed in twain, and undergoing similar agreeable things.

Canton is noted for its many curious and interesting temples. There are over eight hundred temples in the city. The most interesting one I saw during my flying trip was the Temple of the Five Hundred Gods. While there the guide asked me if I was superstitious, and upon my answering in the affirmative, he said he would show me how to try my luck. Placing some joss sticks in a copper jar before the luck-god, he took from the table two pieces of wood, worn smooth and dirty from frequent use, which, placed together, were not unlike a pear in shape. With this wood— he called it the "luck pigeon"— held with the flat sides together, he made circling motions over the smouldering joss sticks, once, twice, thrice, and dropped the luck pigeon to the floor. He explained if one side of the luck pigeon turned up and the other turned down it meant good luck, while if they both fell in the same position it meant bad luck. When he dropped it they both turned the one way, and he knew he would have bad luck.

I took the luck pigeon then, and I was so superstitious that my arm trembled and my heart beat in little palpitating jumps as I made the motions over the burning joss sticks. I dropped the wood to the floor, and one piece turned one way and one the other, and I was perfectly happy. I knew I was going to have good luck.

I saw the Examination Hall, where there are accommodations for the simultaneous examination of 11,616 celestial students, all male. We went to the entrance-gate through a dirty park-like space where a few stunted trees grew feebly and a number of thin, black pigs rooted energetically. Dirty children in large numbers followed us, demanding alms in boisterous tones, and a few women who, by the aid of canes, were hobbling about on their cramped small feet, stopped to look after us with grins of curiosity and amusement. The open space is the principal entrance, then we go through a small gate called the gate of Equity, and later still another called the Dragon gate, which leads into the great avenue. A most strange and curious sight this avenue gives. An open space with a tower on the end known as the watch tower, has a god of literature in the second story. On each side of the open green space are rows of whitewashed buildings, not unlike railway cattle yards in appearance. In these ranges of cells, cells that measure 5-1/2 by 3-2/3 feet, 11,616 pig-tailed students undergo their written examination. On the sides facing the avenue are Chinese inscriptions showing what study is examined in that range. In each cell is a board to sit on, and one a little higher for a desk. This roughly improvised desk must be slid out to allow the student to enter or depart unless he crawls under or jumps over. The same texts are given to all at daylight, and very often when essays are not finished at night the students are kept over night in their cells. The Hall is about 1,380 feet long by 650 feet wide, and is really a strangely interesting place well worth a visit. It is said the examinations are very severe, and from the large number of candidates examined, sometimes only one hundred and fifty will be passed. The place in which the essays are examined is called the Hall of Auspicious Stars, and the Chinese inscription over the avenue translated reads, "The opening heavens circulate literature."

I had a great curiosity to see the leper village, which is commonly supposed to contain hundreds of Chinese lepers. The village consists of numbers of bamboo huts, and the lepers present a sight appalling in its squalor and filth. Ah Cum told us to smoke cigarettes while in the village so that the frightful odors would be less perceptible. He set the example by lighting one, and we all followed his lead. The lepers were simply ghastly in their misery. There are men, women and children of all ages and conditions. The few filthy rags with which they endeavored to hide their nakedness presented no shape of any garment or any color, so dirty and ragged were they. On the ground floors of the bamboo huts were little else than a few old rags, dried grass and things of that kind. Furniture there was none. It is useless to attempt a description of the loathsome appearance of the lepers. Many were featureless, some were blind, some had lost fingers, others a foot, some a leg, but all were equally dirty, disgusting and miserable. Those able to work cultivate a really prosperous-looking garden, which is near their village. Ah Cum assured me they sold their vegetables in the city market! I felt glad to know we had brought our luncheon from the ship. Those lepers able to walk spend the day in Canton begging, but are always compelled to sleep in their village, still I could not help wondering what was the benefit of a leper village if the lepers are allowed to mingle with the other people. On my return to the city I met several lepers begging in the market. The sight of them among the food was enough to make me vow never to eat anything in Canton. The lepers are also permitted to marry, and a surprising number of diseased children are brought into a cursed and unhappy existence.

As we left the leper city I was conscious of an inward feeling of emptiness. It was Christmas day, and I thought with regret of dinner at home, although one of the men in the party said it was about midnight in New York. The guide said there was a building near by which he wanted to show us and then we would eat our luncheon. Once within a high wall we came upon a pretty scene. There was a mournful sheet of water undisturbed by a breath of wind. In the background the branches of low, overhanging trees kissed the still water just where stood some long-legged storks, made so familiar to us by pictures on Chinese fans.

Ah Cum led us to a room which was shut off from the court by a large carved gate. Inside were hard wood chairs and tables. While eating I heard chanting to the weird, plaintive sound of a tom-tom and a shrill pipe. When I had less appetite and more curiosity, I asked Ah Cum where we were, and he replied: "in the Temple of the Dead."

And in the Temple of the Dead I was eating my Christmas luncheon. But that did not interfere with the luncheon. Before we had finished a number of Chinaman crowded around the gate and looked curiously at me. They held up several children, well clad, cleanly children, to see me. Thinking to be agreeable, I went forward to shake hands with them, but they kicked and screamed, and getting down, rushed back in great fright, which amused us intensely. Their companions succeeded after awhile in quieting them and they were persuaded to take my hand. The ice once broken, they became so interested in me, my gloves, my bracelets and my dress, that I soon regretted my friendliness in the outset.

It is customary at the death of a person to build a bonfire after night, and cast into the fire household articles, such as money boxes, ladies' dressing cases, etc., composed of gilt paper, the priests meanwhile playing upon shrill pipes. They claim the devil which inhabits all bodies leaves the body to save the property of the dead, and once they play him out he can never re-enter, so souls are saved.

I climbed high and dirty stone steps to the water-clock, which, they say, is over five hundred years old, and has never run down or been repaired. In little niches in the stone walls were small gods, before them the smouldering joss sticks. The water-clock consists of four copper jars, about the size of wooden pails, placed on steps, one above the other. Each one has a spout from which comes a steady drop-drop. In the last and bottom jar is an indicator, very much like a foot rule, which rises with the water, showing the hour. On a blackboard hanging outside, they mark the time for the benefit of the town people. The upper jar is filled once every twenty-fear hours, and that is all the attention the clock requires.

On our return to the Powan I found some beautiful presents from Consul Seymour and the cards of a number of Europeans who had called to see me. Suffering from a sick-headache, I went to my cabin and shortly we were on our way to Hong Kong, my visit to Canton on Christmas day being of the past.

CHAPTER XIV.
TO THE LAND OF THE MIKADO.

SHORTLY after my return to Hong Kong I sailed for Japan on the Oceanic. A number of friends, who had contributed so much towards my pleasure and comfort during my stay in British China, came to the ship to say farewell, and most regretfully did I take leave of them. Captain Smith took us into his cabin, where we all touched glasses and wished one another success, happiness and the other good things of this earth. The last moment having come, the final good-bye being said, we parted, and I was started on my way to the land of the Mikado.

The Oceanic, on which I traveled from Hong Kong to San Francisco, has quite a history. When it was designed and launched twenty years ago by Mr. Harland, of Belfast, it startled the shipping world. The designer was the first to introduce improvements for the comfort of passengers, such as the saloon amidships, avoiding the noise of the engines and especially the racing of the screw in rough weather. Before that time ships were gloomy and somber in appearance and constructed without a thought of the happiness of passengers. Mr. Harland, in the Oceanic, was the first to provide a promenade deck and to give the saloon and staterooms a light and cheerful appearance. In fact, the Oceanic was such a new departure that it aroused the jealousy of other ship companies, and was actually condemned by them as unseaworthy. It is said that so great was the outcry against the ship that sailors and firemen were given extra prices to induce them to make the first trip.

Instead of being the predicted failure, the Oceanic proved a great success. She became the greyhound of the Atlantic, afterwards being transferred to the Pacific in 1875. She is the favorite ship of the O. & O. line, making her voyages with speed and regularity. She retains a look of positive newness and seems to grow younger with years. In November, 1889, she made the fastest trip on record between Yokohama and San Francisco. No expense is spared to make this ship comfortable for the passengers. The catering would be hard to excel by even a first-class hotel. Passengers are accorded every liberty, and the officers do their utmost to make their guests feel at home, so that in the Orient the Oceanic is the favorite ship, and people wait for months so as to travel on her.

When I first went to the ship the monkey had been transferred from the Oriental. Meeting the stewardess I asked how the monkey was, to which she replied dryly:

"We have met."

She had her arm bandaged from the wrist to the shoulder!

"What did you do?" I asked in consternation.

"I did nothing but scream; the monkey did the rest!" she replied.

I spent New Year's eve between Hong Kong and Yokohama. The day had been so warm that we wore no wraps. In the forepart of the evening the passengers sat together in Social Hall talking, telling stories and laughing at them. The captain owned an organette which he brought into the hall, and he and the doctor took turns at grinding out the music. Later in the evening we went to the dining-hall where the purser had punch and champagne and oysters for us, a rare treat which he had prepared in America just for this occasion.

What children we all become on board a ship! After oysters we were up to all sorts of childish tricks. As we sat around the table the doctor gave us each a word to say, such as Ish! Ash! Osh! Then when we were sure of our word, it coming in rotation around the circle, he told us to shout the words in unison when he gave the signal. We did, and it made one great big sneeze— the most gigantic and absurd sneeze I ever heard in my life. Afterwards a jolly man from Yokohama, whose wife was equally jolly and lively-spirited, taught us a song consisting of one line to a melody quite simple and catching.

"Sweetly sings the donkey when he goes to grass, Sweetly sings the donkey when he goes to grass, Ec-ho! Ec-ho! Ec-ho!"

When eight bells rang we rose and sang Auld Lang Syne with glasses in hand, and on the last echo of the good old song toasted the death of the old year and the birth of the new. We shook hands around, each wishing the other a happy New Year. 1889 was ended, and 1890 with its pleasures and pains began. Shortly after, the women passengers retired. I went to sleep lulled by the sounds of familiar negro melodies sung by the men in the smoking-room beneath my cabin.

CHAPTER XV.
ONE HUNDRED AND TWENTY HOURS IN JAPAN.

AFTER seeing Hong Kong with its wharfs crowded with dirty boats manned by still dirtier people, and its streets packed with a filthy crowd, Yokohama has a cleaned-up Sunday appearance. Travelers are taken from the ships, which anchor some distance out in the bay, to the land in small steam launches. The first-class hotels in the different ports have their individual launches, but like American hotel omnibuses, while being run by the hotel to assist in procuring patrons, the traveler pays for them just the same.

An import as well as an export duty is charged in Japan, but we passed the custom inspectors unmolested. I found the Japanese jinricksha men a gratifying improvement upon those I seen from Ceylon to China. They presented no sight of filthy rags, nor naked bodies, nor smell of grease. Clad in neat navy-blue garments, their little pudgy legs encased in unwrinkled tights, the upper half of their bodies in short jackets with wide flowing sleeves; their clean, good-natured faces, peeping from beneath comical mushroom-shaped hats; their blue-black, wiry locks cropped just above the nape of the neck, they offered a striking contrast to the jinricksha men of other countries. Their crests were embroidered upon the back and sleeves of their top garment as are the crests of every man, woman and child in Japan.

Rain the night previous had left the streets muddy and the air cool and crisp, but the sun creeping through the mistiness of early morning, fell upon us with most gratifying warmth. Wrapping our knees with rugs the 'ricksha men started off in a lively trot to the Pacific Mail and O. and O. Companies' office, where I met discourteous people for the first time since I left the P. & O. "Victoria." And these were Americans, too. The most generous excuse that can be offered for them is that they have held their positions so long that they feel they are masters, instead of a steamship company's servants. A man going into the office to buy a ticket to America, was answered in the following manner by one of the head men:

"You'll have to come back later if you want a ticket. I'm going to lunch now."

I stayed at the Grand Hotel while in Japan. It is a large building, with long verandas, wide halls and airy rooms, commanding an exquisite view of the lake in front. Barring an enormous and monotonous collection of rats, the Grand would be considered a good hotel even in America. The food is splendid and the service excellent. The "Japs," noiseless, swift, anxious to please, stand at the head of all the servants I encountered from New York to New York; and then they look so neat in their blue tights and white linen jackets.

I always have an inclination to laugh when I look at the Japanese men in their native dress. Their legs are small and their trousers are skin tight. The upper garment, with its great wide sleeves, is as loose as the lower is tight. When they finish their "get up" by placing their dish-pan shaped hat upon their heads, the wonder grows how such small legs can carry it all! Stick two straws in one end of a potato, a mushroom in the other, set it up on the straws and you have a Japanese in outline. Talk about French heels! The Japanese sandal is a small board elevated on two pieces of thin wood fully five inches in height. They make the people look exactly as if they were on stilts. These queer shoes are fastened to the foot by a single strap running between toes number one and two, the wearer when walking necessarily maintaining a sliding instead of an up and down movement, in order to keep the shoe on.

On a cold day one would imagine the Japanese were a nation of armless people. They fold their arms up in their long, loose sleeves. A Japanese woman's sleeves are to her what a boy's pockets are to him. Her cards, money, combs, hair pins, ornaments and rice paper are carried in her sleeves. Her rice paper is her handkerchief, and she notes with horror and disgust that after using we return our handkerchiefs to our pockets. I think the Japanese women carry everything in their sleeves, even their hearts. Not that they are fickle— none are more true, more devoted, more loyal, more constant, than Japanese women—but they are so guileless and artless that almost any one, if opportunity offers, can pick at their trusting hearts.

If I loved and married, I would say to my mate: "Come, I know where Eden is," and like Edwin Arnold, desert the land of my birth for Japan, the land of love— beauty— poetry— cleanliness. I somehow always connected Japan and its people with China and its people, believing the one no improvement on the other. I could not have made a greater mistake. Japan is beautiful. Its women are charmingly sweet. I know little about the men except that they do not go far as we judge manly beauty, being undersized, dark, and far from prepossessing. They have the reputation of being extremely clever, so I do not speak of them as a whole, only of those I came in contact with. I saw one, a giant in frame, a god in features; but he was a public wrestler.

The Japanese are the direct opposite to the Chinese. The Japanese are the cleanliest people on earth, the Chinese are the filthiest; the Japanese are always happy and cheerful, the Chinese are always grumpy and morose; the Japanese are the most graceful of people, the Chinese the most awkward; the Japanese have few vices, the Chinese have all the vices in the world; in short, the Japanese are the most delightful of people, the Chinese the most disagreeable.

The majority of the Europeans live on the bluff in low white bungalows, with great rooms and breezy verandas, built in the hearts of Oriental gardens, where one can have an unsurpassed view of the Mississippi bay, or can play tennis or cricket, or loll in hammocks, guarded from public gaze by luxurious green hedges. The Japanese homes form a great contrast to the bungalows. They are daintily small, like play houses indeed, built of a thin shingle-like board, fine in texture. Chimneys and fireplaces are unknown. The first wall is set back, allowing the upper floor and side walls to extend over the lower flooring, making it a portico built in instead of on the house. Light window frames, with their minute openings covered with fine rice paper instead of glass, are the doors and windows in one. They do not swing open and shut as do our doors, nor do they move up and down like our windows, but slide like rolling doors. They form the partitions of the houses inside and can be removed at any time, throwing the floor into one room.

They have two very pretty customs in Japan. The one is decorating their houses in honor of the new year, and the other celebrating the blossoming of the cherry trees. Bamboo saplings covered with light airy foliage and pinioned so as to incline towards the middle of the street, where meeting they form an arch, make very effective decorations. Rice trimmings mixed with sea-weed, orange, lobster and ferns are hung over every door to insure a plentiful year, while as sentinels on either side are large tubs, in which are three thick bamboo stalks, with small evergreen trees for background.

In the cool of the evening we went to a house that had been specially engaged to see the dancing, or *geisha*, girls. At the door we saw all the wooden shoes of the household, and we were asked to take off our shoes before entering, a proceeding rather disliked by some of the party, who refused absolutely to do as requested. We effected a compromise, however, by putting cloth slippers over our shoes. The second floor had been converted into one room, with nothing in it except the matting covering the floor and a Japanese screen here and there. We sat upon the floor, for chairs there are none in Japan, but the exquisite matting is padded until it is as soft as velvet. It was laughable to see us trying to sit down, and yet more so to see us endeavor to find a posture of ease for our limbs. We were about as graceful as an elephant dancing. A smiling woman in a black kimono set several round and square charcoal boxes containing burning charcoal before us. These are the only Japanese stove. Afterwards she brought a tray containing a number of long-stemmed pipes— Japanese women smoke constantly— a pot of tea and several small cups.

Impatiently I awaited the *geisha* girls. In the tiny maidens glided at last, clad in exquisite trailing, angel-sleeved kimonos. The girls bow gracefully, bending down until their heads touch their knees, then kneeling before us murmur gently a greeting which sounds like "Koinbanwa!" drawing in their breath with a long, hissing suction, which is a token of great honor. The musicians sat down on the floor and began an alarming din upon *samisens*, drums and gongs, singing meanwhile through their pretty noses. If the noses were not so pretty I am sure the music would be unbearable to one who has ever heard a chest note. The *geisha* girls stand posed with open fan in hand above their heads, ready to begin the dance. They are very short with the slenderest of slender waists. Their soft and tender eyes are made blacker by painted lashes and brows; their midnight hair, stiffened with a gummy wash, is most wonderfully dressed in large coils and ornamented with gold and silver flowers and gilt paper pom-pons. The younger the girl the more gay is her hair. Their kimonos, of the most exquisite material, trail all around them, and are loosely held together at the waist with an obi-sash; their long flowing sleeves fall back, showing their dimpled arms and baby hands. Upon their tiny feet they wear cunning white linen socks cut with a place for the great toe. When they go out they wear wooden sandals. The Japanese are the only women I ever saw who could rouge and powder and be not repulsive, but the more charming because of it. They powder their faces and have a way of reddening their under lip just at the tip that gives them a most tempting look. The lips look like two luxurious cherries. The musicians begin a long chanting strain, and these bits of beauty begin the dance. With a grace, simply enchanting, they twirl their little fans, sway their dainty bodies in a hundred different poses, each one more intoxicating than the other, all the while looking so childish and shy, with an innocent smile lurking about their lips, dimpling their soft cheeks, and their black eyes twinkling with the pleasure of the dance. After the dance the *geisha* girls made friends with me, examining, with surprised delight, my dress, my bracelets, my rings, my boots— to them the most wonderful and extraordinary things,— my hair, my gloves, indeed they missed very little, and they approved of all. They said I was very sweet, and urged me to come again, and in honor of the custom of my land— the Japanese never kiss— they pressed their soft, pouting lips to mine in parting.

Japanese women know nothing whatever of bonnets, and may they never! On rainy days they tie white scarfs over their wonderful hair-dressing, but at other times they waddle bareheaded, with fan and umbrella, along the streets on their wooden clogs. They have absolutely no furniture. Their bed is a piece of matting, their pillows, narrow blocks of wood, probably six inches in length, two wide and six high. They rest the back of the neck on the velvet covered top, so their wonderful hair remains dressed for weeks at a time. Their tea and pipe always stand beside them, so they can partake of their comforts the last thing before sleep and the first thing after.

A Japanese reporter from Tokyo came to interview me, his newspaper having translated and published the story of my visit to Jules Verne. Carefully he read the questions which he wished to ask me. They were written at intervals on long rolls of foolscap, the space to be filled in as I answered. I thought it ridiculous until I returned and became an interviewee. Then I concluded it would be humane for us to adopt the Japanese system of interviewing.

I went to Kamakura to see the great bronze god, the image of Buddha, familiarly called Diabutsu. It stands in a verdant valley at the foot of two mountains. It was built in 1250 by Ono Goroyemon, a famous bronze caster, and is fifty feet in height; it is sitting Japanese style, ninety-eight feet being its waist circumference; the face is eight feet long, the eye is four feet, the ear six feet six and one-half inches, the nose three feet eight and one-half inches, the mouth is three feet two and one-half inches, the diameter of the lap is thirty-six feet, and the circumference of the thumb is over three feet. I had my photograph taken sitting on its thumb with two friends, one of whom offered $50,000 for the god. Years ago at the feast of the god sacrifices were made to Diabutsu. Quite frequently the hollow interior would be heated to a white heat, and hundreds of victims were cast into the seething furnace in honor of the god. It is different now, sacrifices being not the custom, and the hollow interior is harmlessly fitted up with tiny altars and a ladder stairway by which visitors can climb up into Diabutsu's eye, and from that height view the surrounding lovely country. We also visited a very pretty temple near by, saw a famous fan tree and a lotus-pond, and spent some time at a most delightful tea-house, where two little "Jap" girls served us with tea and sweets. I also spent one day at Tokio, where I saw the Mikado's Japanese and European castles, which are enclosed by a fifty foot stone wall and three wide moats. The people in Tokio are trying to ape the style of the Europeans. I saw several men in native costume riding bicycles. Their roads are superb. There is a street car line in Tokio, a novelty in the East, and carriages of all descriptions. The European clothing sent to Japan is at least ready-made, if not second hand. One woman I saw was considered very stylish. The bodice of a European dress she wore had been cut to fit a slender, tapering waist. The Japanese never saw a corset and their waists are enormous. The woman was able to fasten one button at the neck, and from that point the bodice was permitted to spread. She was considered very swell. At dinner one night I saw a "Jap" woman in a low cut evening dress, with nothing but white socks on her feet.

It would fill a large book if I attempted to describe all I saw during my stay in Japan. Going to the great Shiba temple, I saw a forest of superb trees. At the carved gate leading to the temple were hundreds of stone and bronze lanterns, which alone were worth a fortune. On either side of the gate were gigantic carved images of ferocious aspect. They were covered with wads of chewed paper. When I remarked that the school children must make very free with the images, a gentleman explained that the Japanese believed if they chewed paper and threw it at these gods and it stuck their prayers would be answered, if not, their prayers would pass unheeded. A great many prayers must have been answered. At another gate I saw the most disreputable looking god. It had no nose. The Japanese believe if they have a pain or ache and they rub their hands over the face of that god, and then where the pain is located, they will straightway be cured. I can't say whether it cured them or not, but I know they rubbed away the nose of the god.

The Japanese are very progressive people. They cling to their religion and their modes of life, which in many ways are superior to ours, but they readily adopt any trade or habit that is an improvement upon their own. Finding the European male attire more serviceable than their native dress for some trades they promptly adopted it. The women tested the European dress, and finding it barbarously uncomfortable and inartistic went back to their exquisite kimonos, retaining the use of European underwear, which they found more healthful and comfortable than the utter absence of it, to which they had been accustomed. The best proof of the comfort of kimonos lies in the fact that the European residents have adopted them entirely for indoor wear. Only their long subjection to fashion prevents their wearing them in public. Japanese patriotism should serve as a model for us careless Americans. No foreigner can go to Japan and monopolize a trade. It is true that a little while ago they were totally ignorant of modern conveniences. They knew nothing of railroads, or street cars, or engines, or electric lighting. They were too clever though to waste their wits in efforts to rediscover inventions known to other nations, but they had to have them. Straightway they sent to other countries for men who understood the secret of such things, and at fabulous prices and under contracts of three, five and occasionally ten years duration, brought them to their land. They were set to work, the work they had been hired to do, and with them toiled steadily and watchfully the cleverest of Japanese. When the contract is up it is no longer necessary to fill the coffers of a foreigner. The employé was released, and their own man, fully qualified for the work, stepped into the position. And so in this way they command all business in their country.

Kimonos are made in three parts, each part an inch or so longer than the other. I saw a kimono a Japanese woman bought for the holidays. It was a suit, gray silk crepe, with pink peach blossoms dotting it here and there. The whole was lined with the softest pink silk, and the hem, which trails, was thickly padded with a delicate perfume sachet. The underclothing was of the flimsiest white silk. The whole thing cost sixty dollars, a dollar and a half of which paid for the making. Japanese clothing is sewed with what we call a basting stitch, but it is as durable as it could be if sewed with the smallest of stitches. Japanese women have mirrors in which they view their numerous charms. Their mirrors are round, highly polished steel plates, and they know nothing whatever of glass mirrors. All the women carry silk card cases in their long sleeves, in which are their own diminutive cards.

English is taught in the Japan schools and so is gracefulness. The girls are taught graceful movements, how to receive, entertain and part with visitors, how to serve tea and sweets gracefully, and the proper and graceful way to use chopsticks. It is a pretty sight to see a lovely woman use chopsticks. At a tea-house or at an ordinary dinner a long paper laid at one's place contains a pair of chopsticks, probably twelve inches in length, but no thicker than the thinner size of lead pencils. The sticks are usually whittled in one piece and split only half apart to prove that they have never been used. Every one breaks the sticks apart before eating, and after the meal they are destroyed.

An American resident of Japan told me of his going to see a cremation. The Japanese graveyard is a strange affair, with headstones set close together, leaving the space for the graves less than the size of a baby's grave in America. As soon as the breath has left a body it is undressed and doubled up, head to feet, and is made to go in a very small bamboo box built in imitation of a Japanese house. This house may cost a great deal of money. It is carried along the streets on two poles to the place where it is to be cremated where it is given in charge of the cremator, and the friends go back to their homes until the following day, when they return for the ashes, which are generally placed in an urn and buried. The American, of whom I spoke, made arrangements with a cremator, and, accompanied by a friend, walked to the place in the country and waited out of sight until the mourners had vanished before they dared to draw near enough to see the cremation. They had walked quite a distance, dinnerless, and said, naively, that the odor was like that of veal, and it made him ravenously hungry.

A small hole about three feet long is made in the earth and in it the fire is built. When it was the proper heat the box was set over it, and in an instant it was consumed. The body released from its doubled position straightened out. The lower half being over the fire was soon cremated, excepting the feet and knee joints. The man in charge carefully pulled the upper part of the body over the fire, and with the same large fork put the half-consumed feet and knee-joints under the arms. In less than an hour all that remained of the body was a few ashes in the bottom of the pit. While the cremator was explaining it all to the gentleman he repeatedly filled his little pipe and lit it with the fire from the burning body. At his urgent request the gentleman consented to take tea with him when his task was done. They entered his neat little home while he jumped into a boiling bath in the open garden, from which he emerged later as red as a lobster. Meanwhile his charming and pretty daughters were dispensing the hospitalities of their home to their guests, and the father, desirous of enjoying their society, came and stood in the doorway, talking to them and watching them eat while he wiped his naked body with a towel!

The prettiest sight in Japan, I think, is the native streets in the afternoons. Men, women and children turn out to play shuttle-cock and fly kites. Can you imagine what an enchanting sight it is to see pretty women with cherry lips, black bright eyes, ornamented, glistening hair, exquisitely graceful gowns, tidy white-stockinged feet thrust into wooden sandals, dimpled cheeks, dimpled arms, dimpled baby hands, lovely, innocent, artless, happy, playing shuttlecock in the streets of Yokohama?

Japanese children are unlike any other children I ever saw at play. They always look happy and never seem to quarrel or cry. Little Japanese girls, elevated on wooden sandals and with babies almost as large as themselves tied on their backs, play shuttle-cock with an abandon that is terrifying until one grows confident of the fact that they move with as much agility as they could if their little backs were free from nursemaid burdens. Japanese babies are such comical little fellows. They wear such wonderfully padded clothing that they are as shapeless as a feather pillow. Others may think, as I did, that the funny little shaven spots on their heads was a queer style of ornamentation, but it is not. I am assured the spots are shaven to keep their baby heads cool.

The Japanese are not only pretty and artistic but most obliging. A friend of mine who guided us in Japan had a Kodak, and whenever we came upon an interesting group he was always taking snap shots. No one objected, and especially were the children pleasant about being photographed. When he placed them in position, or asked them to stand as they were, they would pose like little drum-majors until he gave them permission to move.

The only regret of my trip, and one I can never cease to deplore, was that in my hasty departure I forgot to take a Kodak. On every ship and at every port I met others— and envied them— with Kodaks. They could photograph everything that pleased them; the light in those lands is excellent, and many were the pleasant mementos of their acquaintances and themselves they carried home on their plates. I met a German who was spending two years going around the world and he carried two Kodaks, a large and a small size, and his collection of photographs was the most interesting I ever saw. At the different ports he had professional photographers develop his plates.

The Japanese thoughtfully reserve a trade for their blind. They are all taught massage bathing, and none but the blind are allowed to follow this calling. These people go through the streets uttering to a plaintive melody these words:

"I'll give you a bath from head to toe for two cents."

At Uyeno park, where they point out a tree planted by General Grant when on his tour around the world, I saw a most amusing monkey which belonged to the very interesting menagerie. It was very large and had a scarlet face and gray fur. It was chained to the fence, and when one of the young men in our party went up and talked to him the monkey looked very sagacious and wise. In the little crowd that gathered around, quite out of the monkey's reach, was a young Jap, who, in a spirit of mischief, tossed a pebble at the red-faced mystery, who turned with a grieved and inquiring air to my friend.

"Go for him," my friend responded, sympathetically, to the look, and the monkey turned and with its utmost strength endeavored to free itself so it could obey the bidding. The Jap made his escape and the monkey quieted down, looking expressively at the place where the Jap had stood and then at my friend for approval, which he obtained. The keeper gave the monkey its dinner, which consisted of two large boiled sweet potatoes. My friend broke one in two and the monkey greedily ate the inside, placing the remainder with the other potato on the fence between his feet. Suddenly he looked up, and as quick as a flash he flung, with his entire force, which was something terrific, the remaining potato at the head of some one in the crowd. There was some loud screaming and a scattering, but the potato missing all heads, went crashing with such force against a board fence that every particle of it remained sticking there in one shapeless splotch. The Jap who had tossed the pebble at the monkey, and so earned his enmity, quietly shrunk away with a whitened face. He had returned unnoticed by all except the monkey, who tried to revenge himself with the potato. I admired the monkey's cleverness so much that I would have tried to buy him if I had not already owned one.

In Yokohama, I went to Hundred Steps, at the top of which lives a Japanese belle, Oyuchisan, who is the theme for artist and poet, and the admiration of tourists. One of the pleasant events of my stay was the luncheon given for me on the Omaha, the American war vessel lying at Yokohama. I took several drives, enjoying the novelty of having a Japanese running by the horses' heads all the while. I ate rice and eel. I visited the curio shops, one of which is built in imitation of a Japanese house, and was charmed with the exquisite art I saw there; in short, I found nothing but what delighted the finer senses while in Japan.

CHAPTER XVI.
ACROSS THE PACIFIC.

IT was a bright sunny morning when I left Yokohama. A number of new friends in launches escorted me to the Oceanic, and when we hoisted anchor the steam launches blew loud blasts upon their whistles in farewell to me, and the band upon the Omaha played "Home, Sweet Home," "Hail Columbia," and "The Girl I Left Behind Me," in my honor; and I waved my handkerchief so long after they were out of sight that my arms were sore for days. My feverish eagerness to be off again on my race around the world was strongly mingled with regret at leaving such charming friends and such a lovely land.

Everything promised well for a pleasant and rapid voyage. Anticipating this, Chief-engineer Allen caused to be written over the engines and throughout the engine room, this date and couplet:

> "For Nellie Bly,
> We'll win or die.
> January 20, 1890."

It was their motto and was all very sweet to me. The runs were marvelous until the third day out, and then a storm came upon us. They tried to cheer me, saying it would only last that day, but the next day found it worse, and it continued, never abating a moment; head winds, head sea, wild rolling, frightful pitching, until I fretfully waited for noon when I would slip off to the dining-room to see the run, hoping that it would have gained a few miles on the day before, and always being disappointed. And they were all so good to me! Bless them for it! If possible, they suffered more over the prospect of my failure than I did.

"If I fail, I will never return to New York," I would say despondently; "I would rather go in dead and successful than alive and behind time."

"Don't talk that way, child," Chief Allen would plead, "I would do anything for you in my power. I have worked the engines as they never were worked before; I have sworn at this storm until I have no words left; I have even prayed— I haven't prayed before for years— but I prayed that this storm may pass over and that we may get you in on time."

"I know that I am not a sinner," I laughed hysterically. "Day and night my plea has been, 'Be merciful to me a sinner,' and as the mercy has not been forthcoming, the natural conclusion is that I'm not a sinner. It's hopeless, it's hopeless!"

"Don't think so," the purser would beg; "don't be so disheartened; why, child, if by jumping overboard I could bring you happiness and success, I should do so in a moment."

"Never mind, little girl, you're all right," the jolly, happy-hearted captain would laugh. "I've bet every cent I have in the bank that you'll get in before you are due. Just take my word for it, you'll be in New York at least three days ahead of time."

"Why do you try to cheat me? You know we are way behind time now," I urged, longing to be still farther cheated into fresh hope, to which the doctor would say, dryly:

"Look here, Nellie Bly, if you don't stop talking so I'll make you take some pills for your liver."

"You mean wretch, you know I can't help being blue. It's head sea, and head winds, and low runs— not liver!"

And then I would laugh, and so would they; and Mr. Allen, who had been pleading for me to "smile just once, give them but one glimpse of my old, jolly smile," would go away content. This is but a repetition of the way in which I was coaxed out of my unhappiness every day, by those great-hearted, strong, tender men.

At last a rumor became current that there was a Jonah[1] on board the ship. It was thought over and talked over and, much to my dismay, I was told that the sailors said monkeys were Jonahs. Monkeys brought

---

1 A person that brings bad luck to ships, based on the Biblical prophet Jonah

bad weather to ships, and as long as the monkey was on board we would have storms. Some one asked if I would consent to the monkey being thrown overboard. A little struggle between superstition and a feeling of justice for the monkey followed. Chief Allen, when I spoke to him on the subject, told me not to do it. He said the monkey had just gotten outside of a hundred weight of cement, and had washed it down with a quart of lamp oil, and he, for one, did not want to interfere with the monkey's happiness and digestion! Just then some one told me that ministers were Jonahs; they always brought bad weather to ships. We had two ministers on board! So I said quietly, if the ministers were thrown overboard I'd say nothing about the monkey. Thus the monkey's life was saved.

Mr. Allen had a boy, Walter, who was very clever at tricks. One day Walter said he would show that he could lift a bottle merely by placing his open hand to the side of the bottle. He put everybody out of the cabin, as he said if they remained in it broke the influence. They watched intently through the open door as he rolled up his sleeve and rubbed his arm downward, quite vigorously, as if trying to get all the blood in his hand. Catching the wrist with the other hand, as if to hold all the blood there, he placed his open hand to the side of [the] bottle and, much to the amazement of his audience, the bottle went up with his hand. When urged to tell how to do the wonderful trick, he said:

"It's all very easy; all you do is to rub your arm, that's just for show; then you lay hold of your wrist just as if you wanted to keep all the blood in your hand; you keep one finger free— no one notices that— and you take the neck of the bottle between the hand and the finger, and the bottle goes up with the hand. See?"

One evening, when the ship was rolling frightfully, everybody was gathered in the dining-hall; an Englishman urged Walter to do some tricks, but Walter did not want to be bothered then, so he said: "Yes, sir; in a moment, sir," and went on putting the things upon the table. He had put down the mustard pot, the salt cellar and various things, and was wiping a plate. As he went to put the plate down the ship gave a great roll, the plate knocked against the mustard pot and the mustard flew all over the Englishman, much to the horror of the others. Sitting up stiffly, the mustard dotting him from head to knees, he said sternly:

"Walter! What is this?"

"That, sir, is the first trick," Walter replied softly, and he glided silently and swiftly off to the regions of the cook.

But Walter was caught one day. A sailor told him that he could hide an egg on him so no one would be able to find it. Walter had his doubts, but he willingly gave the sailor a test. The egg was hidden and a man called in to find it. He searched Walter all over without once coming upon the egg. The sailor suggested another trial to which Walter, now an interested and firm believer in the sailor's ability, gladly consented. The sailor opened Walter's shirt and placed the egg next to the skin in the region of his heart, carefully buttoning the shirt afterwards. The man was called in, he went up to Walter and hit him a resounding smack where Sullivan hit Kilrain. He found the egg and so did Walter!

Japanese "boys" serve in the dining—hall on the Oceanic, but the sailors are Chinese. They chant in a musical manner when hoisting sails. It sounds as if they say "Ah— Oh— Eh— Oh! Ah— Oh— Eh— Ah— Oh!" The "boys" shake the tablecloths into a plate. They put a plate in the tablecloth which two of them shake once or twice and then slide the plate to the floor. The plate will be seen to have gathered all the crumbs.

One Chinaman and one Japanese traveled first-class coming over. The Chinaman was confined to his cabin with sea-sickness all the time, so we saw very little of him. The Japanese wore European dress and endeavored to ape the manners of the Europeans. Evidently he thought it the custom to use tooth-picks. It is— with some people. After every meal he used a tooth-pick so that the whole table might see, as if wishing to show he was civilized! Then after a great amount of gorging he always placed the tooth-pick pen-like behind his ear where it stayed until the next meal.

But even with low runs our trip was bound to come to an end. One night it was announced that the next day we would be in San Francisco. I felt a feverish excitement, and many were the speculations as to whether there would be a snow blockade to hinder my trip across the Continent. A hopefulness that had not known me for many days came back, when in rushed the purser, his face a snow-white, crying:

"My God, the bill of health was left behind in Yokohama."

"Well— well— what does that mean?" I demanded, fearing some misfortune, I knew not what.

"It means," he said, dropping nerveless into a chair, "that no one will be permitted to land until the next ship arrives from Japan. That will be two weeks."

The thought of being held two weeks in sight of San Francisco, in sight of New York almost, and the goal for which I had been striving and powerless to move, was maddening.

"I would cut my throat, for I could not live and endure it," I said quietly, and that spurred him on to make another search, which resulted in finding the report safely lodged in the doctor's desk.

Later came a scare about a small-pox case on board, but it proved to be only a rumor, and early in the morning the revenue officers came aboard bringing the newspapers. I read of the impassable snow blockade which for a week had put a stop to all railroad traffic, and my despair knew no bounds. While the Oceanic was waiting for the quarantine doctor, some men came out on a tug to take me ashore. There was no time for farewells. The monkey was taken on the tug with me, and my baggage, which had increased by gifts from friends, was thrown after me. Just as the tug steamed off the quarantine doctor called to me that he had forgotten to examine my tongue, and I could not land until he did. I stuck it out, he called out "all right;" the others laugh, I wave farewell, and in another moment I was parted from my good friends on the Oceanic.

CHAPTER XVII.
ACROSS THE CONTINENT.

I ONLY remember my trip across the continent as one maze of happy greetings, happy wishes, congratulating telegrams, fruit, flowers, loud cheers, wild hurrahs, rapid hand-shaking and a beautiful car filled with fragrant flowers attached to a swift engine that was tearing like mad through flower-dotted valley and over snow-tipped mountain, on— on— on! It was glorious! A ride worthy a queen. They say no man or woman in America ever received ovations like those given me during my flying trip across the continent. The Americans turned out to do honor to an American girl who had been the first to make a record of a flying trip around the world, and I rejoiced with them that it was an American girl who had done it. It seemed as if my greatest success was the personal interest of every one who greeted me. They were all so kind and as anxious that I should finish the trip in time as if their personal reputations were at stake. The special train had been waiting for my arrival in readiness to start the moment I boarded it. The Deputy Collector of the port of San Francisco, the Inspector of Customs, the Quarantine Officer and the Superintendent of the O. & O. steamers sat up all the night preceding my arrival, so there should be no delay in my transfer from the Oceanic to the special train. Nor were they the only ones to wait for me. One poor little newspaper woman did not see bed that night so anxious was she for an interview which she did not get. I was so entirely ignorant about what was to be done with me on landing, that I thought I was someone's guest until I was many miles away from San Francisco. Had I known in advance the special train was mine, every newspaper man and woman who cared to should have been my guest.

My train consisted of one handsome sleeping-car, the San Lorenzo, and the engine, The Queen, was one of the fastest on the Southern Pacific.

"What time do you want to reach New York, Miss Bly?" Mr. Bissell, General Passenger Agent of the Atlantic and Pacific system, asked me.

"Not later than Saturday evening," I said, never thinking they could get me there in that time.

"Very well, we will put you there on time," he said quietly, and I rested satisfied that he would keep his word.

It did not seem long after we left Oakland Mole until we reached the great San Joaquin valley, a level green plain through which the railroad track ran for probably three hundred miles as straight as a sunbeam. The road-bed was so perfect that though we were traveling a mile a minute the car was as easy as if it were traveling over a bed of velvet.

At Merced, our second stop, I saw a great crowd of people dressed in their best Sunday clothes gathered about the station. I supposed they were having a picnic and made some such remark, to be told in reply that the people had come there to see me. Amazed at this information I got up, in answer to calls for me, and went out on the back platform. A loud cheer, which almost frightened me to death, greeted my appearance and the band began to play "By Nellie's Blue Eyes." A large tray of fruit and candy and nuts, the tribute of a dear little newsboy, was passed to me, for which I was more grateful than had it been the gift of a king.

We started on again, and the three of us on the train had nothing to do but admire the beautiful country through which we were passing as swiftly as cloud along the sky, to read, or count telegraph poles, or pamper and pet the monkey. I felt little inclination to do anything but to sit quietly and rest, bodily and mentally. There was nothing left for me to do now. I could hurry nothing, I could change nothing; I could only sit and wait until the train landed me at the end of my journey. I enjoyed the rapid motion of the train so much that I dreaded to think of the end. At Fresno, the next station, the town turned out to do me honor, and I was the happy recipient of exquisite fruits, wines and flowers, all the product of Fresno County, California.

The men who spoke to me were interested in my sun-burnt nose, the delays I had experienced, the number of miles I had traveled. The women wanted to examine my one dress in which I had traveled around, the cloak and cap I had worn, were anxious to know what was in the bag, and all about the monkey.

While we were doing some fine running the first day, I heard the whistle blow wildly, and then I felt the train strike something. Brakes were put on, and we went out to see what had occurred. It was hailing just then, and we saw two men coming up the track. The conductor came back to tell us that we had struck a hand-car, and pointed to a piece of twisted iron and a bit of splintered board–all that remained of it–laying alongside. When the men came up, one remarked, with a mingled expression of wonder and disgust upon his face:

"Well, you ARE running like h—!"

"Thank you; I am glad to hear it," I said, and then we all laughed. I inquired if they had been hurt; they assured me not, and good humor being restored all around, we said good-bye, the engineer pulled the lever, and we were off again. At one station where we stopped there was a large crowd, and when I appeared on the platform, one yell went up from them. There was one man on the outskirts of the crowd who shouted:

"Nellie Bly, I must get up close to you!"

The crowd evidently felt as much curiosity as I did about the man's object, for they made a way and he came up to the platform.

"Nellie Bly, you must touch my hand," he said, excitedly. Anything to please the man. I reached over and touched his hand, and then he shouted:

"Now you will be successful. I have in my hand the left hind foot of a rabbit!"

Well, I don't know anything about the left hind foot of a rabbit, but when I knew that my train had run safely across a bridge which was held in place only by jack-screws, and which fell the moment we were across; and when I heard that in another place the engine had just switched off from us when it lost a wheel, then I thought of the left hind foot of a rabbit, and wondered if there was anything in it.

One place, where a large crowd greeted me, a man on the limits of it yelled:

"Did you ride on an elephant, Nellie?" and when I said I had not, he dropped his head and went away. At another place the policemen fought to keep the crowd back; everybody was wanting to shake hands with me, but at last one officer was shoved aside, and the other seeing the fate of his comrade, turned to me, saying: "I guess I'll give up and take a shake," and while reaching for my hand was swept on with the crowd. I leaned over the platform and shook hands with both hands at every station, and when the train pulled out crowds would run after, grabbing for my hands as long as they could. My arms ached for almost a month afterwards, but I did not mind the ache if by such little acts I could give pleasure to my own people, whom I was so glad to be among once more.

"Come out here and we'll elect you governor," a Kansas man said, and I believe they would have done it, if the splendid welcomes they gave me are any criterion. Telegrams addressed merely to "Nellie Bly, Nellie Bly's Train," came from all parts of the country filled with words of cheer and praise at all hours of the day and night. I could not mention one place that was kinder than another. Over ten thousand people greeted me at Topeka. The mayor of Dodge City presented me, in behalf of the citizens, with resolutions of praise. I was very anxious to go to Kansas City, but we only went to the station outside of the limits, in order to save thirty minutes. At Hutchinson a large crowd and the Ringgold Cornet Band greeted me, and at another place the mayor assured me that the band had been brought down, but they forgot to play. They merely shouted like the rest, forgetting in the excitement all about their music.

I was up until four o'clock, talking first with a little newspaper girl from Kearney, Nebraska, who had traveled six hundred miles to meet and interview me, and later dictating an account of my trip to a stenographer, who was sea-sick from the motion of the train. I had probably slept two hours when the porter called me, saying we would soon be in Chicago. I dressed myself leisurely and drank the last drop of coffee there was left on our train, for we had been liberally entertaining everybody who cared to travel any distance with us. I was surprised, on opening the door of my state-room, to see the car quite filled with good-looking men. They were newspaper men, members of the Chicago Press Club, I found a moment later, who had come out to Joliet to meet me and to escort me to their city. Mr. Cornelius Gardener, the vice-president of the club, in the absence of the president, took charge of our little party. Before we were in I had answered all their questions, and we joked about my sun-burnt nose and discussed the merits of my one dress, the cleverness of the monkey, and I was feeling happy and at home and wishing I could stay all day in Chicago.

Carriages were waiting to take us to the rooms of the Press Club. I went there in a coupe with Vice-President Gardener who said, in a published narration of my visit afterwards, that he was strongly tempted to steal me, which clever idea so amused me that had the case been reversed, I know I should have acted on it, much to the confusion of a waiting public in New York. In the beautiful rooms of the Press Club I met the president, Stanley Waterloo, and a number of clever newspaper men. I had not been expected in Chicago until noon, and the club had arranged an informal reception for me, and when they were notified of my speedy trip and consequently earlier arrival, it was too late to notify the members. After a most delightfully informal reception I was escorted to Kinsley's, where the club had a breakfast prepared. And then I learned that, owing to some misunderstanding, none of the men had had anything to eat since the night before. After breakfast the members of the Press Club, acting as my escort, took me to visit the Chicago Board of Trade. When we went in, the pandemonium which seems to reign during business hours was at its height. My escorts took me to the gallery, and just as we got there a man raised his arm to yell something to the roaring crowd, when he saw me, and yelled instead:

"There's Nellie Bly!"

In one instant the crowd that had been yelling like mad became so silent that a pin could have been heard fall to the floor. Every face, bright and eager, was turned up towards us, instantly every hat came off, and then a burst of applause resounded through the immense hall. People can say what they please about Chicago, but I do not believe that anywhere else in the United States a woman can get a greeting which will equal that given by the Chicago Board of Trade. The applause was followed by cheer after cheer and cries of "Speech!" but I took off my little cap and shook my head at them, which only served to increase their cheers.

Shortly afterwards the Press Club escorted me to the Pennsylvania Station, where I reluctantly bade them good-bye, unable to thank them heartily enough for the royal manner in which they had treated a little sun-burnt stranger.

Now I was on a regular train which seemed to creep, so noticeable was the difference in the speed of traveling. Instead of a fine sleeping-car at my disposal, I had but a state-room, and my space was so limited that floral and fruit offerings had to be left behind. In Chicago, a cable which afforded me much pleasure reached me, having missed me at San Francisco.

"Mr. Verne wishes the following message to be handed to Nellie Bly the moment she touches American soil: M. and Mme. Jules Verne address their sincere felicitations to Miss Nellie Bly at the moment when that intrepid young lady sets foot on the soil of America."

The train was rather poorly appointed, and it was necessary for us to get off for our meals. When we stopped at Logansport for dinner, I being the last in the car, was the last to get off. When I reached the platform a young man, whom I never saw before or since, sprang upon the other platform, and waving his hat, shouted:

"Hurrah for Nellie Bly!"

The crowd clapped hands and cheered, and after making way for me to pass to the dining-room, pressed forward and cheered again, crowding to the windows at last to watch me eat. When I sat down, several dishes were put before me bearing the inscription, "Success, Nellie Bly."

It was after dark when we reached Columbus, where the depot was packed with men and women waiting for me. A delegation of railroad men waited upon me and presented me with beautiful flowers and candy, as did a number of private people. I did not go to bed until after we had passed Pittsburgh, and only got up in the morning in time to greet the thousands of good people who welcomed me at Harrisburg, where the Harrisburg Wheelman's Club sent a floral offering in remembrance of my being a wheelman. A number of Philadelphia newspaper men joined me there, and at Lancaster I received an enthusiastic reception.

Almost before I knew it I was at Philadelphia, and all too soon to please me, for my trip was so pleasant I dreaded the finish of it. A number of newspaper men and a few friends joined me at Philadelphia

to escort me to New York. Speech-making was the order from Philadelphia on to Jersey City. I was told when we were almost home to jump
to the platform the moment the train stopped at Jersey City, for that
made my time around the world. The station was packed with thousands of people, and the moment I landed on the platform, one yell
went up from them, and the cannons at the Battery and Fort Greene
boomed out the news of my arrival. I took off my cap and wanted to
yell with the crowd, not because I had gone around the world in seven-
ty-wo days, but because I was home again.

CHAPTER XVIII.
THE RECORD.

I STARTED from Hoboken, on my trip, around the world, November 14, 1889. I finished it in Jersey, January 25, 1890. The itinerary of my trip, published the morning I started, and the itinerary as I found it, were as follows:

PLANNED ITINERARY	ITINERARY AS FOUND
November 14— Leave New York via Augusta Victoria	Nov. 14— Left New York via Augusta Victoria
November 21— Due Southampton. London by rail in three hours	
November 22— Leave Victoria Station, London, 8 P.M. on India Mail	2:30 A.M. Arrived Southampton-London 10:00 A.M. Left London, Charing Cross Station
November 23— Calais, Paris and Turin	1:10 A.M. Left Calais
November 24— Brindisi at 10:14 P.M.	
November 25— Leave Brindisi, steamship Cathay, 9 A.M.	1:30 A.M. Arrived Brindisi 3:00 A.M. Left Brindisi, steamship Victoria
November 27— Ismallia	3:30 P.M. Arrived Port Said
	Nov. 28— 11:00 A.M. Arrived Ismallia 9:00 P.M. Suez
December 3— Aden	11:00 A.M. Arrived Aden

December 10— Colombo (Ceylon)	Dec. 8— 11:00 A.M. Arrived Colombo (Ceylon)
December 16— Penang	7:00 A.M. Arrived Penang
December 18— Singapore	5:00 A.M. Arrived Singapore
December 25— Hong Kong	7:00 A.M. Arrived Hong Kong
December 28— Leave Hong Kong for Yokohama, Japan	2:30 P.M. Left Hong Kong for Yokohama
January 7— Leave Yokohama, via Pacific Mail Steamship	10:55 A.M. Left Yokohama via Occidental and Oriental Steamship
January 22— Due San Fransisco	8:00 A.M. Arrived San Francisco
	7:05 A.M. Arrived Chicago
January 27— Due New York	3:51 P.M. Arrived New York
November 14 to January 27— Seventy-five Days	November 14 to January 25— Seventy-two days

	MILES	HOURS TRAVELLING	HOURS DELAYED
Hoboken to Southampton	3,041	184.50	50
To London	90	2.15	14.25
" Brindisi	1,450	55.30	1.30
" Port Said	930	62.30	3.30
" Aden	1,394	110	6
" Colombo	2,093	138	98.05
" Penang	1,278	89.55	7
" Singapore	381	39	11
" Hong Kong	1,437	111	127.20
" Yokohama	1,597	131.40	104.55
" San Fransisco	4,525	333.05	
" Chicago	2,573	71.05	2.55
" Jersey City	951	29.51	
	21,740	1356.41	377.30

Total time occupied in tour, 1,734 hours and 11 minutes, being 72 days, 6 hours and 11 minutes.

Average rate of speed per hour, exclusive of stops, 22.47 miles.

Average rate of speed, including stops, 28.71 miles per hour.

The names of the steamers and the different routes by which I traveled were the "Augusta Victoria" of the Hamburg American Steamship Line, the London and South Western Railway, the South Eastern Railway, the India Mail, the "Victoria" and the "Oriental" of the Peninsular and Oriental Steamship Line, the "Oceanic," of the Occidental and Oriental Steamship Line, the Southern Pacific Railway, the Atlantic and Pacific Railway, the Atchison, Topeka and Sante Fé Railway and the Pennsylvania Railway.

I spent 56 days 12 hours and 41 minutes in actual travel and lost by delay 15 days 17 hours and 30 minutes.

The second table shows the miles traveled, hours spent in traveling and hours delayed. The "hours delayed" marked by a star shows the time spent in diverging from my original line of travel to visit M. and Mme. Jules Verne at Amiens. I traveled 179-1/2 miles out of my way to visit the great novelist which is not considered in my number of miles traveled, nor do I count the miles traveled at the ports where I was detained, which taken together would not fall short of 1,500 miles.

Up to date, my trip is the fastest on record between San Francisco and Chicago. One run was 250 miles in 250 minutes, and that, counting the minutes lost stopping at a half dozen different towns. Another run was 59 miles in 50 minutes. Between Topeka and Kansas City we ran 13 miles in 11 minutes. Later we ran a mile in 53 seconds, and again 26 miles in 23 minutes. We made 2,566 miles in 69 hours, which is the fastest time, I am informed, that has been made for this distance. Although the Sante Fe route is over 500 miles longer than the Union Pacific, we beat the time of the fastest mail to Chicago by ten hours. If we had had the same distance to travel we would have beaten it twenty-four hours. The Santa Fé had only one day to prepare for my trip, and yet everything was perfect. They tell me when the Palmer-Jarrett "Across the Continent" trip was made they had been preparing for it for six months in advance, and when the start was made a flagman was posted at every switch and crossing between New York and San Francisco, and yet without any preparations my train traveled 500 miles farther and beat their time by 24 hours.

It is not possible to quote my fares and expenses as a criterion for prospective tourists, as I was traveling for a newspaper, and what it cost is their secret. Not counting the extra train, if first-class tickets had been bought from New York to New York it would only have cost $805. By using economy, outside expenses should not exceed $300.

On my tour I traversed the following waters: North River, New York Bay, Atlantic Ocean, English Channel, Adriatic Sea, Ionian Sea, Mediterranean Sea, Suez Canal, Gulf of Suez, Red Sea, Straits of Bab el Mandeb, Gulf of Aden, Arabian Sea, Indian Ocean, Straits of Malacca, China Sea, Pacific Ocean, San Francisco Bay.

I visited or passed through the following countries: England, France, Italy, Egypt, Japan, the United States, and the following British possessions: Aden, Arabia; Colombo, Isle of Ceylon; Penang, Prince of Wales Island; Singapore, Malay Peninsula; and the Island of Hong Kong.

L'Envoi.

To so many people this wide world over am I indebted for kindnesses that I cannot, in a little book like this, thank them all individually. They form a chain around the earth. To each and all of you, men, women and children, in my land and in the lands I visited, I am most truly grateful. Every kind act and thought, if but an unuttered wish, a cheer, a tiny flower, is imbedded in my memory as one of the pleasant things of my novel tour.

From you and from all those who read the chronicle of my trip I beg indulgence. These pages have been written in the spare moments snatched from the exactions of a busy life.

Further Reading

Elizabeth Bisland, *The Life and Letters of Lafcadio Hearn* (1906)

Elizabeth Bisland, *At the Sign of the Hobby Horse* (1910)

Elizabeth Bisland, *Seekers in Sicily: Being a Quest for Persephone by Jane and Peripatetica* (1909)

Elizabeth Bisland, *The Case of John Smith* (1916)

Elizabeth Bisland, *The Secret Life: Being the Book of a Heretic* (1906)

Elizabeth Bisland, *A Candle of Understanding* (1903)

Nellie Bly, *Ten Days in a Mad-House* (1887)

Nellie Bly, *Six Months in Mexico* (1888)

Nellie Bly, *Undercover: Reporting for the New York World 1887-1894* (2014)

Nellie Bly, *Miscellaneous Sketches: Nelly Bly Undercover* (2009)

Matthew Goodman, *Eighty Days: Nellie Bly and Elizabeth Bisland's Historic Race Around the World* (2013)

Jason Marks, *Around the World in 72 Days: The Race Between Pulizer's Nellie Bly and Cosmpolitan's Elizabeth Bisland* (1993)

* 9 7 8 1 9 4 3 1 1 5 2 5 9 *